Imagination
and
Education

Imagination and Education

Kieran Egan
Dan Nadaner

Editors

Teachers College, Columbia University
New York and London

Published by Teachers College Press, 1234 Amsterdam Avenue,
New York, NY 10027

Library of Congress Cataloging-in-Publication Data

Kieran, Egan.
    Imagination and education.

    Bibliography: p.
    Includes index.
    1. Imagination.   2. Creative thinking (Education)
3. Education — Aims and objectives.   I. Nadaner, Dan.
II. Title.
LB1062.K44   1988   370.15'7   87-19147
ISBN 0-8077-2878-0
ISBN 0-8077-2877-2 (pbk.)

Manufactured in the United States of America

93   92   91   90   89   88   1   2   3   4   5   6

◇ Contents

◇ Acknowledgments

We owe a debt of gratitude to Dr. George Ivany and Dr. Jaap Tuinman, who, as successive Deans of the Faculty of Education at Simon Fraser University, supported the conference on "Imagination and Educational Development" at which the idea for this book was born. Some of the pieces in this collection or parts of them have appeared in print before. We are grateful to Times Newspapers for permission to reprint Ted Hughes' "Myth and Education," and to the editors of the *Harvard Educational Review* for permission to reprint part of Kieran Egan's "The Origins of Imagination and the Curriculum" (which appeared as "Literacy and the Oral Foundations of Education"). We also want to thank the editor and publishers of the International Journal of Early Childhood for permission to reprint Otto Weininger's "'What if' and 'As if,'" to Philosophical Studies in Education, 1985, for permission to reprint parts of Karen Hanson's "Prospects for the Good Life," and to the Academic Press for permission to reprint parts of Roger Shepard's "Externalization of Mental Images and the Act of Creation." In his discussions of Arnold Lobel's *Frog and Toad Together*, Barbara Williams' *Albert's Toothache*, William Steig's *Yellow and Pink*, and Natalie Babbitt's *Tuck Everlasting*, Gareth Matthews uses some material that first appeared in his column, "Thinking in Stories," in *Thinking: The Journal of Philosophy for Children*, vols. 2 (1980–1), 5 (1983–5), and 6 (1985–6). We wish to thank the editor of *Thinking* for permission to reuse this material. Thanks are due also to the students who took Dan Nadaner's Mental Imagery and Education course at Simon Fraser University in 1984. We are grateful also to our wonderfully imaginative contributors, who are evidence that high imaginative ability does not necessarily interfere with meeting deadlines and doing in all cases a superb professional job. Our heartfelt thanks to Devi Pabla, whose organizational skills and good humor greatly facilitated the preparation of the manuscript on the word processor. During the editing of this book,

Kieran Egan was the grateful recipient of a Social Studies and Humanities Research Council of Canada Leave Fellowship. And, finally, we would like to thank each other. Rarely has such a collaboration gone so harmoniously.

Kieran Egan
Dan Nadaner

◇ Introduction

KIERAN EGAN and DAN NADANER

This book is about the roles and values of imagination in education and about the dangers of ignoring or depreciating them. Because we think our educational systems at present are profoundly influenced by conceptions of education that ignore or depreciate imagination, we have brought this collection of essays together. They have in common the conviction that imagination is not some desirable but dispensable frill, but that it is the heart of any truly educational experience; it is not something split off from "the basics" or disciplined thought or rational inquiry, but is the quality that can give them life and meaning; it is not something belonging properly to the arts, but is central to all areas of the curriculum; it is not something to ornament our recreational hours, but is the hard pragmatic center of all effective human thinking. Our concern is not to promote imagination at the expense of something else—say, rational inquiry or the foundational "3 Rs"; rather it is to show that any conception of rational inquiry or the foundations of education that depreciates imagination is impoverished and sure to be a practical failure. Stimulating the imagination is not an alternative educational activity to be argued for in competition with other claims; it is a prerequisite to making any activity educational.

That imagination does not occupy a firm niche in education will come as news to no one. The current era in education is one of prescribed objectives, testing, and technical emphases in the curriculum. David Elkind, in his book *The Hurried Child* (1981), has astutely reviewed the nexus of technocratic pressures that often makes school a barren experience. Elkind articulates what many parents see daily: kindergarten children coming home from their "jobs" at school, arithmetic exercises in hand, with stars or care-bear awards for their performance on accelerated reading and writing lessons (or hurt feelings if they did not perform so well). On Friday afternoons, perhaps, the children might cut amusing decorations from a stencil to round out the "humanistic side" of their education. For parents worried by this kind of curriculum there may be an alternative public school or a private school (at great expense) that offers something more or at least something different. Or, more likely, there may be no alternative but to see the child through it. A leading social studies educator, now retired, recently observed that the classrooms of today remind her of the classrooms she first encountered 50 years ago, with their tired workbooks and their habit of replacing real child art with cute decorations. In these surroundings, the imagination is not finding hospitable treatment.

And yet the value of imagination in education remains brilliantly apparent, not only to concerned educators but to any parent or teacher interested in improving the quality of education. When we first set out to think with teachers and parents about imagination, in the form of the conference on "Imagination and Educational Development" sponsored by the Faculty of Education of Simon Fraser University, we were surprised by the depth of need that these parents and teachers brought to the subject. In spite of their own schools' push toward the academic "basics," the conference participants felt the need for a broader perspective in the curriculum as clearly as did the speakers. Teachers at the conference met ideas about imagery and narrative structuring in children's thinking with eagerness to find a place for imagination in education.

FINDING THE IMAGINATION

This book represents our effort to clarify the role of imagination in education. We are stepping aside, for a moment, from the analysis of societal pressures that constrain the curriculum, although this kind of study is also needed. We take the tack that, while curriculum development cannot proceed without efforts to redefine and enhance the role of the school in society, it also cannot proceed without leadership in conceptualizing the curriculum. A clear concept of the imagination is needed if the decline of imagination in the curriculum is to be halted. Assumptions about the imagination, left unexamined, can trivialize its role in education. Notions of fantasy and escape, for example, are often assumed to be part of imagination. Although these may be valid aspects of certain kinds of imagination, they can become meaningless stereotypes if accepted uncritically. Media packages, from Disney through *Star Wars*, can easily meet society's need for glossy fantasies. When imagination becomes a fantasy to be consumed and only a diversion in the life of the individual, it is not perceived as a very important capacity to develop further, and certainly not to be developed during valuable school time.

Brian Sutton-Smith has observed that the idea of the imagination is not very old (it needed the era of rationalism and individualism to precede it), and so its association with education is even more recent. Historically, educators who have addressed the imagination have construed it in limited and specific ways. In its most influential forms, the imagination has been seen as a projection of the unconscious, as creative behavior, as a distracting flight of fancy, or as the imagistic side of cognition. The first extended attempts to discuss the imagination were byproducts of Freud's work. Depth psychology identified and gave significance to the child's unconscious life. In his book *Imagination* (1963), Harold Rugg spoke of the imagination as a way for children to overcome mental blocks and attain moments of spontaneous insight. Rugg's work began in the late 1920s, at the height of the child study movement. Similarly, Frances Wickes, a disciple of Jung, explored the value of projected fantasies and fears in *The Inner World of Childhood* (1927). This kind of imagination, the psychoanalytic version, was central to child-centered education and to the notion of free self-expression in art education.

As the reputations of Freud and Jung declined among educators, so did the status of fantasy in the curriculum. But a close relative of this school of thought, creative behavior, kept a strong following. Creativity was seen both as a state of mind and as a capacity that could accomplish something concrete—like inventing a better spaceship. Rather than an end in itself, creativity was a form of imagination that was attached to making things, especially new and useful things. The term "creative" became so popular in the 1950s and 1960s that it became interchangeable with imagination, and more often with art. The emphasis on creativity, itself a vague term, has left a legacy of vague thinking about the arts, and the inability to distinguish the arts from many other forms of purposeful production.

If writers on creative behavior have attributed only good results to imaginative thinking, philosophers like Gilbert Ryle have seen a darker side. Reacting against Freud and other noted introspectors, analytic philosophers have equated productive thinking with testable propositions, making it difficult to see the value of invisible mental events (that is, the imagination). For the hard-core analytic philosopher, the imagination is at best lovable and curious, and at worst a damaging intrusion upon logic. Ryle (1977) is one of the few of this school to see the role of imagination as a "vanguard of thought," but he also points to its "silly" moments, calling it an intellectual "jay-walker." In this bias for strict order he follows a tradition begun by Hobbes (1881), who saw in dreams only the random crumbling of waking thought. Concepts like these have surely shaped current assumptions about the nature of thought and helped assign low status to nondiscursive forms of thought in education.

Cognitive psychology is the most recent discipline to take an interest in the imagination. A growing breed of cognitivists is finding a place for imagery within thought and is beginning to examine the manifestations of imagery in dreams, daydreams, memory, and perception. Psychologists like Peter McKellar (1957) and Roger Shepard (1978) have been instrumental in the reentry of imagery into psychology, an area where it had been effectively banished since John Watson wrote his behaviorist manifesto in 1914. Watson's legacy remains very influential, however, rendering the implications of behaviorism and experimental psychology the dominant assumptions for education. After a 50-year gap in scholarship, the discussion of imagery in psychology is still a catch-up affair, focusing mainly on ontological questions (for example, does imagery exist, or is it an epiphenomenon of propositional thinking?). A full-bodied description of the imagination, in its diverse narrative and cultural forms, remains far off on the horizon, as does the derivation (from this field) of implications for education.

Sutton-Smith has contributed to this volume an extended and incisive analysis of the several ways the imagination has been construed in Western culture. (We have preserved his essay as spoken at the conference from which the idea for this book began, because the narrative tone enhances his point.) Beyond his effort to clarify meanings, however, what is remarkable in Sutton-Smith's essay is his ability to suggest concretely what the imagination *is*. The same can be said for the essays by Ted Hughes, Maxine Greene, Gareth Matthews, Robin Barrow, and others in this volume. The behaviorists and analytic philosophers were right about one thing, and that is that the imagination is an inner experience, difficult to observe and therefore difficult to describe. Yet methods do exist. Ted Hughes is a poet and classical scholar, a practitioner of the kind of world-integrating thinking he describes. Maxine Greene is an educational philosopher whose phenomenological orientation has been a crucial point of resistance to the more sterile trends in the field. Brian Sutton-Smith has long been known as an authority on children's play, and has achieved prominence not only for his theoretical insights but also for his rich anecdotal knowledge of the subject. The imagination will never be adequately known through laboratory methods or purely dispassionate analysis. It is a cultural event, with a cultural history (or many cultural histories, as Degen-hardt's and McKay's essay reminds us). It is the kind of mental event that can be best known through active identification with it, whether as poet, phenomenologist, teacher, or playroom supervisor. In reviewing these essays, we find ourselves both enchanted and illuminated by the variety of ways in which the authors have combined clear scholarship with an engaged attitude toward their subject.

KINDS OF IMAGINATION

The material in this volume is rich in images, and it would be pointless to try to compress them into a single definition of the imagination and its place in education. It would be fair to conclude, however, that the imagination is diverse. Sutton-Smith, in discussing the relationship of imagination to thinking, argues that that relationship probably takes several strong forms. The imagination may be a thing of narrative, of pure visual imagery, or of abstract relations.

The imagination may also be good or evil. In the context of Maxine Greene's argument, the imagination is an instrument of liberation. It is a way to "become different . . . to choose against things as they are . . . [to live] forward a little." For Ted Hughes, this positive, liberating concept of imagination is also the kind worth incorporating in education, giving the chance to open new roads of understanding and organize reality within a "large, flexible grasp." Without the continued practice of an adequate imagination, Hughes suggests, a kind of intellectual paralysis sets in, making a person susceptible to mass-media definitions of reality and to other demons. Sutton-Smith takes a less value-oriented approach, observing that imagination and liberation, or imagination and romanticism, are not always partners. Dictators, too, have had their imaginations. When we speak of what the role of imagination in education *should* be, then, we have a problem of both defining the imagination and identifying the value of its several different forms.

IMAGINATION AND EDUCATION

Efforts to give imagination a place in education in this century have been sporadic, beginning with Kirkpatrick (1957) and Rugg (1963), and continuing through to Margaret Sutherland's (1971) work on imagery and problem solving in the schools. Significant also have been Ruth Mock's book (1970) and Mary Warnock's impressive *Imagination*

(1976). What has not been accomplished to date is a clear description of the connection between the values of imagination and the nature of education. With the resources that the authors in this book bring to the subject, we feel optimistic that that connection can be seen much more clearly. For Barrow, the imagination is not an entity in itself, but a quality of "unusual and effective" conception, a quality that contributes directly to the educational goals of understanding and critical thought. Sutton-Smith has stated the case for the imagination in education most dramatically, suggesting that the imagination is the very source of thought. More than a "link up" with thinking, the imagination is a unique form of intelligence.

The question, then, of how the imagination can be related to the school curriculum is rich and potent. We feel fortunate that the contributors to this volume have created connections between imagination and education that are strong and specific enough to speak directly to educational practice. Combining conceptual clarity with practical experience in the several subject areas, the chapters in Part III help flesh out the more specific side of the imagination's place in the school. Roger Shepard, for example, offers a provocative look at the role of imagination in scientific discovery, challenging the simplistic notions that science is a matter only of logic and verification. In a delightful and original essay, Gareth Matthews demonstrates the rich store of philosophical thought in children's stories, urging that we see them for the provocative communications that they are, rather than as charming but meaningless tales. Claire Golomb, similarly, identifies the symbolic aspect of young children's artistic efforts, which makes their artwork more than imitation and gives it strong significance in cognitive development.

The imagination takes diverse forms, and in each of its incarnations it is a distinct quality of thought and feeling, a unique human activity. Through the practice of imagination, meanings are given to appearances, emotions intertwine with thoughts, and the mind finds a satisfying occupation. The examples of imagination given throughout the book will, we hope, not only establish the logical links between imagination and education, but also help refurnish the collective vision of what education itself is about.

REFERENCES

Elkind, D. (1981). *The hurried child: Growing up too fast too soon.* Reading, MA.: Addison-Wesley.

Hobbes, T. (1881). *The Leviathan.* Oxford: J. Thornton.

Kirkpatrick, E. A. (1957). *Imagination and its place in education.* New York: Basic Books.

McKellar, P. (1957). *Imagination and thinking: A psychological analysis.* New York: Basic Books.

Mock, R. (1970). *Education and the imagination.* London: Chatto and Windus.

Rugg, H. (1963). *Imagination.* New York: Harper & Row.

Ryle, G. (1977). *On thinking.* Totowa, N.J.: Rowan and Littlefield.

Shepard, R. (1978, February). "The mental image." *American Psychologist, 33*, 125–137.

Sutherland, M. (1971). Everyday imagining and education. London: Routledge and Kegan Paul.

Warnock, M. (1976). *Imagination.* Berkeley, CA.: University of California Press.

Watson, J. B. (1914). *Behavior: An introduction to comparative psychology.* New York: H. Hold.

Wickes, F. (1927). *The inner world of childhood.* New York: Appleton and Co.

PART I

In Search
of the
Imagination

1 ◇ In Search of the Imagination

BRIAN SUTTON-SMITH
University of Pennsylvania

My title, *In Search of the Imagination*, is literal enough although hardly anything else in this chapter will be. The kind of imagination that I am going to describe is the turbulent kind, full of opposites and a fulcrum of historical conflict; it conducts every child uneasily through childhood, in the presence of those who would "read it out" in their own favor, one way or another. I suggest that this view of the imagination makes education much more difficult but also more exciting.

But first, what is the imagination? Is it what Mozart had? Shakespeare? Freud? Einstein? Frank Lloyd Wright? Muhammed Ali? Mata Hari? Or is it what anyone has when they say: "What if?" What if pigs could fly? What if 90 percent of the matter in space were missing? What if the mind is not like a computer, or not like Boolean algebra? What if the imagination is simply the subjunctive mood?

My approach in this chapter will be historical. I will suggest that our current view of the imagination is a patchwork of historically derived textures. I would like to attempt (and it can be only an attempt) to make a little more systematic what some of those textures appear to be. The imagination is a relative newcomer on the stage of history. Its *lineage* is an inheritance of irrationality, mimicry, and dissimulation. Its *currency* is childishness, freedom, and uniqueness. Its *future* might be metagenerative. It has cut enormous ice in the arts the past 200 years, but it has had, as yet, meager influence in education.

THE IMAGINATION AS IRRATIONAL

The first layer of history with which I will deal is that of irrationality. Let's begin with two examples from children. Here first is a story by a four-year-old, cited in my book *The Folkstories of Children* (1981).

> Once upon a time there was a monster named King of Beasts
> and King of Beasts went out for a walk

3

He walked for a hundred and two years and he died
His bones said "wake up, wake up"
And then his bones died and then his spirit said "Wake up,
wake up"
    to his bones
The house became haunted
And then a person went in and the person got scared away and
    his brother bit the body part
His brother died
And then the other brother died in the same house
And then the same thing happened
And then often the same thing happened the same thing happened
    to both of them again and they were really dreaming that
    they died
After they woke up they really died
And then the skeleton said "Wake, wake up" and the spirit
    said "Wake up, wake up" to the skeleton
The end.

I think most people would think this was imaginative, though I do believe we could find plenty of people who would assume that the child who told this story was disturbed, not quite sane. What most of us do when we meet this kind of imagination, however, is attempt to restrain it. We are uneasy with the irrational aspects of the imagination. Parents and teachers in particular like to give such extrusions a didactic twist. The following story, from Judy Dunn, a Cambridge researcher, describes a three-year-old playing with his teddy bear and the way his mother reacts.

GARRY: (playing with teddy bear) He's got to have a rest. He feels much better now, Ted does. He's eating it up. He's gone to sleep now. He's got his pillow for his head. Night night.

MOTHER: Have you read him a story?

GARRY: No, he doesn't want a story.

MOTHER: He doesn't want a story? Ooh, you have a story when you go to bed. Why don't you get your caterpillar book and read him that?

GARRY: He doesn't want a story. He's asleep now . . . . Now he's sitting on the chair. 'Cause he's one of the three bears.

MOTHER: One of the three bears? Where's their porridge? Here's Goldlilocks. Look.

GARRY: This is . . . Goldilocks. She went for a walk. And sat down there. And went for a walk. And Big Father see that (*growls*). And he went to bed with him. And he went

to Goldilocks. And he . . . went in that bed. And it was
too little for him so's he could go in it *(growls)*. So
Daddy Bear tried Baby Bear's. Daddy tried Baby Bear's.
Now he's in Baby Bear's. Baby Bear's tired. Who's this
he says *(growls)*. I'm going to wake her up. And he
smacks Little Ted. War War War. Smack smack . . . .
He doesn't want to go to bed any more. He wants to go
to the toilet. He's doing weewee on the floor.

MOTHER: He'd better not. Go and sit him on the potty.

GARRY: He's done it. Naughty Bear . . . . He's done weewee in
his bed. He's weeing on the floor. He's weeing on the
floor again. He's done it again and again and again. He's
done it on the floor. He's done it on the sofa . . . .
There's Father Bear coming. And Baby wakes up.
Smack him! Smacked his father! And he goes and . . . .
And Father says that's my chair! *(growls)*. And smack!
Smack! Smack! (Dunn, 1984)

To begin with, we need some idea of that condition, which existed in tribal and pre-city life, in which the imagination was a state of
collective possession by irrational forces or by the Gods. As far as we
can tell, in oral cultures the imagination was more often harnessed to
the mnemonic or historical requirements of group preservation. It
looked backwards not forwards. It did not have the freedom that the
modern world has been able to allow it. Today we can put our heritage in libraries and on video and computer tapes and allow a differentiated and even irrelevant individual excess of fantasy, which was
itself unimaginable in prior times. That is not to suggest, however, that
the tribal imagination was not itself bizarre as, for example, many
American Indian folktales attest. I, for example, am always staggered
by the American Indian Winnebago trickster tales, in which the actions of the major figure include "his right arm fighting with his left
arm; telling his anus to watch over roasting ducks as he sleeps; awakening with an erection holding up his blanket and mistaking it for the
chief's banner; scattering villagers by breaking wind; and wading
through his own excrement" (Abrams & Sutton-Smith, 1977, p. 29).

According to Mikhail Bakhtin's (1984) account of our own Middle Ages, carnival and bacchanalian behavior, which we would regard
as degrading, was viewed as a form of revitalization, a participation in
the life and death processes of nature. In their grotesque realism of
body functions, their eroticism, and their scatology, people of medieval times were reuniting nature and culture, the irrational and the rational.

In tribal or medieval accounts, there is not the same sense of control over nature, either impersonal nature or our own personal nature, that we take for granted. To us the trickster of the Winnebago, the fox of the Taba of Argentina, the frog and tortoise tales of the Ibo of Nigeria, the spider of the African Hausa, or Maui of the Polynesians might well support a psychological picture of a poorly socialized, almost psychopathic kind of personality. Their common characteristics of impulsiveness, disregard for feelings, lack of caring relationship, lack of remorse, inability to learn from mistakes, constant use of pretense and trickery, and innocent charm are hardly endearing to moderns. But looking at things in such a psychological way is a modern habit of thought. Rather than psychological diagnoses, these tales are statements about the irrationality of the world out there.

What is "imaginative" in these earlier societies is not a feature of individual minds, but a collective metaphysic on the irrationality of the world. The early Greeks, for example, envisaged life as a divine lottery in which the Gods played heedlessly with the rest of us. We were pawns on their playing boards and they occasionally dropped the pieces on the floor. Our modern imagination supposes itself to be more rational and orderly, even when it is being nonsensical. Our primary modern example of nonsense, *Alice in Wonderland*, is occupied by unsocial eccentrics who are extremely bad mannered or grotesquely incompetent, and yet Alice is always reasonable, self-controlled, and polite. In *Wonderland* she must "adjust herself to a life without laws; in *Looking Glass* to one governed by laws to which she is not accustomed." (Phillips, 1977, p. 9). Even the great irrational and anarchic thermonuclear conflict, which we have with the Russians, is played by both sides according to rules of War Games. The modern world clearly has a strong preference for the notion of an orderly or rational imagination over the notion of a disorderly or irrational one, even when, as in this thermonuclear case, it dallies insanely and randomly with its own survival. To summarize, according to a very primordial notion of the imagination, it is irrational, demonic, or a state of possession, and it is also contexted within the actual cultural life of the people, rather than taking on an abstracted life of its own as in the modern condition of novels and Mr. Picasso.

THE IMAGINATION AS MERE APPEARANCE OR MIMICRY

In Western civilization the Greek philosophers Plato and Aristotle dealt the imagination its first and most fatal blow by distinguishing between those kinds of knowing that have more or less direct access to truth and knowledge (philosophy, logic, and ultimately science) and those kinds that they believed could only mimic the others, such as the arts, literature, and play. With one stroke, as it were, they confined the imagination to 2,000 years of mimicry (Spariosu, 1981). And we still live in the world that they created. It is a mildly harebrained matter to even hold a conference on "Imagination and Educational Development"—consider if you had asked the voting public or Ronald Reagan to support such a project. The hegemony of the sciences is such that the imagination has become a largely implicit process in the modern world, and yet every minute of the day scientists are using their own "what ifs" within the constraints of their own scientific practices and norms of behavior. If the imagination does not mimic the laws of science or of logic, they might say it is merely fanciful. The subtitle of the conference, "What kinds of thinking occur when young children play, dream, tell stories and make art? How can this kind of natural intelligence be put to use in education?" sounds like attempts to find justifications for the imagination by suggesting it has linkages with *thinking* and natural *intelligence*, which are presumably more respectable mental functions. How does imagination mimic thought (and intelligence) is being asked, and Plato would presumably have fully understood that this is the right kind of question.

But what if the imagination is itself the very font of thought? What if the imagination is what permits thought to work by providing it with the images and metaphors that give it direction? What if the imagination is primarily not mere fancy or imitation, but is itself thought's direction? Presumably our educational foci would then be very different. For example, I heard the illustrious neuropsychologist Karl Pribram describe the metaphors that at various periods of his life directed his own research activity on the brain. These included the notion that the brain is a telephone exchange, a thermostat, a computer, and a hologram; he described poignantly how at times he faltered for lack of a metaphor to direct his activity when all others seemed to be no longer empirically fruitful. His point was that the analogical imagination is central both to the history of science and to its future, and he suggested that the imagination is the source of knowledge, not its imitation.

Enough has been said to show that the imagination can be seen, either as providing the derivative appearance of reality or as the source of that reality itself. Once again it seems that the imagination as the pale shadow of reality, as the accessory to social and physical science, not its font, has been the focus in education. The imagination has been used for those supplementary exercises that provide motivation, not for unraveling the sources of knowledge themselves. And yet how can we so limit our view of children? Consider the following four-year-olds at play.

> SALLY: (to Alison) Why don't you go and do your home-work? You got any homework? You want to play with your teddy bear?
>
> ELLEN: No, she's being a bad girl today.
>
> ALISON: No, I didn't.
>
> SALLY: (to Ellen) What did she do?
>
> ELLEN: She picked up a knife. Was trying to kill her dad.
>
> ALISON: (with frown) No, I didn't. I just maked a play one.
>
> ELLEN: (hugging) That's OK then.

Here is a group of girls in a pretend play frame in which one is accused of a pretend attack on her father and successfully defends herself by pointing out she was only pretending within her pretense (Fein, 1984). In short, she does not break the main play frame. She observes the conservation of illusion rule, which, incidentally, seems to precede the conservation of number rule by about three years. But within its logic, she discovers, as did Hamlet, a play within the play to put the accuser at bay. Imagination made out to be mere mimicry seems in these examples to be the source of thought—thought's first practice—not its echo. Vygotsky seems to win over Piaget in this example.

As it happens, this is just where the Platonic issue is currently being argued out—in the arena of symbolic play. I attended a conference (Gottfried & Brown, 1984) on this very issue, where the child's first steps towards *symbolization* in play were a matter of controversy while there was some consensus at the *descriptive level*; that is, children in the second year of life acquire symbolic play and this proceeds from:

1. self-play, to object play, to other play
2. single schemes to multiple schemes
3. substitutions to inventions
4. prototypic to nonprototypic responses
5. with increasing decentralization
6. with increasing abstraction.

There was considerable disagreement about this theoretically, however. Some took sides with Plato and Piaget and saw the steps in symbolic play as a mirror and a map of underlying cognitive operations. They saw play as mere appearance. Others felt that play was sustained by event scripts, that children played at what they could already do. They imitated their own and others' real life experiences.

For me, both of these alternatives are of a copyist nature and imply a doctrine of realism before irrealism that I cannot accept. Babies are neither sober before they are mad, nor mad before they are sober. Each emotion takes its own course.

In early infancy some babies have the good fortune to participate with their parents in a positive feast of exuberant diversity, where faces and bodies and gestures and emotions are framed and reframed, postulated and denied, crescendoed and diminished with all the mad happiness that medieval adults seldom achieved except by carnival and that modern adults seldom achieve perhaps except in love.

In short, we find that there is a sensory-motor or enactive or theater imagination (Sutton-Smith, 1979) that is quite aboriginal with parents who blow "raspberries" on their babies' faces, toss them in the air, tickle them, and play "This little piggy went to market." None of this mimics anything: It originates that revitalization of everyday living that is for me the basic meaning of play, of carnival, of recreation, and of leisure. All those paradoxical frames, all those states of being and non-being, are life's ontological commentary. They are the frames that bring irony to the main frame, the everyday frame. They parody its folly by excesses of nonsense and in so doing revitalize the human spirit. All of our current research—and there is now an abundance—shows that parents who play exuberantly and foolishly with their infants give us children who love life and go at it with will and intelligence.

So much then for the benighted doctrine of the playful imagination as a form of mimicry or mere appearance. May it rest in restlessness. But in case you had forgotten, this is a historical review. We have accepted the view of play as irrational, but not as mere mimicry. It mimics mimicry, but it doesn't foster it.

THE IMAGINATION AS DECEPTIVE

The notion of the imagination as the source of, at worst, what is deceptive, or, at best, what is flexible, seems to have had its genesis in the Renaissance and in the individualism we associate with that period. The great parodies of the sixteenth and seventeenth centuries by Rabelais, Erasmus, and Cervantes focus on the differences among behavior that is an absurdly rigid imitation of the ceremonial life or of the life of the ancients, the church, or feudal honor, and a life played with both more practicality and more flexibility. In the writings of Machiavelli and Castiglione in the early 1500s, one is taught to play one's roles in public life for the sake of expediency. Not to be such a player is to be a foolish person who mistakes his or her own mask for reality. When 100 years later Shakespeare's Polonius advocates that:

> This above all: to thine own self be true
> And it doth follow, as the night the day
> Thou canst not then be false to any man.

It is already too late. Shakespeare knows we must play many selves, live by many mirrors, be socially mobile, have a private world of our own. How can we be true to some self that underlies all the others, to some deep structure of self that will later be discovered perhaps by Freud or perhaps by Lacan or perhaps not at all? And yet apparently we do truly believe that there is some real self lying behind all our other masks. After all, the villain in these early years was the dissembler, who appears like an ordinary man, but is underneath an evil person—the hypocrite and villain. The 1600s were also the period of autobiography. The 1600s were the time of puritan plain speaking and the 1700s the time of the novel. "Historians of European culture are in substantial agreement that, in the late sixteenth and early seventeenth centuries, something like a mutation in human nature took place," says Lionel Trilling (1971), p. 19.

So what do we do with the imagination that has made all this possible? We laud flexibility, but we seldom expect it in schoolrooms and we certainly give little encouragement for its bipolar mates, deception and hypocrisy; and yet, according to some analysts, the very hegemony of authoritarian routines creates the duplicity that children must learn. Even if they didn't learn it in the classroom, their life with the savages on the playground certainly would teach them. Playground learning is a learning of politics, of gullibility, of dissimulation, of parody and mockery, of how to acquire prestige and power. We are all familiar with this in the form of children's folklore in the works of the British Iona and Peter Opie (1968) and the Americans Knapp and Knapp (1976); and yet in a sense we seldom connect our awareness with education. Yet deceit is probably the inevitable issue of the imagination itself, not only historically as I have been arguing but also genetically. To be able to imagine is to be able to be free of conventional appearances. Here are some examples from Knapp and Knapp (1976):

You can jeer at others with distortions of reality

I see London, I see France.
I see Laura's underpants.

They ain't black, they ain't white.
Oh, my God, they're dynamite.

Liar Liar pants on fire.
Nose as long as a telephone wire.

Copy catter, dirty ratter.
Stick your face in monkey splatter.

Hasten Jason, bring the basin.
Urp Slop. Too late, bring the mop.

I'm going to cut you so low that if they stood a dime on its edge they'd need a parachute to get you down.

The sexes can scorn each other with distortions of decency

Boys are zipped:
Is somebody in your family dead? No. Well, your flag's half mast.

Girls' bras are snapped:
Are you a turtle? No. How come you snap then (bras)?

Children trick each other for gullibility

What would happen if a girl ate bullets?
She would grow bangs.

What's long and green and lives in a trunk?
Elephant snot.

What do you call a friendly helpful monster?
A failure.

What did the mother bullet say to the father bullet?
We're going to have a beebee.

What's long and white and lies on the bottom of the ocean?
Moby's Dick.

They can parody commercials

Pepsi cola hits the spot.
Ties your belly in a knot.
Tastes like vinegar, looks like ink.
Pepsi cola is a stinky drink.

Winstons taste bad, like the last one I had.
No filter, no flavor, just plain toilet paper.

Everything tastes better
With Blue Vomit on it.

Nursery rhymes and therefore childhood itself are parodied

Little Miss Muffet, sat on a tuffet, eating her curds and whey.
Along came a spider and sat down beside her, and said
What's in the bowl, bitch?

Mary had a little lamb,
The doctor was surprised.
But when McDonald had a farm,
The doctor nearly died.

The birth of the imagination makes alternative appearance, alternative thinking, and alternative dissembling possible.

Once again, just as in education we have generally been opposed to the imagination as a force of an irrational kind or as a primary form of knowledge to be advocated, so we are ill at ease with flexibility and particularly with one of its issues, deception. We force the deceptive under the desk and into the playground. We are just as uncomfortable as Rousseau, who was uncomfortable even with the "arts" of deception, in particular theater. Like Rousseau, we do not mind games and sports, because in them people confront other players directly. But theater is something else. We seldom allow it much access to our curriculum. Rousseau felt that actors are required to practice deception as their art form, and that we the audience learn such self-alienation simply by watching them. While in general few today would agree with Rousseau's view of the desirable noble savage self, nevertheless in practice our unease with the theater in the classroom means we severely restrict that kind of imagination.

And yet if we follow the symbolic interactionist branch of social science theory from George Mead (1934) to Erving Goffman (1959), we are, all of us, all the time, busy constructing our worlds by being role players, by presenting ourselves to others in favorable lights. Consider that at this moment I am playing the role of keynote speaker at an academic conference, and you are playing the role of diligent audience. We construct this scene by our flexible adoption of the masks expected in this kind of place, and if in fact we are bored stiff, either you or I, we try to dissemble, me by showing enthusiasm for the subject, you by putting your hands over your face, in an apparently contemplative, but actually somnolent, pose. In Goffman's eyes, every piece of interaction in human society can be peeled apart to show the way in which the members contribute to the upkeep of interaction by intense concern, by intense strategy, and by feigning—most of it, of course, done in a quasi-conscious fashion.

What this means is that our very social institutions keep going because of our imaginative maintenance of them. They do not run by themselves. And yet, why is this awareness kept from education? Do we secrete it from children because we disguise it from ourselves? Would we fall into disrepute if we treated our rigid myths as flexible and imaginative constructions for carrying on life in the meantime? Is it possible to be flexible with existence, or do we prefer the rigid deceits we call "reality"?

THE IMAGINATION AS CHILDISH, AS INNOCENCE, AS TRIVIAL, AND AS USELESS

That some learning is useful and some useless is the dichotomy imposed on us both by puritanism and industrialization. These two together take the Greek notion of knowledge and appearance, and compound it with the distinctions between good and evil, between work and idleness. Concomitantly, the world of childhood developed as a useless subculture, set aside from the major forces of work life. By the 1800s there was a substantial number of beings in the new category called childhood in the Western world, newly equipped with special clothes, special books, special toys, and special schools. Educational toys become distinct from mere entertainments; educational games like sports, from idle scrub play; organized drill, from ethnic street games. Childhood itself as a time outside the work force came to be seen as increasingly disjunctive from adult life and, therefore, increasingly useless or trivial unless devoted to some imitation of the useful occupations of the larger world. Childhood, and womanhood for that matter, were set to one side from economic life and—like natives everywhere are both trivialized and colonized—both subordinated and idealized. Child play was seen as a trivial, even if fanciful, pursuit. Children's literature, after its early days of direct indoctrination, became a vehicle largely for a form of bowdlerized adult fancifulness. Here all the dionysian forces of child life were transformed into prettiness and respectability. Imagination became the vapid combination of powerlessness and hysteria that one could equate with the subordination of both children and women in the past 100 years. It was an idealized, fanciful thing, apparently not to be taken very seriously by anyone. In some ways this concept of the imagination, in its very powerlessness and fancifulness, is the greatest enemy of all. Through many brilliant authors from Lewis Carroll onwards, it has been created as a kind of eunuch and unique power in its own substitive world. It has come to stand for the modern meaning of the "imagination" among many adults and, therefore, a substitute for thinking about the imagination in terms of some of its other, more dynamic possibilities.

And yet what is fanciful doesn't have to be powerless. Our own century has the view that the imagination is most finely manifest in self-contained worlds like those of Joyce, Beckett, Nabokov, and Barthes: worlds that are unlike real worlds and run only according to their own laws; worlds that, as Michael Holquist (1969) says, borrowing from Lewis Carroll, are "a Boojum" rather than an allegory. To quote: "An immaculate fiction . . . that resists the attempts of readers, and especially those readers who write criticism, to turn it into an allegory, a system not equitable with already existing systems in the non fictive world." Thus in the Snark, in *Through the Looking Glass*, Humpty Dumpty says in a famous passage: 'When I use a word . . . it means just what I choose it to mean—neither more nor less.' 'The question is,' said Alice, 'Whether you can make words mean so many different things.' 'The question is,' said Humpty Dumpty, 'Which is to be master—that's all' " (Phillips, 1977, p. 151).

Consider another story by my four-year-old genius. It is certainly a Boojum, certainly fanciful, childish, trivial, and innocent, but hardly powerless. Stories by children quickly make much of those told them by adults.

> Once there was a dragon who went poo poo on a house
> And the house broke
> Then when the house broke, the people died
> And when the people died their bones came out and broke
> And got together and turned into a skeleton
> And then the skeleton came along and scared the people
> Out of town.
> And when all the people got scared out of the town
> Then the skeleton babies were born
> And then everyone called it skeleton town
> And then when they called it skeleton town
> The people came back
> And then they got scared again
> And then when they all got scared away again the skeleton died
> No one came to the town
> So there was no people in that town ever again.

Monsters who walk for 100 years, bones that speak, and dead that come to life, brothers who bite body parts—these are irrational, innovative, yet childish, but are neither innocent nor trivial events. Nevertheless it is my conclusion, unfortunately, after many years that a "keep innocent, be bright and lively, optimistic and wonderful" notion of the imagination is a predominant force in much modern adult control of child life. By making the imagination trivial as a personal force, it can be deprived of its life-giving power—when it is deprived of irrationality, of knowledge, and of flexibility.

THE IMAGINATION AS FREE, AS AGENCY, AS POETIC, AND 'AS IF,' HEURISTIC THINKING

I have been moving ahead in my historical treatment to show prejudice and make indictments, but as yet have not given birth to the subject matter itself. I mean it was not until about 1800 that something called "faculty of the imagination" appeared on the Western philosophical scene as an important conceptualization of the individual psyche. It took the earlier individualism of the Renaissance and 100 years more to lead people to the kind of reductionism that has become the major tradition in modern psychological thinking. When Descartes said in 1640, "I think, therefore I am," he announced a major revolution in human history. It was a solipsistic, egocentric, narcissistic, and alienated postulate. And yet most of our modern psychological thought, which seeks to reduce human behavior to homunculi in human heads, I.Q.s, traits, conflicts, egos, and SAT profiles, is of that kind.

Thinking about the world in this way and trying to understand how anything can exist out of the human mind, which he reduced to the individual senses, Hume, in 1740, was forced to acknowledge uneasily that object constancy can hardly be maintained unless there is some other property of the human mind that "imagines" the objects to be there when we are not looking at them. We not only feign the idea of their constancy, he said, but we believe it. The empiricist Hume was forced logically to such a position, given that he believed true knowledge came only through the senses, but he was full of distaste for it. He said, "I cannot conceive how such trivial qualities of the fancy, conducted by such false suppositions, can ever lead to any solid and rational system" (Warnock, 1976, p. 25).

Through this concession of the great empiricist, the German idealistic philosophers, Kant and Schiller, drove a whole cartload of epistemological and a priori categories equally supposed to exist in the individual mind. Unlike Hume, however, they were also reactive, it seems, to the plight of contemporary humanity in an increasingly industrial, impersonal, technological, and secular world. Given the contemporary disenfranchisement of scholars from political power, of artists from patronage and academies, and of apparently everyone from craftsmanship and beauty, they sought to find a source in the individual himself of what was hopeful, beautiful, and good in the everyday world. For Kant, the faculty of the imagination unites our direct experience with our reason. For Schiller, the imagination or play gives rise to art, and art makes possible sound moral judgment. But, more importantly, it is because of this intrinsic activity of the imagination that we are made free and autonomous. The imagination is the source of our freedom, and freedom was the key concept in the Romantic period. Wordsworth announced in 1800 that poetry is the "spontaneous overflow of powerful feelings." John Stuart Mill in 1833 praised the lyrical over the epic, the spontaneous over the belabored, the subjective over the objective, and the soliloquy over the theatric. These were to be key features of the way in which the imagination was described in the next 200 years. It is interesting to note, for example, in the recent *Handbook of Child Psychology* in the chapter on play, which is supposedly being defined in an objective way, these same Romantic emphases are used (Rubin, Fein, & Vandenberg, 1983). Play is seen as intrinsically motivated, guided by organism-dominated questions, free from externally imposed rules, and characterized by active engagement (Vol. IV, pp. 698–700). Most moderns believe this is the way to define play, and yet the historical and anthropological evidence shows quite clearly that such concepts are not universal. Much of what looks like play to us takes place in an obligatory sacral context and is often savage and brutal (Sutton-Smith and Kelly-Byrne, 1984).

But back to Romanticism. We can, if we wish, derive almost everything that has happened in art since from this same spirit of romantic defiance of the industrial world and of the conformism of middle class behavior. The varying exuberance, the anarchy, the nostalgia, the fantasia, the aestheticism, the Byronism, and the fictionalism of modern art can all be seen as an estrangement from the technological and mass-media world that has overtaken Western society in the past two centuries.

I think you are all familiar with the auxiliary notion that children's art is such a manifestation of freedom and should not be tampered with, and also familiar with the laudatory quality of many of the references made to it in our time: "Once I drew like Raphael," says

Picasso, "but it has taken me a whole lifetime to learn to draw like a child." Franz Cizek, the father of child art, initiated the method of reducing adult influence to a minimum. As he said: "The child who is not influenced has the strong type of art. Therefore, the child from three to nine or ten years of age should be encouraged to make what he feels he must 'bring out of himself'" (Viola, 1936, p. 29). We have, consequently, in this century a great deal of undirected child art, within which many children did indeed have the satisfactions of freedom, but within which very few learned how to either draw or paint except by accident or their own insistence.

Still, my point at the moment is that as an antithesis to modern technology and homogenization, we have come so strongly to think of the imagination as the font of our freedom, and even of anarchic freedom, that in general we also think of it as a fairly irresponsible force. Being of the kind that made Picasso famous, it is not surprising that the general public views it with some alarm. Perhaps our belief in imagination as a rather feeble and fanciful kind for children is itself a reflex to our fear of its more blatant and anarchic manifestations in the world of the arts. Certainly no one would accuse the schools of the Western world of giving much freedom to the imagination except in the sheltered world of preschoolers or in the fanciful forms of children's literature or school "challenge" programs.

THE IMAGINATION AS NOVEL

There may be yet another modern polarity of the imagination of more recent vintage, within which it is argued that novelty is a form of creativity and that, therefore, the production of novelty is itself a register of the imagination. This has had some vogue in psychology and in so-called creativity tests. The other pole says that the world of children is overwhelmed with an endless stream of trivial novelties through advertising, television, and so on, and furthermore that this incessant distraction actually inhibits the real development of creativity by constantly distracting the children from one stimulus to the next, preventing the concentration and familiarity that creativity requires.

I find it hard to assess the role of these two arguments in the imaginative life of children. They are both so averse to our older idea of the imaginative life as something focused, concentrated, or solitary even, that they are much harder to reckon with. Children's distractibility, their need for constant novel and trivial stimuli, is the bane of all teachers. If you are a Marxist, you might see in this a new kind of opiate, a part of mass-media culture keeping the natives contented while they remain enslaved. But even on the positive side, it's perhaps not easy to understand how the modern sea of novelty contributes to the imagination, except perhaps by providing an increasing scale of metacommunicative insights, unless you assume—as some do—that we have arrived at a period in history where contemporary novelties are the sum and substance of the imaginative life, as in pop culture, minimal art, and so forth.

I will leave this last historical layering of the imagination incomplete: The story is not yet over. The permutations of computers stand on the fringe of everyday life as a novel and exciting invitation to escalating imaginative grasp. They offer a new kind of meta-intelligence and are likely to be as profound in their effect as the invention of printing 500 years ago. What threatens us all is the speed with which children enter these newly imaginative worlds and the slowness with which we ourselves accept them. For the first time in history, our children, who have often escaped us in impulse and kinesis, threaten to escape us in intelligence.

In summary, my historical picture shows four *substantive* layers: irrationality, role flexibility, "as if" states, and uniqueness, and two evaluative layers: mimicry and childishness.

IMPLICATIONS

It should not be surprising after this historical review if I now proceed to say that I do not see the imagination as an absolute, for-all-time, function, except for some minimal and universal subjunctivizing, or "what if-ing." Nor should it be surprising if I say that the imagination is:

> relative
> multiple
> differentiated
> contrary
> power oriented.

The most important implication of my account to this point is that there is no single function that we might call the faculty of the imagination. What we mean by that phrase at any time is historically construed and historically contexted. I have argued that in the Western educational tradition there has been a preference for the rational over the irrational usages, for scientific imaginative knowledge over literary imaginative knowledge, for stable over flexible usages, for educational over entertainment usages, and for conformist over unique usages. We prefer to think of the imagination as poetic, but we are not comfortable with its irrational dionysian aspects.

I would prefer you to think of the imagination basically not in haloed or deranged terms derived from historical Romanticism, but as you might think of any other mental function, like memory or attention or language, which are neither good nor bad in themselves but become so within the context of particular values. Hitler was imaginative and so was Shakespeare. The difference doesn't lie in the function of "what if-ing" but in the ends to which it was devoted. The subjunctive mood of mind may be different from the indicative and the imperative, but it is just as universal. With that in mind, what are the implications of this historically relative picture that I have been trying to paint?

Cultural Relativity of Imagination

First there is the *cultural relativity of the imagination*. Although most of us speak as if the children we teach are or are not imaginative, in general we mean by that only the literate kind of free-floating, future-oriented, individualistic imagination that has become a part of the literacy of the Western world and has its source in inventors, novels, film makers, and so on. There has been an argument among educators that many minority and ethnic children who come to school are not imaginative, or have a deficient imagination. But cross-cultural research indicates that we cannot act as if whole groups are deficient in imagination, any more than we can say they are deficient in intelligence or memory, though there will of course be individual differences within groups in these mental functions (Schwartzman, 1978). What has often been viewed as a deficiency in imagination within schoolrooms turns out on closer examination to arise because of cultural differences in its deployment. The literate kind of imagination, which we consider to be *the* imagination and which has developed most fully as a general idea of the imagination in the past few hundred years, assumes that the imagination can float free of its social context, that its author can be anonymous, and that its creatures can be totally imaginary and have only a very direct reference to current affairs. The earlier description of Carroll's "Boojum" was an extreme form of this theory of the imagination, and skeleton town and the King of Beasts were perfect examples. What we tend to think of as imaginative is a highly culturally relative picture (Sutton-Smith & Heath, 1981).

Throughout history, particularly oral history, the imagination has been tightly harnessed to many other needs of the particular social group. It has had to carry the load of memory, and it has had to directly reinforce the prestige of the speaker at the time of telling, beyond the content of the speech. In oral cultures, for example, traditional narratives (as one form of imagination) often include reference to the actual speaker and the actual audience at the time, and may incorporate visitors in an imaginative manner. Today in classrooms we differentiate between personal narratives, which deal with real life events (and are scripts), and fictional narratives, which are fanciful. We use the personal pronoun with the first (I went shopping yesterday) and the third-person character and markers with the second (once upon a time Cinderella did so and so). Very young children mix these two together; oral cultures also mix them together. When personal reference continues to be an important element in one's hierarchies and there are no other, more impersonal means (money, clothes, housing, grades) of pegging one's status, then these older usages of the imagination continue. Here is a story by a twelve-year-old minority child, which illustrates these points:

Ya' don't know me, but you will. I'm Terry Moore. Ya' might think I look sissy sittin' in dat class ackin' like I'm working, ya' know. But I'm de tough one around here, and I done been down to Mr. Brown's office mor'n you kin count. Ya' know, I'm da onliest one what can stand up to dat paddle of his. He burn me up. I'ma tell you 'bout dat (pause). One day I was walkin' down the hal, now you ain't 'posed to do dat, less'n you got a pass, and I ain't had no pass on my ass. And all of a sudden I hear somebody comin', and dere was a feelin' like my ass was caught for like he knowed I was dere. I took out runnin' (pause) now don't ever run 'less 'n ya' know you don't hafta stop. Dat was my mistake. It was good while it lasted. I run all the way down Main, but my feet 'n legs start hurtin' and then I got me a strain, but den I saw a power like Spider Man, and I look back, and dis web fall all over Mr. Brown, and he struggle (pause), and he struggle (pause), and he struggle. 'n den dis big old roach come outta de walls of dem ol' building on Main, and that roach start eatin' his head (pause), his fingers (pause), 'n his toes (pause) 'n he holler, 'n he holler, 'n I come to de end of Main, and I stop to watch.
Hey Terry lisn'n, hep me.
Yea, I hep you, you gonna do what I say?
I do it, I do it. Just get me outta here.

I just hold my sides laughing, and him getting madder and madder. So after I had me a good laugh, I say,

You gonna burn dat paddle up?

He say, You kin have it, you kin have it.

So I let 'im up, and call off dat roach and dat spider web, and we went back to school. But he didn't do what he say. He git me, 'n he took dat paddle to me, and toh me up (long pause). But somewhere out dere, old Spider Man, he know I'm takin' it for him, and he hep me out next time. (Sutton-Smith & Heath, 1981, p. 43)

What we have here is clearly an allegory rather than a Boojum, and presumably many minority children have difficulty in schools because, among other things, their chosen forms of narrative are not recognized as fictions but are seen merely as lies. When the cultural concept of individuality is different, so is the form of allowable imagination. When Descartes secluded himself from the world in a hot Bavarian stove to keep warm and said "I think, therefore I am," he forecast the kind of alienation from others that lies behind the modern tradition of the imagination and that has been alien to most of the rest of the world throughout history. It is to the credit of educator Shirley Heath of Stanford University that in her work with South Carolina children she understood this cultural difference in the usages of fantasy and had her children spend much more time in personal accounts of their own neighborhoods and ways of life. She emphasized social scripts, not personal fantasies (Heath, 1983).

Multiple Relationships between Imagination and Intelligence

The second implication is that *the relationships of the imagination to thinking and intelligence are multiple*, not singular. For a start, if we are to follow Howard Gardner in his 1983 imaginative work *Frames of Mind*, there are seven kinds of intelligence:

logico-mathematical
linguistic-narrative
spatial
musical
kinesthestic
interpersonal
intrapersonal.

Putting aside whether Gardner's new version of Thurstone's original multiple and specific abilities has really put to rest the old argument of unity versus diversity in this area, we can, I think, concede that how one imagines in each of these domains will clearly be different and will need different tutoring. Thinking subjunctively in science or literature or architecture or music or sports or socially or intuitively can hardly be very much alike, at least not in ways that are directly useful across all disciplines. Every subject matter requires its own "what if" speculation, its own plane of imagination.

More importantly at this time, however, I want to take up a theme that many of us have been advocating in recent years—that the mind is, among other things, a narrative concern (Sutton-Smith, 1983). Dreams are universal and so are stories. In trying during this century to discover what the mind is, we have used analogies from strategy games, from chance games (probability), and from computers, but have seldom used analogies from narrative, which is clearly much more universal and ancient than the others. One consequence is that when we think about thinking as Piaget and most other scientists have, we largely assume that the fundamental character of thinking is either logical or prelogical; it takes place in terms of categorization. So that when we are asked to focus on the role of thinking in imagination, I strongly suspect that it is with Piaget's kind of logico-mathematical thinking in mind. And that kind of imagination has to do with number games, magic puzzles, logical riddles, and the like. The power of science has made us believe that this is the only kind of thinking.

Fortunately, the discovery in recent developmental psychology research (Bretherton, 1984) that children remember their scripts better than their categories has turned more attention to the fact that the mind works better as a narrator than as a categorizer. As a result, we are suddenly at liberty to realize that the imagination as narrative is contributing to the linguistic mode of intelligence just as much as the imagination as logic is contributing to the logical mode of intelligence. The logical mode of mind draws away from the world into its sphere of impersonal and objective postulates and predictions, with mathematics as its apotheosis and verification as its ultimate proof. The narrative mode of mind, on the other hand, must be thoroughly contextualized if it is to be understood. It presupposes that the listeners understand the world to which the story teller refers as well as the teller does; this is true whether it is a personal or a fictional narrative (though, as we have seen, they also have their differences). Further, the narrative mode has little to do with objectivity, predictions, and verifications; rather, it has to do with consensual support, impartial readings, and verisimilitude. The science that derives from physics and mathematics is a science of verification; the science that derives from linguistics and narratives is a science of interpretation. I am not even going to speculate on the science derived from music, space, and so on—my point is only to indicate the pluralistic burden that we must sustain.

Differentiating Imagination from Play

Another implication of this study of imagination is that we must *differentiate the imagination from other symbolic forms*. Our culture constantly conflates together play, the imagination, daydreams, reverie, and so forth. I would like to make a plea for clarity over the difference between the imagination and play. When one adopts the subjective mood and says, "What if I piled these blocks one on top of the other, would they fall over?" That, to me, is not play. The child's intelligence, like that of the adult, is constantly exploring in such analytic and constructive ways, but we, in our disregard, call them play. In fact, they are direct acts of intelligent exploration, discovery, imitation, mastery, construction, and imagination. None of this is play, unless the children cease to be concerned with a solution to the problem and instead become concerned with the paradox of their own actions, in which case they frolic and exaggerate to show they don't mean it, or with the paradox of their ideas, in which case they say quite clearly they are only pretending. (There is much more to be said about this and I recommend my books *The Masks of Play* [1984] and *Toys as Culture* [1985] for a fuller account.)

What I am stressing is that, by saying that play is imagination or imagination play, we deprive both of their natural rights. If we call imagination play we deprive the imagination of its verbal applications and trivialize it ("they are only playing"); or if we call play imagination, we confine it to schoolroom contexts and prevent it from its true and necessary exuberance and hilarity far from the classroom crowd. To confuse the two is just the kind of bowdlerizing romanticism of which I have spoken earlier that trivializes and destroys both.

The Conflictual Nature of Imagination

The historical survey presented earlier makes a powerful argument for still another implication—that we should *take oppositions seriously* in our understanding of the vital role of the imagination. Ours is a century of unmasking our surface stories about ourselves. Think of all the scholars and artists who have told us that we are not what we think we are (Trilling, 1971). Freud is the primary example, and he has argued that our lives are grounded in ambivalence. We hate those we love, we are desperate for both complete autonomy and complete union, we can't say yes and we can't say no. The history of modern art in its turn is a history of disorientation, disabling our conventional views of what we should expect. Morse Peckham (1967) has described the career of modern art as *Man's Rage for Chaos*, and has suggested that only by contemplating chaos artistically can we be ready in effect for the unrehearsed and unexpected. Without this drive for the irrational we would be caught unprepared in our drive for safety, survival, and comfortable habit. Gregory Bateson (1972) has argued that it is because they do not have negatives that animals must play. It is only through play that they can signify that what they are doing does not mean what it seems; that the nip connotes the bite but not what the bite connotes—I must make sure you understand my signal that I am at play, or my playful punch at you will get me a sock in the jaw. Kenneth Burke (1966) has pointed out that there are no negatives in nature; they are generated only by symbolic systems, of which play is the first. In *belief* we oppose thou shall, with thou shalt not. In *logic* we oppose the proposition that it is with the proposition that it is not. In *language* we oppose prose with paradox or parody, iteration with irony and sarcasm, and everything with comedy and burlesque. Man is, according to Burke, the inventor of the negative.

In sociology, the conventional requirements of everyday culture cause you to fantasize their inversion, says Georg Simmel (1950). Given that you must do this or that, you immediately imagine what it would be like if you didn't do it or if you did something else. Out of this universal disposition arises the antistructure of society, the clubs, the redlight district, the peer groups, the myriad ways in which humans group together to express their antithetical impulses. Anthropologists like Levi-Strauss (1966) and Victor Turner (1974) emphasize the conflictual and binary nature of culture, and the way in which imaginative events like festivals, games, rituals, and ceremonies arise as partial solutions to deep-seated conflicts that would otherwise lead to war, division, or litigation. In these theories the imagination gives rise to imaginary solutions that do in fact palliate and sometimes solve the bitterness of inevitable social division.

Usually those festivals or games themselves seem to take on something of the binary nature of the cultural situation from which they emerge. Games deal in order and disorder, stability and vertigo, winning and losing, approaching and avoiding, playing carefreely and playing deeply, as if these and myriad other social conflicts can be assuaged by being captured in these imaginary forms. To state the conflict in imaginary form is to inform our minds and relieve our actions. The young child tells me the story:

> This is a story about a jungle. Once upon a time there was a jungle. There were lots of animals, but they weren't very nice. A little girl came into the store. She was scared. Then a crocodile came in. The end. (*girl, age five*)

Or:

> The boxing world. In the middle of the morning everybody gets up, puts on boxing gloves and fights. One of the guys gets socked in the face and he starts bleeding. A duck comes along and says, "Give up." (*boy, age five*) (Sutton-Smith, 1981).

These children have solved nothing in their stories; but like the patient who goes to the therapist, or the friend who tells his predicament, or the church goer who sings a hymn, the telling itself, despite its lack of resolution, is, in the human situation, resolution enough. Perhaps the answer to how people can use imagination to relieve themselves is given us in its own jolting way by the quasi-delinquent in *Learning to Labour* by Paul Willis. He gets his relief from what he sees as a miserable school life by what he calls "laffing."

> I think fuckin' laffing is the most important thing in fuckin' everything. Nothing ever stops me laffing (. . .) I remember once, there was me, John, and this other kid, right, and these two kids cum up and bashed me for some fuckin' reason or another. John and this other kid were way, off (. . .) I tried to give 'em one, but I kept fuckin' coppin' it . . . so I ran off, and as I ran off, I scopped a handful of fuckin' snow up, and put it right over me face, and I was laffing me bollocks off. They kept saying, 'You can't fuckin' laff.' I should have been scared but I was fuckin' laffin (. . .).
> (. . .) I don't know why I want to laff, I dunno why it's so fuckin' important. It just is (. . .) I think it's just a good gift, that's all, because you can get out of any situation. If you can laff, if you can make yourself laff, I mean really convincingly, it can get you out of millions of things (. . .). You'd go fuckin' berserk if you didn't have a laff occasionally. (Willis, 1977, p. 29)

I would suggest that the imagination is a form of laffing, though seldom as violent as this example might indicate. Alternatively, laffing is a matter of imagining that things are not really what they seem: They are really totally absurd. Laffing is the imagination of the absurd.

Imagination and Power

The final implication is that the central and major use of imagination by children in the modern world is to remove from themselves
the stigma of their powerlessness, their detachment from the real
world, their lack of apprenticeship, and their subordination.

This is the major opposition that they seek to controvert in all
their own imaginative works and in the imaginative works they admire. Whether they are enjoying the disordering of adult reality with
Mother Hubbard's dog, Bugs Bunny cartoons, or Sendak's Wild Ones,
they are incessantly reaching out for their own control and their own
heroism in this world of winners into which they are born temporary
losers. Here is a seven-year-old boy's story of how he defeated ex-
President Nixon.

Once upon a time there were two babies. They loved, they hated spinach. So once their mother gave them a big pot of spinach, each with one
fried egg on it. And they hated it *so much*, they threw it at their mother.
She gave them another pot of spinach with *two* eggs on it this time and
they were even madder and they threw it at their father this time. Then
their mother gave them two pots of spinach with six fried eggs on it.
They threw it at their sister. Then, when Nixon heard of this, he called
them "The Fried Egg Family." But the baby was angry at Nixon. So
when Nixon came to their house, they did nothing to him. But as he was
walking out the door, the baby saw him and then stuck out their weenies and then they put their weenies to work. And when Nixon saw these
things, he flipped. But then, they pulled in their weener and put two buns
on top of them and put some catsup and spinach and then Nixon got right
back up and he started to bit. All of a sudden, the babies went pissing
and shot their X-Y-Z. And Nixon was so upset he almost, his heart almost cracked. But then, they had more strategy.
So when he was walking over the mountain, they made flying hamburgers and then Nixon screamed, "We're being invaded by flying hamburgers!" And then the babies made flying hamburgers shoot out missile
hotdogs and then Nixon had a very good idea! And he ate it—the hotdogs. But Nixon was so dumb, those hotdogs were solid metal and when
he bit on them, they cracked his teeth and he was so upset. And then a
lady came and said, "Will you help me across the street?" And Nixon
said, "Whaaaaaaaaaaaaah." "You are weird, Man," the lady said. And
then the babies had little bit more strategy. They started shooting spinach with fried eggs on top. And then New York called Nixon "The Fried
Egg President." That's all. The end. (Sutton-Smith, 1981)

If we put the children back into the world of work—and perhaps
we will in the new computer age—then this particular dialectic of the

imagination might not have to occur. Or we can repress this kind of expression as we usually do. Or we can permit it and civilize it into even more magnificent stories, or we can use it as a spur to all those other grammatical accomplishments we usually take so much more earnestly. Or we can take all of this much more seriously and ask how schools can be planned to allow for their continuous reconstruction at the service of their imaginative members. Many imaginative alternatives are clearly possible to imaginative people.

CONCLUSION

I have presented you with a turbulent imagination, with a concept whose history is filled with contradictions. The imagination has been seen as irrational or rational, as knowledge or mere appearance, as flexible or stable, deceptive or rigid, useful or useless, educational or trivial, idealized or gross, free or conformist, focused or distractible. In addition, I have suggested that the imagination is relative, being deployed differently in different cultures and subcultural groups; that it is plural, being used differently in the intelligences of logic, language, space, music, and the body or those of a social or intuitive kind; that it should be differentiated from play and other forms of intelligent activity; and finally that it is deeply connected to the antithetical strains of human culture, because it is after all the playground of the subjective, the domain where the opposites and the alternatives can be faced or feted.

Clearly, I have made opposition both the center of my description and the fulcrum of my historical contentions. Social conflicts find their way into the history of the imagination; and those who would deal with imagination in the classroom, I am arguing, must allow them into its informative and assuaging management, if they are to use its full power. The margin of life can be festooned with the mimicries of respectable knowledge or they can be made bright with its inversion.

REFERENCES

Abrams, D., & Sutton-Smith, B. (1977). "The development of the trickster in children's narratives." *The Journal of American Folklore*, *90*, pp. 29–48.

Bakhtin, M. (1984). *Rabelais and his world*. Bloomington, IN.: Indiana University Press.

Bateson, G. (1972). *Steps to an ecology of mind*. New York: Ballantine.

Bretherton, I. (1984). *Symbolic play*. New York: Academic Press.

Burke, K. (1966). *Language as symbolic action*. Berkeley, CA.: University of California Press.

Castiglione, B. (1968). *The book of the courtier*. London: Penguin Books.

Cervantes, M. (1938). *Don Quixote*. New York: Heritage Press.

Dunn, J. (1984). Pretend play in the family. In A. W. Gottfried & C. C. Brown (Eds.), *Play interactions,* pp. 149–162. Lexington, MA.: D. C. Heath.

Erasmus, D. (1969). *The praise of folly*. Princeton, N. J.: Princeton University Press.

Fein, G. (1984). The affective psychology of play. In A. W. Gottfried & C. C. Brown (Eds.), *Play interactions,* pp. 31–50. Lexington, MA.: D. C. Heath.

Gardner, H. (1983). Frames of mind. New York: Basic Books.

Goffman, E. (1959). The presentation of self in everyday life. New York: Doubleday.

Gottfried, A. W., & Brown, C. C. (1984). Ways with words. Cambridge: Cambridge University Press.

Heath, S. B. (1983). *Ways with words*. Cambridge: Cambridge University Press.

Holquist, M. (1969). What is a Boojum? In P. Brooks (Ed.), *The child's part*. Boston: Beacon Press.

Knapp, M., & Knapp, H. (1976). *One potato, two potato*. New York: Norton.

Levi-Strauss, C. (1966). *The savage mind*. Chicago: University of Chicago Press.

Machiavelli, N. (1947). *The prince*. New York: Crofts Classics.

Mead, G. H. (1934). *Mind, self and society*. Chicago: University of Chicago Press.

Opie, I., & Opie, P. (1968). *The lore and language of school children*. New York: Oxford University Press.

Peckham, M. (1967). *Man's rage for chaos*. New York: Schocken.

Phillips, R. (1977). *Aspects of Alice*. New York: Vintage Press.

Piaget, J. (1951). *Play, dreams and imitation in childhood*. New York: Norton.

Rabelais, F. (1955). *Gargantua and Pantagruel*. London: Penguin Books.

Rubin, K., Fein, G., & Vandenberg, B. (1983). Children's play. In E. M. Hetherington (Ed.), *The Carmichael handbook of children's psychology,* pp. 693–774. New York: Wiley.

Schiller, F. (1965). *On the aesthetic education of man*. New York: Frederick Ungar.

Schwartzman, H. (1978). *Transformations: The anthropology of children's play*. New York: Plenum.

Simmel, G. (1950). *The sociology of G. Simmel*. (Transl. K. Wolf). Glencoe, IL.: The Free Press.

Spariosu, M. (1981). Literature and play: History, principles, method. In M. Spariosu (Ed.), *Literature, mimesis and play,* pp. 13–52. Tubingen, West Germany: Gunter Narr Verlag.

Sutton-Smith, B. (1979). *Play and learning*. New York: Gardner Press.

Sutton-Smith, B. (1981). *The folkstories of children*. Philadelphia, PA.: University of Pennsylvania Press.

Sutton-Smith, B. (1983). The origins of fiction and the fictions of origin. In E. Bruner (Ed.), *Story, play, text*. Proceedings of the American Ethnological Association, Washington, D.C.

Sutton-Smith, B. (1986). *Toys as culture*. New York: Gardner Press.

Sutton-Smith, B., & Heath, S. B. (1981). Paradigms of pretense. *Quarterly Newsletter of the Laboratory of Comparative Human Cognition*, *3*, pp. 41–45.

Sutton-Smith, B., & Kelly-Byrne, D. (Eds.) (1983). *The masks of play*. West Point, N. Y.: Leisure Press.

Sutton-Smith, B., & Kelly-Byrne, D. (1984). The idealization of play. In P.K. Smith (Ed.), *Play in animals and humans*. London: Blackwell.

Trilling, L. (1971). *Sincerity and authenticity*. Cambridge, MA.: Harvard University Press.

Turner, V. (1974). *The Ritual Process*. Chicago: Aldine Pub. Co.

Viola, W. (1936). *Child art and Frank Cizek*. Vienna: Austrian Junior Red Cross.

Warnock, M. (1976). *Imagination*. Berkeley, CA.: University of California Press.

Willis, P. (1977). *Learning to labour*. London: Gower.

2 ◇ Myth and Education

TED HUGHES
Devon, England

In *The Republic*, where he describes the constitution of his ideal state, Plato talks a little about the education of the people who will live in it. He makes the famous point that quite advanced mathematical truths can be drawn from children when they are asked the right questions in the right order, and his own philosophical method, in his dialogues, is very like this. He treats his interlocutors as children and by small, simple, logical, stealthy questions gradually draws out of them some part of the Platonic system of ideas—a system that has in one way or another dominated the mental life of the Western world ever since.

Nevertheless he goes on to say that a formal education—by which he means a mathematical, philosophical, and ethical education—is not for children. The proper education for his future ideal citizens, he suggests, is something quite different: It is to be found in the traditional myths and tales of which Greece possessed such a huge abundance.

Plato was nothing if not an educationist. His writings can be seen as a prolonged and many-sided debate on just how the ideal citizen is to be shaped. It seemed to him quite possible to create an elite of philosophers who would also be wise and responsible rulers, with a perfect apprehension of the Good. Yet he proposed to start their training with the incredible fantasies of these myths.

Everyone knows that the first lessons, with human beings just as with dogs, are the most important of all. So what would be the effect of laying at the foundations of their mental life this mass of supernatural figures and their impossible antics? Later philosophers, throughout history, who often enough have come near to worshipping Plato, have dismissed these tales as absurdities. So how did he come to recommend them?

They were the material of the Greek poets. Many of them had been recreated by poets in works that became the model and despair of later writers. Yet we know what Plato thought about poets. He

30

wanted them suppressed—much as it is said he suppressed his own poems when he first encountered Socrates. If he wanted nothing of the poets, why was he so respectful of the myths and tales that formed the imaginative world of the poets?

He had no religious motives. For Plato, those gods and goddesses were hardly more serious, as religious symbols, than they are for us. Yet they evidently did contain something important. What exactly was it, then, that made them in his opinion the best possible grounding for his future enlightened, realistic, perfectly adjusted citizen?

Let us suppose he thought about it as carefully as he thought about everything else. What did he have in mind? Trying to answer that question leads us in interesting directions.

Plato was preceded in Greece by more shadowy figures. They are a unique collection. Even what fragments remain of their writings reveal a cauldron of titanic ideas, from which Plato drew only a spoonful. Wherever we look around us now, in the modern world, it is not easy to find anything that was not somehow prefigured in the conceptions of those early Greeks.

And nothing is more striking about their ideas than the strange, visionary atmosphere from which they emerged. Plato is human and familiar; he invented that careful, logical, step-by-step style of investigation, in which all his great dialogues are conducted, and that almost all later philosophers developed, until it evolved finally into the scientific method itself. But his predecessors stand in a different world. By comparison they seem like mythical figures, living in myth, dreaming mythical dreams.

And so they were. We find them embedded in myth. Their vast powerful notions emerge, like figures in half-relief, from the massif of myth, which in turn lifts from the human/animal darkness of early Greece.

Why did they rise in Greece and not somewhere else? What was so special about early Greece? The various peoples of Greece had created their own religions and mythologies, more or less related but with differences. Further abroad, other nations had created theirs, again often borrowing from common sources, but evolving separate systems, sometimes gigantic systems.

Those seemingly supernatural dreams, full of conflict and authority and unearthly states of feeling, were projections of man's inner and outer world. They developed their ritual, their dogma, their hierarchy of spiritual values in a particular way in each separated group. Then at the beginning of the first millennium they began to converge, by one means or another, on Greece.

They came from Africa via Egypt, from Asia via Persia and the Middle East, from Europe, and from all the shores of the Mediterranean. Meeting in Greece, they mingled with those rising from the soil of Greece itself. Wherever two cultures, with their religious ideas, are brought sharply together, there is an inner explosion. Greece had become the battleground of the religious and mythological inspirations of much of the archaic world. The conflict was severe, and the effort to find solutions and make peace among all those contradictory elements was correspondingly great.

And the heroes of the struggle were those early philosophers. The struggle created them, it opened the depths of spirit and imagination to them, and they made sense of it. What was religious passion in the religions became in the philosophers a special sense of the holiness and seriousness of existence. What was obscure symbolic mystery in the mythologies became in the philosophers a bright, manifold perception of universal and human truths. In their works we see the transformation from one to the other taking place. And the great age that immediately followed them, in the fifth century B.C., was the culmination of the activity.

It seems proper, then, that the fantastic dimension of those tales should have appeared to Plato as something very much other than frivolous or absurd. We can begin to guess, maybe, at his objective, in familiarizing children with as much as possible of that teeming repertoire.

To begin with, we can say that an education of the sort Plato proposed would work on a child in the following way.

A child takes possession of a story as what might be called a unit of imagination. A story that engages, say, earth and the underworld is a unit correspondingly flexible to the child's imagination. It contains not merely the space and in some form or other the contents of those two places; it reconciles their contradictions in a workable fashion and holds open the way between them. The child can reenter the story at will, look around him or her, find all those things, and consider them at leisure.

In attending to the world of such a story there is the beginning of imaginative and mental control. There is the beginning of a form of contemplation. To begin with, each story is separate from every other story. Each unit of imagination is like a whole separate imagination, no matter how many the head holds.

If the story is learned well, so that all its parts can be seen at a glance, as if we looked through a window into it, then that story has become like the complicated hinterland of a single word. It has become a word. Any fragment of the story serves as the "word" by which the whole story's electrical circuit is switched into consciousness, and all its light and power brought to bear.

As a rather extreme example, take the story of Christ. No matter what point of that story we touch, the whole story hits us. If we mention the Nativity, or the miracle of the loaves and fishes, or Lazarus, or the Crucifixion, the voltage and inner brightness of the whole story is instantly there. A single word of reference is enough, just as you need to touch a power line with only the tip of your finger to feel its energy.

The story itself is an acquisition, a kind of wealth. We only have to imagine for a moment individuals who know nothing of it at all. Their ignorance would shock us, and, in a real way, they would be outside our society. How would they even begin to understand most of the ideas that are at the roots of our culture and appear everywhere among the branches?

To follow the meanings behind the one word *crucifixion* would take us through most of European history and much of Roman and Middle Eastern too. It would take us into every corner of our private life. And before long, it would compel us to acknowledge much more important meanings than merely informative ones, openings of spiritual experience, a dedication to final realities, which might well stop us dead in our tracks and demand of us personally a sacrifice that we could never otherwise have conceived.

A word of that sort has magnetized our life into a special pattern. Behind it stands not just the crowded breadth of the world, but all the depths and intensities of it too. Those things have been raised out of chaos and brought into our ken by the story in a single word. The word holds them all there, like a constellation, floating and shining, and though we may draw back from tangling with them too closely, nevertheless they are present. These depths and intensities remain part of the head that lives our life, and they grow as we grow. A story can wield so much! And a word wields the story.

Imagine hearing, somewhere in the middle of a poem being recited, the phrase "The Crucifixion of Hitler." The word *Hitler* is as much of a hieroglyph as the word *crucifixion*. Individually, those two words bear the consciousness of much of our civilization. But they are meaningless hieroglyphs, unless the stories behind the words are known. We could almost say it is only by possessing these stories that we possess that consciousness.

In those who possess both stories, the collision of those two words, in that phrase, cannot fail to detonate a psychic depth-charge.

Whether we like it or not, a huge inner working starts up. How can Hitler and crucifixion exist together in that way? Can they or can't they? The struggle to sort it out throws up ethical and philosophical implications that could absorb our attention for a very long time. All our static and maybe dormant understanding of good and evil and of what opens beyond good and evil is shocked into activity. Many unconscious assumptions and intuitions come up into the light to declare themselves and explain themselves and reassess each other.

For some temperaments, those two words paired in that way might well point to wholly fresh appraisals of good and evil and the underlying psychological or even actual connections between them. Yet the visible combatants here are two stories.

Without those stories, how could we have grasped those meanings? Without those stories, how could we have reduced those meanings to two words? The stories have gathered up huge charges of reality, illuminated us with them, and given us their energy, just as those colliding myths of gods and goddesses in early Greece roused the philosophers and the poets.

If we argue that a grasp of good and evil has nothing to do with a knowledge of historical anecdotes, we have only to compare what we felt of Hitler's particular evil when our knowledge of his story was only general, with what we felt when we learned more details. It is just those details of Hitler's story that have changed the consciousness of modern man. The story hasn't given us something that was never there before; it has revealed to us something that was always there.

And no other story, no other anything, ever did it so powerfully, in the same way as it took the story of Christ to change the consciousness of our ancestors. The better we know these stories as stories, the more of ourselves and the world is revealed to us through them.

The story of Christ came to us first of all as two or three sentences. That tiny seed held all the rest in potential form, like the blueprint of a city. Once we laid it down firmly in imagination, it became the foundation for everything that could subsequently be built and exist there. The same is true of the story of Hitler.

Are those two stories extreme examples? They would not have appeared so to the early Greeks, who had several Christs and several Bibles and quite a few Hitlers to deal with. Are Aesop's fables more to our scale? They operate in exactly the same way. Grimm's tales are similar oracles.

But what these two stories show very clearly is how stories think for themselves, once we know them. They not only attract and light up everything relevant in our own experience; they are also in continual private meditation, as it were, on their own implications. They are little factories of understanding. New revelations of meaning open out of their images and patterns continually, stirred into reach by our own growth and changing circumstances.

Then at a certain point in our lives, they begin to combine. What happened forcibly between Hitler and the Crucifixion in that phrase, begins to happen naturally. The head that holds many stories becomes a small early Greece.

It does not matter, either, how old the stories are. Stories are old the way human biology is old. No matter how much they have produced in the past in the way of fruitful inspirations, they are never exhausted. The story of Christ, to stick to our example, can never be diminished by the seemingly infinite mass of theological agonizing and insipid homilies that have attempted to translate it into something more manageable. It remains, like any other genuine story, irreducible, a lump of the world, like the body of a newborn child.

There is little doubt that, if the world lasts, pretty soon someone will come along and understand the story as if for the first time. That person will look back and see 2,000 years of somnolent fumbling with the theme. Out of that, and the collision of other things, he or she will produce, very likely, something totally new and overwhelming, some whole new direction for human life. The same possibility holds for the ancient stories of many another deity.

Why not? History is really no older than that newborn baby. And every story is still the original cauldron of wisdom, full of new visions and new life.

What do we mean by "imagination"? There are obviously many degrees of it. Are there different kinds?

The word *imagination* usually denotes not much more than the faculty of creating a picture of something in our heads and holding it there while we think about it. Since this is the basis of nearly everything we do, clearly it's very important that our imagination should be strong rather than weak. However, education neglects this faculty completely. How is the imagination to be strengthened and trained? A student has imagination, we seem to suppose, much as he or she has a face, and nothing can be done about it. We use what we've got.

We realize that imagination can vary enormously from one person to the next, and from almost nonexistent upwards. Of people who simply cannot think what will happen if they do such and such a thing, we say they have no imagination. They have to work on principles, on orders, or by precedent, and they will always be marked by extreme rigidity, because they are, after all, moving in the dark.

We all know such people, and we all recognize that they are dangerous since, if they have strong temperaments in other respects, they end up by destroying their environment and everybody near them. The terrible thing is that they are the planners, and ruthless slaves to the plan—which substitutes for the faculty they do not possess. And they have the will of desperation: Where others see alternative courses, they see only a gulf.

Of people who imagine vividly what will happen if they act in a certain way, and then turn out to be wrong, we say they are dealing with an unpredictable situation or, just as likely, they have an inaccurate imagination. Lively, maybe, but inaccurate. There is no innate law that makes a very real-seeming picture of things an accurate picture.

Those people will be great nuisances, and as destructive as the others, because they will be full of confident schemes and proof, which will simply be false, because somehow their sense of reality is defective. In other words, their ordinary perception of reality, by which the imagination regulates all its images, overlooks too much or misinterprets too much. Many disturbances can account for some of this, but simple inattentiveness accounts for most of it.

Those two classes of people comprise the majority of us for much of the time. The third class of people is quite rare. Or our own moments of belonging to that class are rare. Imagination that is both accurate and strong is so rare that somebody who appears in possession of it is regarded as something more than human. We see it in the few great generals in history. Normally, it occurs patchily, because accurate perceptions are rarely more than patchy. We have only to make the simplest test on ourselves to reconfirm this. And where our perceptions are blind, our speculations are pure invention.

This basic type of imagination, with its delicate wiring of perceptions, is our most valuable piece of practical equipment. It is the control panel for everything we think and do, so it ought to be education's first concern. Yet, who has ever spent half an hour in any classroom trying to strengthen it in any way? Even in the sciences, where accurate perception is recognizably crucial, is this faculty ever deliberately trained?

Sharpness, clarity, and scope of the mental eye are all important in our dealings with the outer world, and they are plenty. If we were machines, it would be enough. But the outer world is only one of the worlds we live in. For better or worse, we have another—the inner world of our bodies and everything pertaining to it. It is closer than the outer world, more decisive, and utterly different.

So here are two worlds, which we have to live in simultaneously, and because they are intricately interdependent at every moment, we can't ignore one and concentrate on the other without accidents, possibly fatal accidents. But why can't this inner world of the body be regarded as an extension of the outer world? In other words, why isn't the sharp, clear, objective eye of the mind as adequate for this world as it is for the other, more obviously outer world? And if it isn't, why isn't it?

The inner world is not so easily talked about because nobody has ever come near to understanding it. Though it is the closest thing to us—indeed, it is us—we live in it as on an unexplored planet in space. It is not so much a place, either, as a region of events. And the first thing we have to confess is that it cannot be seen objectively.

How does the biological craving for water turn into the precise notion that it is water that we want? How do we "see" the make-up of an emotion that we do not even feel—though electrodes on our skin will register its presence? The word "subjective" was invented for a good reason, but under the vaguest of general terms lies the most important half of our experience.

After all, what exactly is going on in there? It is quite frightening, how little we know about it. We can't say there's nothing—that "nothing" is merely the shutness of the shut door. And if we say there's something—how much more specific can we get?

We quickly realize that the inner world is indescribable, impenetrable, and invisible. We try to grapple with it, and all we meet is one provisional dream after another. It dawns on us that in order to look at the inner world "objectively" we have had to separate ourselves from what is an exclusively "subjective" world, and that it has vanished. In the end, we acknowledge that the objective imagination and the objective perceptions—those sharp clear instruments that cope so well with the outer world—are of very little use there.

By speculating backwards from effects, we can possibly make out a rough plan of what ought to be in there. The incessant bombardment of raw perceptions must land somewhere. We have been able to notice that any one perception can stir up a host of small feelings, which excite further feelings—not necessarily so small—in a turmoil of memory and association.

We do have some evidence, we think that our emotional and instinctive life, which seems to be on a somewhat bigger scale and not so tied to momentary perceptions, is mustering and regrouping in response to outer circumstances. But these bigger and more dramatic energies are also occasionally yoked to the pettiest of those perceptions and driven off on some journey. Now and again we are made aware of what seems to be an even larger drama of moods and energies that are hard to name—psychic, spiritual, cosmic. Any name we give them seems metaphorical, since in the inner world everything is relative, and we are never sure of the scale of magnification or miniaturization of the signals.

We can guess, with a fair sense of confidence, that all these interinvolved processes, which seem like the electrical fields of our body's electrical installations—our glands, organs, chemical transmutations, and so on—are striving to tell about themselves. They are all trying to make their needs known, much as thirst imparts its sharp request for water. They are talking incessantly, in a dumb, radiating way, about themselves, about their relationships with each other, about the situation of the moment in the main overall drama of the living, growing, and dying body in which they are assembled, and also about the outer world, because all these dramatis personae are really striving to live, in some way or other, in the outer world.

That is the world for which they have been created, the world that created them. And so they are highly concerned about the doings of the individual behind whose face they hide, because they are that individual. They want that person to live in the way that will give him or her the greatest satisfaction.

This description is bald enough, but it is as much as the objective eye can be reasonably sure of—and then only in a detached way, the way we think we are sure of the workings of an electrical circuit. For more intimate negotiations with that world, for genuine contact with its powers and genuine exploration of its regions, it turns out that the eye of the objective imagination is blind.

We solve the problem by never looking inward. We identify ourselves and all that is wakeful and intelligent with our objective eye, saying, "Let's be objective." That is really no more than saying "Let's be happy." We sit, closely cramped in the cockpit behind the eyes, steering through the brilliantly crowded landscape beyond the lenses, focused on details and distinctions.

In the end, since all our attention from birth has been narrowed into that outward beam, we come to regard our body as no more than a somewhat stupid vehicle. All the urgent information coming towards us from that inner world sounds to us like a blank, or at best the occasional grunt, or a twinge. This is because we have no equipment to receive and decode it. The body, with its spirits, is the antenna of all perceptions, the receiving aerial for all wavelengths. But we are disconnected. The exclusiveness of our objective eye, the very strength and brilliance of our objective intelligence, suddenly turn into stupidity—of the most rigid and suicidal kind.

That condition certainly sounds extreme, yet most of the people we know, particularly older people, are likely to regard it as ideal. It is a modern ideal. The educational tendencies of the last 300 years, and especially of the last 50, corresponding to the rising prestige of scientific objectivity and the lowering prestige of religious awareness, have combined to make it so. It is a scientific ideal and a powerful ideal; it has created the modern world. Without it, the modern world would fall to pieces: Infinite misery would result. The disaster is that the world is heading straight toward infinite misery, because it has persuaded human beings to identify themselves with what is no more than a narrow mode of perception. The more rigorously the ideal is achieved, the more likely it is to be disastrous: a bright, intelligent eye, full of exact images, set in a head of the most frightful stupidity.

The drive toward this ideal is so strong that it has materialized in the outer world. A perfect mechanism of objective perception has been precipitated: the camera. Scientific objectivity, as we all know, has its own morality, which has nothing to do with human morality. It is the morality of the camera. This is the prevailing morality of our time. It is a morality utterly devoid of any awareness of the requirements of the inner world. It is contemptuous of the "human element." That is its purity and its strength. The prevailing philosophies and political ideologies of our time subscribe to this contempt, with a nearly religious fanaticism, just as science itself does.

Some years ago in an American picture magazine I saw a collection of photographs that showed the process of a tiger killing a woman. The story behind this was as follows: The tiger, a tame tiger, belonged to the woman. A professional photographer had wanted to take photographs of her strolling with her tiger. Something—maybe his incessant camera—had upset the tiger; the woman had tried to pacify it, whereupon it attacked her and started to kill her. So what did that hero of the objective attitude do then?

Jim Corbett's stories about tigers and leopards that eat human beings describe occasions when such an animal with a terrifying reputation was driven off its victim by some other person, or by a girl who beat the animal over the head with a digging stick. But this photographer—we can easily understand him because we all belong to this modern world—had become his camera. Whatever his thoughts were, he went on taking photographs of the whole procedure while the tiger killed the woman. The pictures were there in the magazine, but the story was told as if the photographer were absent, as if the camera had simply gone on doing what any camera would be expected to do, being a mere mechanical device for registering outward appearances.

The same paralysis comes to many of us when we watch television. After the interesting bit is over, what keeps us mesmerized by that bright little eye? It can't be the horrors and inanities and killings that jog along there between the curtains and the mantelpiece after supper. Why can't we move? Reality has been removed beyond our participation, behind that very tough screen, into another dimension.

Our inner world of natural impulsive response is safely in neutral gear. Like broiler killers, we are reduced to a state of pure observation. Everything that passes in front of our eyes is equally important, equally unimportant. As far as what we see is concerned, and in a truly practical way, we are paralyzed.

Even people who profess to dislike television fall under the same spell of passivity. They can free themselves only by a convulsive effort of will. The precious tool of objective imagination has taken control of us there. Materialized in the camera, it has imprisoned us in the lens.

In England, not very long ago, the inner world and Christianity were closely identified. Even the conflicts within Christianity only revealed and consolidated more inner world. When religious knowledge lost the last rags of its credibility, earlier this century, psychoanalysis appeared as if to fill the gap. Both attempt to give form to the inner world, but with a difference.

When it came the turn of the Christian Church to embody the laws of the inner world, it made the mistake of claiming that they were objective laws. That might have passed, if science had not come along, whose laws were so demonstrably objective that it was able to impose them on the whole world.

As the mistaken claims of Christianity became scientifically meaningless, the inner world that it had clothed became incomprehensible, absurd, and finally invisible. Objective imagination, in the light of science, rejected religion as charlatanism, and the inner world as a bundle of fairy tales, a relic of primeval superstition. People rushed toward the idea of living without any religion or any inner life whatsoever as if toward some great new freedom—a great final awakening. The most energetic intellectual and political movements of this century wrote the manifestos of the new liberation. The great artistic statements have recorded the true emptiness of the new prison.

The inner world, of course, could not evaporate just because it no longer had a religion to give it a visible body. A person's own inner world cannot fold up its spiritual wings, shut down all its tuned circuits, and become a mechanical business of nuts and bolts, just because a political or intellectual ideology requires it to. As religion was stripped away, the defrocked inner world became a waif, an outcast, a tramp. Denied its one great health—acceptance into life—it fell into a huge sickness, a huge collection of deprivation sickness. And this is how psychoanalysis found it.

The small piloting consciousness of the bright-eyed objective intelligence had steered its body and soul into a hell. Religious negotiations had formerly embraced and humanized the archaic energies of instinct and feeling. They had conversed in simple but profound terms with the forces struggling inside people and had civilized them, or attempted to.

Without religion, those powers have become dehumanized. The whole inner world has become elemental, chaotic, continually more primitive, and beyond our control. It has become a place of demons. But of course, insofar as we are disconnected from that world anyway, and lack the equipment to pick up its signals, we are not aware of it. All we register is the vast absence, the emptiness, the sterility, the meaninglessness, the loneliness. If we do manage to catch a glimpse of our inner selves by some contraption or mirrors, we recognize it with horror—it is an animal crawling and decomposing in a hell. We refuse to own it.

In the last decade or two, the imprisonment of the camera lens has begun to crack. The demonized state of our inner world has made itself felt in a million ways. How is it that children are so attracted toward it?

Every new child is nature's chance to correct culture's error. Children are most sensitive to the inner world, because they are the least conditioned by scientific objectivity to life in the camera lens. They have a double motive, in attempting to break from the lens. They want to escape the ugliness of the despiritualized world in which they see their parents imprisoned, and they are aware that this inner world we have rejected is not merely an inferno of depraved impulses and crazy explosions of embittered energy. Our real selves lie down there. Down there, mixed up among all the madness, is everything that once made life worth living. All the lost awareness and powers and allegiances of our biological and spiritual being are there. The attempt to reenter that lost inheritance takes many forms, but it is the chief business of the swarming cults.

Drugs cannot take us there. If we cite the lofty religions in which drugs did take the initiates to where they needed to go, we ought to remember that here again the mythology was crucial. The journey was undertaken as part of an elaborately mythologized ritual. It was the mythology that consolidated the inner world, gave human form to its experiences, and connected them to daily life. Without that preparation a drug carries its user to a prison in the inner world as passive and isolated and meaningless as the camera's eye from which he or she escaped.

Objective imagination, then, important as it is, is not enough. What about a "subjective" imagination? It is only logical to suppose that a faculty developed specially for peering into the inner world might end up as specialized and destructive as the faculty for peering into the outer one.

Besides, the real problem comes from the fact that outer world and inner world are interdependent at every moment. We are simply the locus of their collision: two worlds, with mutually contradictory laws, or laws that seem to us to be so, colliding afresh every second, struggling for peaceful coexistence. And whether we like it or not, our life is what we are able to make of that collision and struggle.

What we need, evidently, is a faculty that embraces both worlds simultaneously. A large, flexible grasp, an inner vision that holds wide open, like a great theater, the arena of contention, and that pays equal respects to both sides—that keeps faith, as Goethe says, with the world of things and the world of spirits equally.

This really is imagination. This is the faculty we mean when we talk about the imagination of the great artists. The character of great works is exactly this: that in them the full presence of the inner world combines with and is reconciled to the full presence of the outer world. And in them we see that the laws of these two worlds are not contradictory at all: They are one all-inclusive system; they are laws that somehow we find it all but impossible to keep, laws that only the greatest artists are able to restate.

They are the laws, simply, of human nature. People have recognized all through history that the restating of these laws, in one medium or another, in great works of art, are the greatest human acts. They are the greatest acts and they are the most human. We recognize these works because we are all struggling to find those laws, as an individual on a tightrope struggles for balance, because they are the formula that reconciles everything and balances every imbalance.

So it comes about that once we recognize their terms, these works seem to heal us. More important, it is in these works that humanity is truly formed. It has to be done again and again, as circumstances change, and the balance of power between outer and inner world shifts, showing everybody the gulf.

The inner world, separated from the outer world, is a place of demons. The outer world, separated from the inner world, is a place of meaningless objects and machines. The faculty that makes the human being out of these two worlds is called divine. That is only a way of saying that it is the faculty without which humanity cannot really exist. It can be called religious or visionary. More essentially, it is imagination that embraces both outer and inner worlds in a creative spirit.

Laying down blueprints for imagination of that sort is a matter of education, as Plato divined. The myths and legends, which Plato proposed as the ideal educational material for his young citizens, can be seen as large-scale accounts of negotiations between the powers of the inner world and the stubborn conditions of the outer world under which ordinary men and women have to live. They are immense and at the same time highly detailed sketches for the possibilities of understanding and reconciling the two. They are, in other words, an archive of draft plans for the kind of imagination we have been discussing.

Their accuracy and usefulness, in this sense, depend on the fact that they were originally the genuine projections of genuine understanding. They were tribal dreams of the highest order of inspiration and truth, at their best. They gave a true account of what really happens in that inner region where the two worlds collide. This has been attested over and over again by the way in which the imaginative people of every subsequent age have had recourse to their basic patterns and images.

But the Greek myths were not the only true myths. The unspoken definition of myth is that it carries truth of this sort. These big dreams become the treasured property of a people only when they express the real state of affairs. Priests continually elaborate the myths, but what is not true is forgotten again. So every real people has its true myths. One of the first surprises of mythographers was finding how uncannily similar these myths are all over the world. They are as alike as the lines on the palm of the human hand.

Plato implied that all traditional stories, big and small, were part of his syllabus. Indeed the smaller stories come from the same place. If a tale can last, in oral tradition, for two or three generations, then it has either come from the real place or found its way there. The small tales are just as vigorous educational devices as the big myths.

There is a long tradition of using stories as educational implements in a far more deliberate way than Plato seems to have proposed. Rudolf Steiner has a great deal to say about the method. In his many publications of Sufi literature, Idries Shah (*The Way of the Sufi*, 1969) indicates how central to the training of the sages and saints of Islam are the traditional tales. Sometimes they are no more than small anecdotes, sometimes lengthy and involved adventures such as were collected into the Arabian Nights.

As I pointed out, using the example of the Christ story, the first step is to learn the story, as if it were laying down the foundation. The next phase rests with the natural process of the imagination.

The story is, as it were, a kit. Apart from its own major subject—obvious enough in the case of the Christ story—it contains two separable elements: its pattern and its images. Together they make that story and no other. Separately they set out on new lives of their own.

The roads they travel are determined by the brain's fundamental genius for metaphor. Automatically, it uses the pattern of one set of images to organize quite a different set. It uses one image, with slight variations, as an image for related and yet different and otherwise imageless meanings.

In this way, the simple tale of the beggar and the princess begins to transmit intuitions of psychological, perhaps spiritual, states and relationships. What began as an idle reading of a fairy tale ends by simple natural activity of the imagination as a rich perception of values of feeling, emotion, and spirit that would otherwise have remained unconscious and languageless.

The inner struggle of worlds, which is not necessarily a violent and terrible affair, though at bottom it often is, is suddenly given the perfect formula for the terms of a truce. A simple tale, told at the right moment, transforms a person's life with the order its pattern brings to incoherent energies.

While the tale's pattern proliferates in every direction through all levels of consciousness, its images are working, too. The image of Lazarus is not easily detached by a child from its striking place in the story of Christ, but once it begins to migrate, there is no limiting its importance. In all Dostoevsky's searching adventures, the basic image, radiating energies that he seems never able to exhaust, is Lazarus.

The image does not need to be so central to a prestigious religion for it to become so important. At the heart of *King Lear* is a very simple little tale—the Story of Salt. In both of these we see how a simple image in a simple story has somehow focused all the pressures of an age—collisions of spirit and nature and good and evil and a majesty of existence that seem uncontainable. But it has brought all that into a human pattern, and made it part of our understanding.

3 ◇ What Happened to Imagination?

MAXINE GREENE
Teachers College, Columbia University

In the recent proliferation of reports on education and calls for reform, there has been little or no mention of imagination. There seems to be a general association of imagination with the noncognitive, with the intuitive, or with the merely playful; and none of these are granted relevance for serious learning or for mastery. The neglect and the distortion trouble me. They appear to signify an acquiescence to existence within boundaries or frames: a contained, systematized way of living closed to alternative possibilities.

I think of all those (poets, painters, mathematicians, philosophers) who have recognized that a "one-dimensional" life (Marcuse, 1964) is a life of confinement to one of the multiple realities available to human beings. What we know as "reality" is, after all, interpreted experience; to limit learners to a single dominant mode of interpreting their experience may be to frustrate their individual pursuits of meaning—and, consequently, their desires to come to know, to learn. It may involve (it probably does involve) the imposition of a predefined conception of the "given," which these days is a largely technical rendering of the world.

It is not simply the idea of confinement that troubles me. It is the idea that young people are not encouraged to look *through* the windows of the actual on occasion, to regard things as if they could be otherwise. They are given few opportunities to gather what the poet Hart Crane called "reflections," which might enable them to perceive such relationships as that between "a drum and a street lamp—via the unmentioned throbbing of the heart and nerves of a distraught man . . . " (October 1926, pp. 34–5). Young people are given few opportunities to discover the kinds of connections Lewis Thomas made visible when he described, in *The Lives of a Cell*, what he called the

45

music of the spheres (1975) and the rearrangements associated with the process of entropy.

> If there were to be sounds to represent this process, they would have the arrangement of the Brandenburg Concertos for my ear, but I am open to wonder whether the same events are recalled by the rhythms of insects, the long, pulsing runs of birdsong, the descants of whales, the modulated vibrations of a million locusts in migration, the tympani of gorilla breasts, termite heads, drumfish bladders. A "grand canonical ensemble" is, oddly enough, the proper term for a quantitative model system in thermodynamics borrowed from music by way of mathematics. (p. 25)

Not only is Thomas able to move back and forth through the multiple provinces of meaning; he recognizes the ways in which experience can be expanded through the entertainment of associations and alternative possibilities. For Mary Warnock, imagination is one of the powers of cognition, allowing for the sense "that there is always *more* to experience and *more in* what we experience than we can predict" (1976, p. 203). It seems to me that Thomas' writing is an example of this, even as is the wonder-struck inquiry of a young student made aware that there is always something beyond.

The notion of something beyond reminds me of Wallace Stevens, who once called imagination "the power that enables us to perceive the normal in the abnormal, the opposite of chaos in chaos" (1965, p. 153). In one of his poems, a blue guitar becomes a metaphor for what he means. There is a man with a blue guitar charged with not playing things as they are. The man replied, "Things as they are/ Are changed upon the blue guitar . . ." (1969, p. 165). Those around him object; they want him to play a tune about things "exactly as they are." Later on, he tells them: "Throw away the lights, the definitions/ And say of what you see in the dark/ That it is this or that it is that./ But do not use the rotted names" (p. 183). He seems to be asking that his listeners break with their stock responses, their fixed ideas of the actual; that they see for themselves beyond even what familiar names disclose. And, at length, he says, "You as you are? You are yourself. The blue guitar surprises you." Surprise, yes, and the unpredictable. And, as importantly, an open self in the process of creation. It seems evident enough that the self, so conceived, can neither be measured nor predefined. Given the emphasis today on young people as "human resources" to be trained for productivity in the technological society, I am inclined to believe that such a rendering of a human being may seem inappropriate to those concerned about efficiency and manageability. It may suggest one of the reasons for thrusting imagination aside.

Clearly, Wallace Stevens was no more a spokesman for education than for the values associated with good management; but certian of his metaphors summon up (at least for me) a whole range of ideas relating to knowledge and the life of meaning. The last stanza of his "Six Significant Landscapes" (1969, p. 183), for instance, embodies an entire argument for a way of being and attending other than what is taken for granted today. He wrote:

> Rationalists, wearing square hats,
> Think, in square rooms,
> Looking at the floor,
> Looking at the ceiling.
> They confine themselves
> To right-angled triangles.
> If they tried rhomboids,
> Cones, waving lines, ellipses—
> As, for example, the ellipse of the half-moon—
> Rationalists would wear sombreros.

Each time I read that verse, I find myself experiencing a true shock of recognition and, at once, an actual release from confinement. In this case, it is a confinement to the logical and linear, and to a particular kind of academic order that imposes its own forms on what is felt and perceived. Unexpectedly, every time I read the verse, the triangles begin to reform themselves and actually become rhomboids; and then there is an opening to a multiplicity of anticipated shapes and forms. The surprise comes with the move to the half-moon, which can only become visible through a window the rationalists (with their solemn mortarboards) did not suspect was there. And then there is the other, comical surprise at the image of those mortarboards somehow curving into sombreros. Why not? They are not required to give up their work in the square rooms; but they are offered new possibilities of vision, new extensions of consciousness. That is what imagination can do: create new domains, new vistas, expansions of ordinary awareness. For me, this seems profoundly important in a time of formulated pieties and glittering reassurances that stun audiences into silence and make it difficult to believe that anything is susceptible any longer to critical examination or to change.

Violence, conspiracy, and arms-trading preoccupy us on the one hand; homelessness, hunger, pollution, racism, and the AIDS epidemic tear at us on the other. Private interests overtake what was once a public space. On all sides, people withdraw into enclaves, if they are not simply letting themselves be absorbed in the television "reality." In the face of all this, the educational messages have largely to do with technical expertise, with measurable achievements, with economic competitiveness, with a "cultural literacy" grounded in the most ancient of verities. Of course, there are remembered voices that some of us try to keep audible: John Dewey's, speaking of intelligence and deliberation; Hannah Arendt's, speaking of "newcomers" and a common world; Jerome Bruner's, speaking of life-stories, models, and discoveries; other voices, summoning up images of growth and open-endedness, of nurturing and repairing and keeping things alive. There are contemporary voices like that of Donald A. Schon, shaping images of a "reflective practitioner" seeking a technology that will "help students become aware of their own intuitive understandings, to fall into cognitive confusions and explore new directions of understanding and action" (1983, p. 333), or that of Theodore R. Sizer, saying that inspiration and hunger are "the qualities that drive good schools" (1984, p. 221).

They feed my desire to speak of a kind of education that recognizes imagination as fundamental to learning to learn, essential to the feeling that life is more than a futile, repetitive, consuming exercise. The idea of beginnings is central to this: Hannah Arendt's view that "it is in the nature of beginning that something new is started which cannot be expected from whatever happened before. This character of startling unexpectedness is inherent in all beginnings . . . . The new always happens against the overwhelming odds of statistical laws and their probability, which for all practical everyday purposes, amounts to certainty; the new therefore always appears in the guise of a miracle" (1958, pp. 177–8). To talk about beginnings and the improbable where teaching and learning are concerned is to presume that, somewhere in the background, there is the sound of a blue guitar.

Also, it is to conceive of both teaching and learning as modes of action, not behaviors, since action is what signifies the taking of initiatives, the starting up of something new. From the vantage point of the initiator or the agent, all sorts of things seem possible; things can become different from "the way they are." A space of freedom may open up; the individual, conscious of others around, may experience (unexpectedly, perhaps) a power to choose, to move towards what is not yet, while he or she looks at things (the classroom, the faces of the students, the books open on the desks, the abstracted eyes, the attentive eyes, the view outside the window) as if they could be otherwise. Or we might shift to the vantage point of the student, perhaps deciding to undertake his or her own action to find out, to teach himself or herself something new. It appears that few persons are likely to feel that way or act in that way if they are not nourishing an image of what it would be like "if only . . . " or some image of what is not yet.

To learn, after all, is to become different, to see more, to gain a new perspective. It is to choose against things as they are. To imagine is to look beyond things as they are, to anticipate what might be seen through a new perspective or through another's eyes. Or (to return to George Herbert Mead and his work on human interactions) it might be to take the view of the "generalized other," what is seen as the community's attitude (1948, p. 154), and discover something unexpected in what it happens to disclose. The cruical point has to do with the capacity to break somehow with what is merely given, to summon up some absent or alternative reality. John Dewey once wrote that imagination is the "gateway" through which meanings derived from prior experiences feed into and illuminate present experiences. Imagination may also be viewed as the source of a future vantage point from which to consider what is lacking in the present or the now. In any case, Dewey went on to say that experience becomes conscious only when accumulated meanings enter in; and he made it eminently clear that, as he saw it, imagination had an essential role to play in the development of mind. Without it, without consciousness, Dewey said, "there is only recurrence, complete uniformity; the resulting experience is routine and mechanical . . . " (1934, p. 272).

This only becomes meaningful, however, from the perspective of someone who has overcome the feeling of being a functionary or a mere cog in a system, who sees himself or herself as attaining a sense of agency. We have only to recall some of our own experiences with beginning things, the consequences of which could not be predetermined. When Dewey described deliberation, it will be recalled, he called it "a dramatic rehearsal in imagination of various competing possible lines of action . . . " (1916, p. 188). He meant a kind of thinking or reflectiveness very different from the predictive or the calculative. He meant the kind that leaves possibilities open, that allows for the unexpected or surprise. The issue may be as simple as turning aside from the discussion of a story in an English class to give students an exercise in paragraph construction. It may be as complex as deciding, in the face of some climactic public event, to try to bring into being a space of dialogue within the classroom. Often we take initiatives that are unexpected even for us (unless we insist upon thinking of ourselves as technicians working in terms of instrumental generalizations). Rehearse in imagination as we may, we often discover that the resultant action is seldom precisely what we had in mind. ("The blue guitar surprises you." Of course it does. Every time.)

To highlight what can be involved in that approach to teaching, it is well to compare it with the approach of certain administrators who feel themselves bound to take the vantage point of the system rather than that of the practitioner engaged in new beginnings. Very frequently they speak and report in terms of cause–effect or input–output relations, tendencies, trends, or probabilities. They focus on observable and usually measurable behaviors resulting in or failing to result in desired end products or prespecified performances. Their preoccupations tend usually to be with endpoints and products, not beginnings; and they look back from the end points when they make their judgments about "mediocrity" and the absence of excellence. They do not ponder alternatives or possible lines of action in the way Dewey described when discussing specific teaching situations. For many officials, for all their occasional acknowledgment of the random and the uncontrollable, freedom (like imagination) seems to be an irrelevance. It is at odds with statistical probability, with prediction, with regularity. It is not only inefficient; it is disruptive to take into account.

I have difficulties with this, apart from my difficulties with the constriction of experience to which it may lead, the confinement of human beings to some version of "square rooms." The notion of normalization arises too easily: Individuals of all sorts are treated as creatures who are to be "normalized," thrust into acceptable boxes or molds, and judged accordingly. It becomes, then, less and less likely that teaching and learning will be thought of as situation-specific; and there will be (indeed, there presently are) principles and regulations to be applied to schooling in general, with an eroding sense of alternative possibilities. I do not mean that the public's representatives or the system's administrators ought to keep their hands off particular schools. It is troubling that guarantees are sought that cannot be given: guarantees of protection against drugs and adolescent pregnancy and "secular humanism." It is particularly troubling that the current malaise and powerlessness so often find expression in scapegoating public schools.

To view the school as defensive against what are perceived to be social evils or as simply reactive to outside forces is to suffer, as Sizer says, a "paralysis of imagination" (1984, pp. 218ff.). It is undoubtedly the case that many members of the public view the role of education to be one of supporting and sustaining the status quo, no matter what its flaws. They see the schools as primarily obligated to prepare the young to fill available occupational and professional slots, to initiate them into the mainstream *ethos*, to equip them with the manners and habits required for acceptability in the community. Their objections to what the schools accomplish are usually a function of the degree to which the schools seem to fail in responding to their concrete demands. In a period when America is ostensibly "feeling good" and proud of itself again, it is difficult to gauge the precise degree of restiveness and dissatisfaction with the public schools at large; and, consequently, it is difficult to know whether the capacity of imagination can be enlisted in pondering what ought to be within and around the schools. Obviously, there are members of the public who feel intensely the deficiencies in their communities and an erosion of those values once believed to be the ground of the nation's commitment: equity, freedom, decency, concern, and even some mode of "excellence." Such people are more likely to create a vision of a better order of things and, indeed, more responsive and liberating schools. For that reason, they are likely to be more sensitive to and articulate about what they perceive to be lacking in the world around them. Often, the sense of lack and deficiency stimulates the imaginative capacity. People begin experiencing the limitations of the status quo; they summon up images of what is absent, of what is not yet achieved.

When I ponder the uses of imagination in social and political spheres, I think about the importance of public dialogue (in multiple voices) having to do with the purposes of education in a democracy. There is a sense in which such a dialogue may become exemplary, particularly if it has to do with the domain in which the lives and futures of the young mesh with the nature and future of what is thought to be the common world. Hannah Arendt has written:

> Education is the point at which we decide whether we love the world enough to assume responsibility for it and by the same token save it from that ruin which, except for renewal, except for the coming of the new and the young, would be inevitable. And education, too, is where we decide whether we love our children enough not to expel them from our world and leave them to their own devices, not to strike from their hands their chance of undertaking something new, something unforeseen by us, but to prepare them in advance for the task of renewing a common world. (1961, p. 196)

If there is substance to what Arendt has said, if the underlying questions might somehow arouse the interest of members of a presently inarticulate public, we would find that both social intelligence and imagination are needed if responses are to be found. Even to ponder what it signifies to ''love the world'' is to move beyond the ordinary into domains where poets ordinarily venture. And to save the world from ruin, to cherish it, must involve those who attend in metaphorical thinking: the linking of what is apparently unlike, bringing together disparate ideas, enriching and expanding both. Then, of course, Arendt introduces the idea of ''something new, something unforeseen,'' clearly something that can only be imagined, that cannot (as she herself wrote) be settled by empirical science.

To think this way along with others would inevitably engage people in a quest for possibility. They would be moving outwards if they did this, risking, trying (with newcomers and beginnings in mind) to become what they might become for the sake of renewing, for the sake of loving a deeply resistant world. To express human agency in this fashion with a concrete sense of what is wrong and what is possible nourishes and complicates my vision of what it might mean to educate in dark times like our own. I remember Rilke writing to ''the young poet'' (1934, pp. 3–4) about inconsiderable things that must be loved, about how they become ''big and beyond measuring.'' And then he reminded the young poet that he was young, and continued: ''I want to beg you, as much as I can, dear sir, to be patient towards all that is unsolved in your heart and to try to love *the questions themselves* like locked rooms and like books that are written in a very foreign tongue. Do not now seek the answers, that cannot be given you because you would not be able to live them. And the point is, to live everything. *Live* the questions now. Perhaps you will then gradually, without noticing it, live along some distant day into the answer.''

If teachers and parents, along with the young, could love the questions and live the questions with the ''distant day'' somehow in sight, the spaces in which they lived would be infused with wonder and imagination both. Teachers might be more prone to create the kinds of situations in which the young would be empowered to learn in such a way that they might find themselves appearing before others—other free people—provoking one another to move forward in the name of loving and renewing, in the name of care for the least and the most among them. It is a question of opening subject matters as possible perspectives on the shared world, a question of releasing people for their own pursuits of meaning, their own searches for answers, their own efforts to name and to articulate what they live.

Imaginative literature is replete with derelict figures and silenced creatures, with persons struggling for moments of wide-awakeness, struggling out of objecthood towards spaces of freedom in their worlds. Who cannot but think of Bartleby and Huckleberry Finn, of Lily Bart and Isabel Archer, of Stephen Daedalus and Ivan Ilyitch, of Dorothea Brooke and Sula Peace and the Underground Man and Dr. Rieux, of Alice Walker's Celie and Ralph Ellison's Invisible Man? It is not only that readers must release their imagination in order to engage with the perspectives of each work and constitute an illusioned world out of the materials of their own consciousness and social experience. It is, more often than not, that the "as–if" so constituted confronts the reader with ambiguities, gaps, voids that must be dealt with imaginatively— and always without guarantees. An individual's experience reveals itself as otherwise than it usually does; it is defamiliarized. Opportunities are provided to see through the taken-for-granted, to disrupt the normal, to see reality anew.

All this suggests a variety of reasons for using the arts when the values of imagination are acknowledged in private life or in public dialogue. Paintings, works of music, dance performances—when made accessible, all have the potential to conjure up new experiential possibility, to make audible a blue guitar. It is not a matter of making people "better," or of initiating them into some elite community where individuals are reputed to be more sensitive, more intimately engaged with the arts. My commitment is to do what can be done to enable as many people as can be reached to crack the old forbidding codes, to break through the artificial barriers that have so long served to exclude. The idea is to offer opportunities to release imagination as all sorts of energies move outwards to the Cezanne or the Haydn or the Balanchine work. The idea is to challenge awed passivity or a merely receptive attitude or a submergence in pleasurable reverie. If people can choose themselves as imaginative beings present to particular works, if they can attend in some "space" they have carved out in their own experience, the works will emerge in their particularity, and new dimensions of the perceiver's lived world may be disclosed.

There are always new beginnings with the arts, the kinds of beginnings spoken of before. That means there are always untapped possibilities, always an element of the unpredictable. I do not mean that what may appear or be summoned up will always be beautiful or pleasant or even significant; not being able to measure or predict, one never can be sure. I do know, however, that whenever I read or see or listen to something as familiar to me as Shakespeare's *Romeo and Juliet* or Handel's *Water Music* or the Cezanne still life with the "pepper bottle," I am likely to discover some dimension, some shape or sound or glint of light or meaning I do not remember having recognized before. There have been works (Philip Glass' music, for example) that I did not originally "like" and, after listening over and over, after learning to notice more of what was there to be noticed, have come to relish for the utterly unexpected break through a familiar horizon of sound (and sometimes even form). Each time new resonances are awakened, new connections disclosed, I am made aware of the uses of imagination and its place in helping me penetrate the "world."

A great deal, of course, depends upon how much I can perceive in the work with which I am trying to engage. A peculiar kind of attentiveness is required to take heed of, say, the shapes and nuances and sounds in a Bergman film like *Fanny and Alexander* or in a ballet as well known as *Giselle*. The more I can perceive, the wider and more complex becomes the field over which my imagination can play; the more details there are to be integrated; the more richness and fecundity there may be to grasp, even (strangely) in a so-called "minimal" work like Barnett Newman's *Stations of the Cross*. Melvin Rader has written that, in witnessing *Hamlet* or *King Lear*, we cannot actually grasp the interplay between the motifs or appreciate the playing of characters against one another if, say, we identify ourselves with any single character. In some way, imagination must intervene, so that we allow those characters to have their full existence in an illusioned world. We must focus on them, take them as somehow self-contained in a world that is outside the actual, that is extraordinarily "real." "We linger," said Rader, "we savor and enjoy. We then elaborate the experience on the basis created by the tranquillizing and focusing of attention. The elaboration is a moody and imaginative mode of vision for the enrichment of the intrinsic perceptual value of the object" (1974, p. 136); and, I would add, for the enrichment of our experience in its depth and the opening of what lies beyond.

Aesthetic education offers opportunities to find such openings and such elaborations. It can do so by moving people to learn to know, to see, to hear more by exploring the languages and gestures out of which plays (as an example) are made; and by acquainting them with the range of conceivable interpretations and the choices that have to be made, with the craft demanded, and with the persistence of the unexpected, no matter how carefully a work is honed. Each time I realize how multiple are human languages and modalities for addressing the world, I recognize again how cheated we are and how subject to manipulation when no one helps us realize how many possibilities exist within our own experience living in the world.

A concern for imagination—and passion and possibility—ought not lead any of us to forget the links between the development of individual selves and the situation of society. There is some recognition, even among educators, that if one cuts the tie between consciousness and politics, one is left with an ideal of a self as realizable in private life alone. Confronting the significance of dialogue, of encounter, of live transaction within a school, we cannot but keep reaffirming the importance of overcoming the silences in the public spaces, the product language, and the technological rationality—all of which eat away at community. Indeed it takes imagination to bring people together in these times in speech and action, to provoke them to try to understand each other's perspectives, to tap into others' desires, even others' dreams. To me, one of the possibilities (one of the imaginative possibilities before us) is that of drawing diverse people together to project, to reach out towards a more humane and fulfilling order of things. The order ought to be many-faceted, formed in diverse ways, depending upon vantage point and biography; but, in the very exploring, in the very imagining, those who come together may come upon what is remediable. It may seem insupportable that there is no playground in the neighborhood, no day care center, no arts program. It may seem unacceptable that dislocated families are living in dangerous and inhumane hotels. It may come to seem wholly wrong that young people, alienated by talk of "rigor" and "high standards," drop out of schools that attempt indifferently to "normalize" the excluded and the poor. Perhaps, if imaginative possibilities are made dramatically visible, more people may act together to repair certain of the reparable deficiencies, to do something about the flaws. In so doing, they may create values in their own lives, make commitments that are new, invent ways of acting that may radiate through the community and beyond.

What happened to imagination? It has been discouraged by literalism, by complacency, by technical rationality, by obsessions with predictable results. But I believe that the work we do in our classrooms, in our clinics, still may remain open-ended in our encounter with continuing newcomers. It can still become an affair of beginnings, of thinking about what is not—and what eventually might be. They call to us—the artists, the prophets, the community organizers, the hard-working teachers—to break through the fixities of our age. They call to us to imagine—to look at things as if they truly could be otherwise.

REFERENCES

Arendt, H. (1961). *Between past and future*. New York: The Viking Press. (1958). *The human condition*. Chicago: University of Chicago Press.

Crane, H. (October 1926). *Poetry XXIX*.

Dewey, J. (1934). *Art as experience*. New York: Minton, Balch. (1916). *Democracy and education*. New York: Macmillan.

Marcuse, H. (1964). *One-dimensional man*. Boston: Beacon Press.

Mead, G. H. (1948). *Mind, self, and society*. Chicago: University of Chicago Press.

Rader, M. (Winter 1974). "The imaginative mode of awareness." *Journal of Aesthetics and Art Criticism*, *33*.

Rilke, R. M. (1934). *Letters to a young poet*. New York: Norton.

Schon, D. A. (1983). *The reflective practitioner*. New York: Basic Books.

Sizer, T. R. (1984). *Horace's compromise*. Boston: Houghton Mifflin.

Stevens, W. (1969). *Collected poems*. New York: Alfred A. Knopf.

Stevens, W. (1965). *The necessary angel*. New York: Vintage Books.

Thomas, L. (1975). *The lives of a cell*. New York: Viking Press.

Warnock, M. (1976). *Imagination*. Berkeley: University of California Press.

4 ◇ How the Graminivorous Ruminating Quadruped Jumped over the Moon: A Romantic Approach

JUNE STURROCK
Simon Fraser University, Canada

Industrial England's dark, satanic mills evidently cast their shadows over its writers. Industrialization and consequent urbanization, with their train of ugliness, suffering, and confinement for many, and great wealth for a few, provoked a rapid and intense reaction from English novelists and poets. "The rich have become richer, and the poor have become poorer," said Shelley in his *Defence of Poetry*, as a result of "the unmitigated exercise of the calculating faculty" (Reiman & Powers, 1977, p. 501). Like many other artists, he sought to redress the balance. The literary insistence during that era on the prime importance of the human imagination, and therefore on the educated imagination, springs partly from anger at these hard material facts and partly from a rejection of the intellectual fashions that accompanied these changes and were sometimes used as a justification for them. Growing materialism and acceptance of the scientific and empirical approach took many forms, including a desire for a total rationalization of all human concerns, from measurement to law. Legal reforms in post-revolutionary France, for instance, did indeed provide, in Blake's words, "one law for the lion and the ox" (Erdman, 1982, p. 44). Meanwhile, Jeremy Bentham was developing the doctrines of Utilitarianism, which treated even human happiness as a measurable commodity.

The fiercest reaction to the supreme rule of reason and the reduction of human energy into a matter of "man-hours" is perhaps Blake's in his prophetic books, with their certainty that "Vision or Imagination is a Representation of what externally exists" (Erdman, 1982, p. 554) and that "Energy is Eternal Delight" (Erdman, 1982, p.

34). For Blake, imagination was the essential part of the intellect, while reason, though necessary, was secondary. But Blake had no formal education, no children, nothing to force his attention on education. His views on imagination and education are implicit, while the views of his great contemporaries, Wordsworth and Coleridge, and his great successors, like Shelley, are quite evident and quite concrete, as were those of many of the great nineteenth century novelists, such as Charlotte Bronte, George Eliot, and especially Charles Dickens.

The following discussion arises partly from a concern with literature as a response to social and political events and conditions, but also from a strong sense of the lasting significance of the beliefs of those great Romantic writers, Wordsworth, Coleridge, and Dickens, for our own children, our own students, and indeed our own continuing growth in an age of a new industrial revolution. Indeed many modern writers on education, perhaps without being aware of it, echo the writings of their more entertaining predecessors. Mary Warnock in her book *Imagination* (1976, p. 202) concludes that "if we think of imagination as a part of our intelligence, universally, then we must be ready to admit that, like the rest of human intelligence, it needs educating." She reaches this conclusion through a discussion of the phenomenologists and Ryle, Sartre, and Wittgenstein, but comes back eventually to "where Wordsworth led us" (p. 194). Indeed Wordsworth returns again and again to the education of the intelligence and the feelings. Like Mary Warnock's book, this chapter is concerned with Wordsworth (and others) and with beliefs about the imagination and education, but it deals with the practical implications of such beliefs rather than their epistemological basis.

Indeed, "where Wordsworth led us" is into the human mind, "my haunt and the main region of my song," as he says himself (in the Preface to *The Excursion*). The subtitle of his great autobiographical poem, *The Prelude*, is after all *The Growth of a Poet's Mind*, while the group of poems that he called "Poems of the Imagination" all deal in some way with the mind's development or with modes of perception: the imagination working transformation. His concern for the education of the imagination lasted into his old age: When he was 75, he was still arguing that a child's prime intellectual needs were freedom for "intercourse with nature" and for "books of imagination which are eminently useful in calling forth intellectual power" (letter to H.S. Tremenheere, December 16, 1845).

His perception of these two needs was throughout his life the basis of his concept of intellectual freedom. But it is useful perhaps to look first at what he rejected in the educational theories that were current in his day and could be seen in schools organized on the Bell or Lancaster system.

Wordsworth felt a contemptuous pity for the intellectual and moral prodigy that such educationalists aimed at creating:

> This model of a child is never known
> To mix in quarrels; that were far beneath
> His dignity. . . .
> . . . .
> A miracle of scientific lore
> . . . .
> He knows the policies of foreign lands;
> Can string you names of districts, cities, and towns
> The whole world over . . . .
> . . . he sifts, he weighs;
> All things are put to question; he must live
> Seeing that he grows wiser everyday
> Or else not live at all, and seeing too
> Each little drop of wisdom as it falls
> Into the dimpling cistern of his heart:
> For this unnatural growth the trainer blame,
> Pity the tree. (*The Prelude*, V, ll. (298–329)

What Wordsworth deplores in such an education is the loss of freedom and spontaneity for such a carefully educated child, as well as the acute self-consciousness and self-centeredness of one who lives "within the pinfold of his own Conceit" (V, 336). The word "pinfold" is significant: The Romantic artist's concern with freedom appears in Wordsworth's work with particular force when he is writing about children, whether children in general, his own six children, or his own childhood, which, despite the early loss of his parents (his mother died when he was eight years old, his father when he was thirteen), he feels to have been ideal for the growth of the imagination because of his early freedom in a sublime landscape; he says he was "much favoured by my birthplace" (*The Prelude*, I, 303). He pictures his dead mother as a mother hen content to be at the center of her half-grown brood, leaving them free to "straggle from her presence" and return again. He blesses her lack of anxiety, which left him free to wander "through Vales/Rich with indigenous produce, open ground/Of fancy/ Happy pastures ranged at will" (*The Prelude*, V, 235–237), while the unfortunate little victim of the educational theorist is "stringed like a poor man's heifer at his feed."

Educational theories have changed, but over-anxiety remains.

The successors of the virtuous little prodigies are presumably the babies who are made to play with flash cards so that they can read when they are two years old. And it is not parents alone who become so enamored of nice tidy theories that they forget the untidy variety of human nature. Wordsworth fears that a child taught thus is robbed of childhood: One version of Book V of *The Prelude* includes the line, ''The child is lost, but see for recompense/The noontide shadow of a man complete'' (de Selincourt, 1959, p. 530). He differs strongly from Rousseau in this emphasis on the necessity of freedom, although the two writers are similar in their concern with childhood.

The freedom that Wordsworth prescribes for children is clearly both mental and physical. Presumably, the totally ignorant have a kind of mental freedom, but this is hardly what Wordsworth, who loved Euclid as well as Cervantes, would have advised, especially in a poem dedicated to the polymath Coleridge. Intellectual freedom for Wordsworth is the freedom of the imagination to roam, the freedom involved in self-forgetfulness, and the freedom given by the imagination's ability to apprehend and accept what the reason cannot grasp: His most serious poems are often attempts to communicate what is almost beyond the boundaries of rational discourse. The role of early contact with the grandeur or beauty of the natural world is emphasized throughout *The Prelude*, but when he talks of childhood education in more detail in Book V, he also makes great claims for the role of books—not encyclopedias or textbooks, but the old stories:

> O give us once again the wishing cap
> Of Fortunatus, and the invisible coat
> Of Jack the Giant-Killer, Robin Hood
> And Sabra in the forest with St. George!
> The child, whose love is here, at least doth reap
> One precious gain, that he forgets himself. (V, 341–346)

Wordsworth saw books as second only to nature (coupled in his later years with Biblical revelation) in their power of developing the child's understanding (*The Prelude*, V, 221–222). As an adult he still loved fantastic stories of magic and adventure, though by then, instead of reading ''Jack the Giant-Killer,'' he was reading Ariosto's *Orlando Furioso*, Spenser's *Faerie Queen*, and Tasso's *Gerusalemme Liberata*. He felt that such extraordinary romances enlarged the mind of child and adult alike. The storybooks of his childhood—and he speaks especially of his love for the Arabian Nights—helped rid him of some of the anxieties and strange terrors of childhood.

Like Bruno Bettelheim (1975, *passim*) 150 years later, Wordsworth wrote of the way that fairy tales enable children to deal with their feelings and their changing lives, and felt that fairy tales had prepared him for the terrors of real events. He wrote of his feelings when he saw a suicide fished up from the lake:

> A spectre shape
> Of terror, yet no soul-debasing fear,
> Young as I was, a child not nine years old,
> Possessed me, for my inner eye had seen
> Such sights before, among the shining streams
> Of fairyland, the forest of romance.
> Their spirit hallowed the sad spectacle
> With decoration of ideal grace. (V, 450–457)

He seemed to feel that the space, the strangeness, the exotic quality of fairy stories and romances—the potency of magic—all help the child to experience mental freedom despite the increasing limitations of human existence.

> Ye dreamers, then,
> Forgers of daring tales! We bless you then,
> Imposters, drivellers, dotards as the ape
> Philosophy will call you: *then* we feel
> With what, and how great might ye are in league,
> Who make our wish, our power, our thought a deed
> An empire, a possession,—ye whom time
> And seasons serve; all Faculties:—to whom
> Earth crouches, the elements are potter's clay,
> Space like a heaven filled up with northern lights,
> Here, nowhere, there, and everywhere at once. (V, 523–533)

The child, according to Wordsworth, needs the fantastic, the impossible, the unnecessary. Play is generally regarded as the proper activity of childhood: What education must do is give the child a sense of how ''play,'' in the sense of activity that is not necessary for survival, and a continuing need for the unnecessary will continue into adult life. Education's role in fitting children eventually to provide food and shelter for themselves is generally acknowledged; it must do more, though, for a fully human life must involve more than the gratification of animal needs.

Paradoxically, although Wordsworth thus recognizes the need for fantasy and romance, he was to a great degree the poet of the ordinary and an advocate of the ordinary. Wordsworth's sense of his poetic vocation and his confidence in his poetic gift filled him with a sense

of mission, a sense that it was his special task to revoluntionize poetry, to change radically the current poetic conventions, as they applied both to poetic diction and to poetic content. His Preface to the
Lyrical Ballads shows clearly his wish to use in poetry the language
of ordinary people rather than the conventional poetic diction of many
eighteenth-century poets, while the verse Prologue to *Peter Bell* is a
strong statement of his own wish to bring ordinary life into the realms
of the poetic and to transform humble and commonplace objects
through the light of the imagination:

> The common growth of mother-earth
> Suffices me—her tears, her mirth.
> Her humblest mirth and fears. (V, 132–135)

Wordsworth's love for the fantastic tales that he read both as a child
and as an adult was combined with an intense love for the ordinary.
He has often been satirized for this, both in his lifetime and after his
death, most successfully by Lewis Carroll, whose "aged, aged man a-
sitting on a gate" (in *Through the Looking-Glass*) is the first cousin of
Wordsworth's Leechgatherer. Although Wordsworth detested hostile
criticism of any kind, and knew that his "low" subject matter exposed him to jeers and misunderstanding, he never recanted on this
subject. He kept till the end of his life a sense that the ordinary can be
transformed by the imagination and that the poet's task is to show this.

More recently, Philip Larkin rejected a different poetic tradition—the magic and finery of Yeats and his successors—for a poetry
that, like photography, "records/dull days as dull, and hold-it smiles
as frauds/And will not censor blemishes/Like washing-lines." As the
poet Craig Raine said in an obituary of Larkin (*Guardian Weekly*, December 8, 1985, p. 5), "In Larkin's poetry, the prose and the passion
are not merely connected, they are inseparable, as they are for all of
us."

Both Larkin and Wordsworth in their different ways felt an urgent need to illuminate the ordinary, to tell a new truth. Of course, it
is a general human concern, so that good teachers and parents, too,
work for this sense of the transformation of the everyday, to ensure
that their children and students do not grow up virtually deaf and blind
and numbed to their ordinary experiences. Mary Warnock regards the
education of the imagination as essential in preventing feelings of the
pettiness and dreariness of ordinary life: The main purpose of education, she says, is "to give people the opportunity of not ever being, in
this sense, bored [that is, lacking the sense that there is more to experience and more in what we experience than we can predict]; of not
ever succumbing to a feeling of futility, or to the belief that they have

come to an end of what is worth having" (1976, p. 203). Wordsworth feels that without a developed imagination custom and habit can turn everyday experience into "a universe of death" (*The Prelude*, XIV, 160); he is voicing one of the universal concerns of the Romantic artist, the fear of the deadening effects of habit. Schiller's *Ode to Joy*, for instance, celebrates the magical power of joy to bring together what custom has divided; for Coleridge too (in *Dejection, An Ode*, stanza IV), joy alone has the power to transform "that inanimate cold world allowed/To the poor loveless ever-anxious crowd." (Coleridge, 1912, p. 365). For Shelley, it is poetry that "strips the veil of familiarity from the world, and lays bare the naked and sleeping beauty, which is the spirit of its forms" (Reiman & Powers, 1977, p. 505). Whatever it is named, it is the mind's creative power that transforms the object of perception. The imagination, seen thus, is salvation: Those who can live in its light "need not extraordinary calls/To rouse them; in a world of life they live" (*The Prelude*, XIV, 104–105).

This is a high claim, but Wordsworth sees entry into the world of life not only as a matter of "a leading from above, a something given" (de Selincourt, 1949, Vol. II, p. 237), but as something that can be either barred or opened by early experience, and thus by parents and teachers. For example, some of the ways in which adults can encourage children to retain their clarity of vision are demonstrated in an account of the transformation of village school life given in Sybil Marshall's *An Experiment in Education*. Her experiment began with a new stress on the visual arts, to bring the children a clear awareness of their surroundings: "To begin on a purely practical level, the attempt to reproduce any well known object has the effect of making the child look closer, of training 'the seeing eye' " (1970, p. 114). The extraordinary and the ordinary should work together to enlarge and deepen the child's mind. The "seeing eye" is what eventually gives life to what Wordsworth calls "that inward eye/Which is the bliss of solitude" (de Selincourt, 1949, Vol. II, p. 217).

Despite Wordsworth's high claims for the nature of childhood experience, he should not be seen as idealizing childhood. He is realistic enough about chidren's notions of pleasure ("vulgar joy" he calls it), such as playing card games, skating, gathering nuts, birdsnesting, rowing, imitating birdcalls, and so on, but he sees these pleasures as leading the child unawares into higher and more lasting pleasures. The "Boy of Winander," who imitates the owl's cry and makes owls and echoes answer him, experiences a sudden silence:

> Then sometimes in that silence while he hung
> Listening, a gentle shock of mild surprise
> Has carried far into his heart the voice

Of mountain torrents; or the visible scene
Would enter unawares into his mind,
With all its solemn imagery, its rocks,
Its woods, and that uncertain heaven, received
Into the bosom of the steady lake. (V, 281–288)

(Coleridge [de Selincourt, 1959, p. 530] said of these last two lines that he would have recognized them as Wordsworth's if he had met them in the Arabain desert). In the next line, the Boy of Winander is dead before the age of 12, so this education of the imagination has led to nothing; except that this seems to be part of Wordsworth's point, that experience should not be sought for what it may lead to, but enjoyed as a thing in itself and not as a means to something else. For in a way, all human learning, all human enterprise, is wasted in the grave. Although Keats saw Wordworth's poetry as tending too much to have "a palpable design on us" (letter to J. H. Reynolds, February 3, 1818), in fact, Wordsworth was like Coleridge in wishing to avoid crude moralizing. This is another reason why he deplored the prim and edifying tales that at this period were seen as "suitable for children."

During the most richly fertile years of their lives, the thought of Wordsworth and Coleridge was strongly related. Wordsworth writes of Coleridge and himself as "Twins almost in genius and in mind," "Predestin'd, if two Beings ever were/To seek the same delights and have one health/One happiness." Warnock (1976, p. 118) indicates how close they were then in their beliefs about the active power of the mind, their belief that "there is creation in the eye/Not less than in the other senses." Their more specific ideas about education are also very close; Coleridge, too, believed in the value of fairy tales and wrote to Thomas Poole (October 16, 1797): "I know no other way of giving the mind a love of the Great and the Whole" (Katzin, 1972, p. 13).

On the individual level, they apparently shared the view that Wordsworth's childhood was the more blessed in its freedom in nature, while Coleridge as a pupil of Christ's Hospital was shut up in dreary London with only the sky and his own wild imagination providing him with the freedom he needed. They also shared the feeling that Coleridge's unfortunate confinement had been harmful to his overexcitable mind, which was according to Wordsworth "the self-created sustenance of a mood/Debarred from Nature's living images/Compelled to be a life unto itself/And unrelentingly possessed by thirst/Of greatness love and beauty" (*The Prelude*, VI, 311–316). Coleridge, feeling that his long years of urban confinement were unhappy and uncreative, desired for his own children an education more like

Wordsworth's. In *Frost at Midnight*, addressing his infant son, Hartley, cradled by his side, Coleridge wrote:

> For I was reared
> In the great city, pent 'mid cloisters dim,
> And saw naught lovely but the sky and stars.
> But thou my babe! shalt wander like a breeze
> By lakes and sandy shores, beneath the crags
> Of ancient mountains, and beneath the clouds,
> Which image in their bulk both lakes and shores
> And mountain crags: so shalt thou see and hear
> The lovely shapes and sounds intelligible
> Of that eternal language which thy God
> Utters who from eternity doth teach
> Himself in all, and all things in himself
> Great Universal Teacher! he shall mould
> Thy spirit and by giving make it ask." (1912, p. 242)

Hartley Coleridge grew up to be the kind of man generally described
as nobody's enemy but his own, but giving did make his spirit "ask":
He found the beauty he was reared in necessary to him and made his
home among the lakes and mountains, watched over by the Wordsworth family and drinking himself silly every two or three months
(Moorman, 1968, pp. 426–427).

Coleridge's Berkeleian belief in the experience of the natural
world as the language of God is close in many ways to Wordsworth's
"Wisdom and Spirit of the Universe," which guides the child allowed
to run free in a natural environment. Few professional educators in
Western society have been able to put this aspect of Wordsworth's
teaching on imagination into practice. Some privileged parents, however, can provide a similar freedom: Even miles away from lakes and
mountains the child can still be given the freedom of unorganized time
in an unorganized environment. The child may lack contact with "visions of the hills" but can inhabit a nonhuman world that extends
mental boundaries and can be enthralled by ants busy on a piece of
broken concrete as well as streams rushing down a mountainside.
Many nineteenth-century thinkers saw the value to young children of
"groping in the dirt," that is, making mud pies; this is partly why such
reformers as Octavia Hill fought to save every scrap of wasteland in
London for the people of London, a battle that continues to be fought
and continues to be worth fighting. In schools, art classes can have a
similar function insofar as they give the child freedom to ruminate and
digest the ideas, facts, and feelings implanted in other lessons.

Wordsworth wrote disparagingly of Dickens as "that Man" and considered his immense popularity as a possible reason for the decline in book sales in the 1840s (letter to Edward Moxon, April 1842). Dickens, unlike Wordsworth, was certainly very much an urban creature, and his popularity is surely based partly on his Londoner's sense of the rich and prolific muddle of city life. Yet Dickens in his different way shared in Wordsworth's profound concern with the education of the imagination. Although he was largely indifferent to nature, being essentially an urban creature, he shared Wordsworth's views on literature for children as well as Coleridge's bitter feeling of educational deprivation. Dickens' deprivation would probably be more universally recognized as such. His humiliation at being sent out to work in a shoeblacking warehouse at the age of ten was intense: "No words can express the secret agony of my soul," he wrote (Johnson, 1952, p. 34). The shame lasted into his adult life: Despite his extraordinary success and his extraordinary genius, he felt the need to hide that episode from all but his wife and his close friend (and later biographer) Forster. But *David Copperfield* records the misery of the experience, the strong feeling of anger at being deprived of an education, the sense of yearning for both knowledge and status.

Perhaps his own suffering is one reason for Dickens' anger at the multiple educational abuses of his England, abuse sometimes of the body (most notably at Dotheboys Hall), but more often of the growing imagination. As suggested earlier, the Romantic artist was compelled by anger at extending rules, weight, and measure outside the laboratory and the market-place: "Bring out number, weight & measure in a year of dearth," wrote Blake (Erdman, 1982, p. 36), while Wordsworth expressed contempt for an education in which the child is taught "to sift, to weigh, to question all things" (*The Prelude*, V, 322–323). Dickens portrayed the result of such an upbringing in Arthur Clennam of *Little Dorrit*, a good but somehow enfeebled man, whose passions had been dispersed and vitiated: He was, significantly, "the only child of parents who weighed, measured and priced everything." Different though they were, these Romantic writers were united in this belief that the scientific or materialistic approach is inappropriate to many human concerns. This does not imply that they thought that the scientific or materialistic approach had no value in education, or that disciplined work was inessential. Dickens, at least, knew at first hand the value of tolerating boredom. Like David Copperfield, he spent hours painfully acquiring the perfect shorthand that made him such an excellent parliamentary reporter and led him into his writing career. He knew that perseverance through occasional boredom is essential

to many of the more intense human pleasures: How else would anyone be able to love opera or to stay married?

Of course, Dickens' longest and most detailed account of the
over-rational approach to education is *Hard Times*. His subject is the
human suffering of the wretched industrial cities of the north and
the midlands of England as epitomized in his "Coketown," but he was
concerned to trace roots as well as branches, which explains his concern with education throughout this novel. He writes of middle class
education in such cities as being just as destructive and inhuman as
working class education: The mill-owner's children, Tom and Louisa
Gradgrind, are as starved of food for their imagination as are
M'Chaokumchild's unfortunate working class pupils. The words of
their father, the elder Thomas Gradgrind, open the novel, exposing
immediately the root of much of the human suffering and human waste
portrayed in a novel that nowadays might easily be interpreted as
springing largely from Dickens' love of the grotesque and the exag-
gerated, but that actually had a solidly factual foundation in the schools
of industrial towns. Those schools were run on the Lancaster system,
by which a thousand children at a time were taught by rote, super-
vised by monitors (Craig, 1969, p. 23). Thomas Gradgrind's opening
words are like a banner inscribed with the Coketown philosophy:

> Now, what I want is, Facts. Teach these boys nothing but Facts. Facts
> alone are wanted in life. Plant nothing else and root out everything else.
> You can only form the minds of reasoning animals upon facts: nothing
> else will ever by of any service to them. This is the principle on which
> I bring up my own children, and this is the principle on which I bring up
> these children. Stick to facts, Sir.

The results of such early teaching are shown in the novel to be
disastrous, especially to Gradgrind's own children. Louisa Gradgrind,
who knows almost nothing of the human heart because she has been
educated in statistics rather than in literature or history, marries for
her brother's sake a man whom she has always disliked and comes to
hate, and almost drifts into adultery. At this point Dickens is surpris-
ingly close to Jane Austen in *Mansfield Park*: Maria Rushworth, who
has been expensively educated and could list before the age of ten the
Kings of England, the Roman emperors, and all the metals, semi-
metals, planets, and distinguished philosophers, marries a man she
despises and in a few months runs away with another man. Although
Jane Austen is often regarded as an anti-Romantic contemporary of the
Romantics, her view of education is similar to theirs: Like Words-

worth, she abhors an education that never disturbs the student's complacency. And like Jane Austen, who compares Maria with her poor relation Fanny Price, who has through force of circumstances acquired humility and a knowledge of her own heart, Dickens implicitly compares Louisa with Sissy Jupe, the poor circus girl, who has experienced the importance of love and who comes too late to the school of facts to acquire its deadly approach to life. The difference is that Jane Austen is primarily concerned with the way a defective upbringing affects the individual and the family, whereas Dickens is concerned both with the individual and with society as a whole. His canvas is large, not the "little bit of ivory" on which Jane Austen half-ironically claimed to work.

Dickens sees a stunted imagination as even more destructive socially than it is individually. Through the development of Louisa's understanding and character, he is able to show how the inhuman working conditions of industrial towns were perpetuated. Louisa, though she is the daughter of a factory owner, is a married woman when she first goes into the house of a factory hand, and she is distressed and shaken by the encounter with an existence so very different from her own. Her education had encouraged her to think of poor people as statistics rather than as suffering human beings. Her father and her husband had taught her to think of the millhands as they did:

> Something to be worked so much and paid so much . . . . Something that increased at such a rate of percentage . . . something wholesale of which vast fortunes were made; something that rose like a sea and did some harm and waste (chiefly to itself) and fell again; this she knew the Coketown hands to be. But she scarcely thought more of separating them into units, than of separating the sea itself into component drops. (Craig, 1969, p. 188)

Dickens here clearly demonstrates what Shelley had argued, that a disproportionate "cultivation of the mechanic arts" at the expense of the "creative faculty" aggravated "the inequality of man" (*Defence*, p. 503): They both realized that a certain kind of education leads to social evils. The mill-owning class cannot imagine the workers as human beings, because they cannot imagine. The kind of education they support encourages people to think of others merely as economic statistics and not to imagine or investigate their real feelings and real difficulties.

Such blindness to the reality of other people's lives and suffering survived the nineteenth century: It enables, for instance, Canadian tobacco farmers to ask their government to set up a tobacco marketing board, saying of the health risk, "People are going to die anyway. So what's the difference if you die younger?" (*The Globe and Mail*, December 10, 1985). This surely arises from defective imagination, not from defective reason. The star pupil of Gradgrind's school, the albino Bitzer, is equally heartless, having learned so thoroughly the lesson that "every inch of the existence of mankind, from birth to death, was to be a bargain across a counter," that for the sake of the reward he is prepared to stop Tom Gradgrind, the son of his former patron, for theft. Dickens presents this betrayal as being poetic justice, for he has shown Mr. Gradgrind busy proving that "the Good Samaritan was a Bad Economist" (p. 238).

In *Hard Times*, Dickens writes of the imagination as a vital part of the intellect that must be educated and that needs food, or fuel. He repeatedly suggests that the "fancy" cannot be totally suppressed, and that if it is neglected and unrecognized it will become corrupted and destructive. M'Choakumchild at work in his classroom cramming each child with facts so as to kill the fancy in each little mind is compared with Morgiana (in the story of Ali Baba) pouring boiling oil into the 40 jars that held the 40 thieves. Dickens suggests, however, that "the robber Fancy" will not always be killed, but rather will be maimed and distorted (Craig, 1969, p. 53). In the case of Tom Gradgrind, his murdered but ghostly fancy leads him into crime and debauchery: He is described as "a young gentleman whose imagination had been strangled in its cradle," but nevertheless he is haunted by "its ghost in the form of grovelling sensualities" (p. 165). Again and again in *Hard Times* and frequently in other novels, Dickens repeats the assertion that the fancy is a necessary part of the human psyche, needing wholesome food, and that in nineteenth-century industrial England it was too often more than half starved. He asks with rather heavy irony whether it is possible "that there was any Fancy in [the workers] demanding to be brought into healthy existence instead of struggling in convulsions" (Craig, p. 67). He writes of the need of the workers of Coketown for play, of their craving for "some relaxation encouraging good humour and good spirits and giving them a rest" and asserts bluntly that this craving "must and would be satisfied right, or must and would inevitably go wrong until the laws of the creation were repealed" (p. 68). Wordsworth proclaims an identical belief in the need to acknowledge and nourish the human imagination: "Dumb yearnings, hidden appetites are ours/And they *must* have their food" (*The Prelude*, V, 506–507). The emphasis is not mine, but that of the older Wordsworth.

Dickens is occasionally startlingly close to Blake, too, in his belief that a proper use of reason depends upon a properly educated imagination, that reason is properly a part of the human intellect and not the whole of it. Dickens uses very Blakean language when he writes that Louisa would have been far happier if her education had been more balanced, if

> first coming upon Reason through the tender light of Fancy, she had seen it as a beneficient god, deferring to gods as great as itself: not a grim idol, cruel and cold, with its victims bound hand to foot, and its big dumb shape set up with a sightless stare, never to be moved by anything but so many calculated tons of leverage . . . . Her remembrances of home and childhood, were remembrances of the drying up of every spring and fountain in her young heart as it gushed out. (p. 223)

Dickens' remedy for this aridity is much like Wordsworth's. Wordsworth suggested Fortunatus and Sabra and the Arabian Nights, while Dickens regarded Thom Thumb and the Man in the Moon as the essential ingredient so disastrously lacking in the education of the little Gradgrinds. Although Sissy Jupe, the circus girl, had read about the fairies, they were forbidden to Louisa and Tom:

> No little Gradgrind had ever seen a face in the moon . . . . No little Gradgrind had ever learnt the silly jingle, Twinkle, twinkle little star; how I wonder what you are! No little Gradgrind had ever known wonder on the subject, each little Gradgrind having at five years old dissected the Great Bear . . . . No little Gradgrind had ever associated a cow in a field with that famous cow with the crumpled horn . . . or with that yet more famous cow who swallowed Tom Thumb: it had never heard of these celebrities, and had only been introduced to a cow as a graminivorous ruminating quadruped with several stomachs. (p. 54)

Philip Collins in *Dickens and Education* (1963) points out Dickens' distaste for the Benthamite approach to education. Certainly he sets up as a counterbalance to the utilitarian beliefs of the Gradgrinds and Bounderby the least utilitarian of human institutions—the circus. It is Mr. Sleary, the proprietor of the circus, who speaks (lispingly) the proper language of humanity and unquestioningly shelters Tom Gradgrind when his father's protegé would have turned him over to the police. Sleary believes "that there ith a love in the world, not all Thelf-interest after all but something very different" (p. 308). And it is the child of the circus, Sissy Jupe, who brings comfort to the Gradgrinds in their misery and humiliation. Like his great predecessors, like Shakespeare as well as Wordsworth, Dickens understands that what is apparently useless and frivolous can be what is most profoundly needed, that play is as vital as work.

Human beings thirst for what is not necessary, for play, as much as they thirst for water: A child who is shut up for hours in a car or plane and then released clearly craves unorganized play as much as food or drink. The need for the apparently unnecessary is part of the human condition.

> O, reason not the need! Our basest beggars
> Are in the poorest thing superfluous.
> Allow not nature more than nature needs,
> Man's life's as cheap as beast's. (*King Lear*, II, 4, 259–262)

The craving for the pretentious, the extraordinary, the redundant, and the rococo may take the form of dreams of the top of Mount Everest or playing the scherzo so fast that the orchestra can't keep up: or else *Dynasty* and *Life Styles of the Rich and Famous*. For although a properly exercised imagination may liberate from what Iris Murdoch calls fantasy (that self-aggrandizing, self-justifying mutter at the back of one's mind), a weakened and starved imagination will fatten on second-hand and second-rate fantasies.

In *Hard Times*, the exercise of the childish fancy is shown as eventually providing a possible foundation for a mature faith:

> The dreams of childhood—its airy fables; its graceful, beautiful, humane, impossible adornments of the world beyond: so good to be believed in once, so good to be remembered when outgrown, for then the least among them rises to the stature of a great Charity in the heart, suffering little children to come in the midst of it. (p. 223)

A different kind of remedy for the social and personal ills caused by undervaluing the role of the imagination is also suggested by *Hard Times*. While children need fairy stories and nursery rhymes and their parents need Defoe and Goldsmith (p. 90), their teachers need a very different kind of teacher training. In 1854, when *Hard Times* was first published, teacher-training colleges were very new: In fact, the first group of students were sent out into the schools in 1853 (Craig, 1969, pp. 319–320), and Dickens was certainly not alone in his criticisms of this new brand of teachers. He suggested that like their little pupils, they had been robbed of their human individuality and spontaneity by their education. They served factory owners and taught the young of factory workers as the products of a factory.

> M'Choakumchild . . . and some one hundred and forty other school masters, had been lately turned at the same time, in the same factory, on the same principles, like so many painoforte legs—Orthography,

etymology, syntax, and prosody, biography, astronomy, geography and general cosmography, the sciences of compound proportion, algebra, land-surveying and levelling, vocal music and drawing from models, were all at the end of his ten chilled fingers . . . . If he had only learnt a little less, how infinitely better he might have taught much more. (p. 53)

Philip Collins points out (1963, p. 144) that M'Choakumchild is not evil like Wackford Squeers, but full of good intentions, as is Dr. Blimber of *Dombey and Son*; nevertheless their teaching is deadly— literally so in the case of Dr. Blimber and little Paul Dombey. Their teaching ignores the complexities and realities of human nature. Dickens expressed a similar view of the kind of education provided in the great public schools of his day. When Richard Carstone of *Bleak House* leaves Winchester, he is highly skilled at making Greek and Latin verses but has no idea about his own particular bent. Esther Summerson as narrator voices Dickens' own feelings: "I did doubt whether Richard would not have profited by someone studying him a little instead of him studying them [the classics] so much" (Page, 1971, p. 218). Richard, of course, drifts from profession to profession, lacking all real sense of his own identity. Dickens, despite a liking for strict order, which must have made him an uncomfortable father and husband, was profoundly interested in the individual and, as a good (if latish) Romantic, in the spontaneous. Inevitably he was angry at the abuses of theories that encouraged uniformity and suppressed vitality.

As Philip Collins says (1963, p. 77), Dickens' most vigorous writing tends to come out of anger and relish of his own anger, and certainly his awful schools and teachers are much more fully imagined than, say, Dr. Strong's good school in *David Copperfield*. But if he is weak in presenting positive images in education, and, indeed, if Mary Warnock's final chapter, applying her excellent detailed historical discussion to present day needs, seems to scamper to a very generalized conclusion (more or less that "imagination needs education"), it is perhaps hardly surprising. Inevitably, the Romantic view of education stresses the need for freedom and spontaneity, and sees education as an interaction between individuals. It is not easy to prescribe for countless individuals. Organizations and institutions always tend to ossify, and yet they must be flexible enough to provide freedom for individual students and teachers.

It is there, probably, that the most serious problem lies, because the urbanization that had begun before Wordsworth's days and was well-established by the time Dickens began to write has by now turned our cities into anthills manageable only by standardization—or so the administrators would argue: The computer, one hears in the bank, the registrar's office, or the department store, will not allow for individual cases. All the same, teachers must adjust their curriculum enough to ensure that their students' differences are acknowledged, so that, for instance, a child capable of reading many adult books is not obligated to answer the imbecile "comprehension questions" in a reader consisting almost entirely of simple and compound sentences. This is obvious: The child's need to be treated as an individual is generally acknowledged.

Fewer people, however, pay even lip service to the corollary of this statement, which is that educators (parents, teachers, teachers of teachers) also need to recognize and use their own individuality. Conscientious people and people concerned with matters of conscience alike tend to treat good as if it were a matter of observing a code, both of prescriptions and prohibitions. A good mother, for instance, does not beat her child; a good mother provides a varied diet. True enough; but good is also a matter of recognizing and using one's own particular sources of energy. To this I would add that a good mother continues to be what she was: The good that children get out of their education is often brought to life by the warmth of a parent's or teacher's spontaneous delight or enthusiasm. While a good teacher refrains from bullying a child, it is not refraining that makes a good teacher, but involvement in whatever is taught. *An Experiment in Education* (1970), for instance, records Sybil Marshall's extraordinary success in teaching children through the visual arts; her own educated delight in painting, not just her conscientious concern with her duty as a teacher, is what fostered the growth of these village children. Dickens' M'Choakumchild is a bad teacher because he is in the business of mass-production both as product and as producer. And the pattern child that Wordsworth described is pitiable just because he is a *pattern* child.

Dickens' relish of his own sincere anger at the general but varied failure of education in nineteenth-century England certainly does not indicate a belief that no education is better than a bad education. He knew perfectly well the dangers of ignorance: One reason why Jo, the crossing sweeper in *Bleak House*, is made a repulsive as well as a pathetic spectacle is that the boy, as he himself says, "knows nothing." In *Hard Times*, too, Dickens writes that the respect the illiterate workers showed to a printed placard would have been ludicrous "if any aspect of public ignorance could ever be otherwise than threatening and full of evil" (p. 267). Although *A Christmas Carol* has become part of the picturesque seasonal clutter, like poinsettias and the Sugar Plum Fairy, it too was written out of anger, and one of its darkest moments is when the spirit of Christmas Present produces from beneath his

cloak two dirty emaciated children, the girl Want and the boy Ignorance. It is the boy whom Dickens sees as the darkest threat: "Most
of all beware this boy, for on his brow I see that written which is
doom." Perhaps he would still see the boy as a dark threat, although
he might now be portrayed as being rosy, well-fed, carefully dressed,
and beaming with complacency.

The perception that most students in the 1980s fit into the pattern just described and are interested only in good grades is widespread enough to have become the subject of a *Doonesbury* comic strip
(January 19, 1986). Even allowing for exaggeration, this perception is
saddening. But some other aspects of the failure of imagination are
worse than saddening.

Wordsworth (never afraid of seeming a bore) tells in *The Prelude*
(Book V) of a dream that embodied his fears concerning the destruction of the works of the human intellect and imagination because of the
frailty of books. He sleeps on the seashore and dreams of an Arab (who
is also, after the nature of dreams, Don Quixote) riding along carrying
a stone and a shell, which the dreamer knows to represent Euclid and
poetry; he is saving them from destruction by the coming flood. The
dreamer awakens to hear the roar of the tide coming in. Many people
are haunted now by fears of a cataclysm, fears that spring from a
drearier reality than the roar of the sea. I have sometimes been
ashamed of my concern that our destructive capacity not only could
kill my children and all children, but could thereby kill, say, Little Red
Riding Hood: It would be a relief to dream of a Quixote carrying a
stone and a shell. Perhaps the education of the imagination—"in which
our present systems of education fail, where they do fail," says Mary
Warnock (p. 9)—is now more urgent than ever because the human
imagination could perhaps prevent the destruction of all the works of
human imagination and all their potential creators.

REFERENCES

Bettelheim, B. (1975). *The uses of enchantment: The meaning and importance of fairy tales*. New York: Random House.
Coleridge, E.H. (Ed.). (1912). *The Complete Poetical Works of Samuel Taylor Coleridge*. Oxford: Clarendon Press.
Collins, P. (1963). *Dickens and education*. London: Macmillan.
Craig, D. (Ed.). (1969). *Hard times* by Charles Dickens. Harmondsworth,
Middlesex: Penguin Books.
de Selincourt, E. (Ed.). (1939). *The letters of William and Dorothy Wordsworth: The later years, 1841–1850*, Vol. III. Oxford: Clarendon Press.

de Selincourt, E., and Darbishire, H. (Eds.). (1949). *The poetical works of William Wordsworth*, 5 vols. Oxford: Clarendon Press.

de Selincourt, E. (Ed.). (1959). *William Wordsworth's "The Prelude,"* 2nd Ed. Oxford: Clarendon Press.

Erdman, D.V. (Ed.). (1982). *The Complete Poetry and Prose of William Blake*. Berkeley: University of California Press.

Johnson, E. (1952). *Charles Dickens: His tragedy and triumph*. Boston: Little, Brown & Co.

Katzin, M. (1972). *Dickens and the fairy tale*. Bowling Green, OH.: Bowling Green Popular Press.

Marshall, S. (1970). *An experiment in education*. Cambridge: Cambridge University Press.

Moorman, M. (1968). *William Wordsworth, A biography: The later years, 1803–1850*. Oxford: Oxford University Press.

Page, N. (Ed.). (1971). *Bleak house* by Charles Dickens. Harmondsworth, Middlesex: Penguin Books.

Raine, Craig (December 8, 1985). *Guardian Weekly*. London.

Reiman, D.H. and Powers, S.B. (Eds.). (1977). *Shelley's Poetry and Prose: Authoritative Texts and Criticism*. New York: W.W. Norton & Co.

Trilling, L. (Ed.). (1951). *The Selected Letters of John Keats*. New York: Farrar Straus & Young.

Warnock, M. (1976). *Imagination*. London: Faber & Faber.

PART II

Imagination
in
Education

5 ◇ Some Observations on the Concept of Imagination

ROBIN BARROW
Simon Fraser University, Canada

I shall argue that the fostering of imagination in students is an important aspect of a satisfactory education and that imagination is a quality that can be purposively developed only indirectly, as a result of teaching certain kinds of curriculum subjects in a particular kind of way. I shall also argue that imagination is by no means exclusively a concern of the arts, still less the specifically creative, plastic, or visual arts. However, the core of this chapter consists of an attempt at a basic analysis of the concept of imagination, since educational claims are often made about imagination without it being very clear exactly what imagination is supposed to be. Also, the concept of imagination has had little direct attention from analytic philosophers.

I have already referred to imagination as if it were some kind of tangible or otherwise locatable entity. This, of course, is not unusual. Everyday language tends to refer to the imagination as if it were some kind of mental organ, akin to physical organs such as the liver and heart, just as it refers to other mental concepts such as intelligence and creativity. Not so long ago, what was known as faculty psychology reinforced and lent academic respectability to the notion of mental concepts as the names of parts of the brain. On the other hand, nearly 40 years ago Gilbert Ryle (1949) argued persuasively against any such view. He maintained that intelligence, creativity, imagination, and so forth were not in any way the names of entities, but abstract nouns dependent upon the adverbial labels we apply to people insofar as they perform various mental acts in a certain kind of way. One does not literally possess intelligence, or have a center of intelligence, as muscular people are so called because they have muscles; rather, intelligence is attributed to people insofar as they act or think in an intelligent manner. There is no part of the brain that is the intelligence.

It is probably fair to say that faculty psychology, in the crude sense referred to, is no longer fashionable. However, Ryle himself has not been without critics, and the idea that intelligent or imaginative people have some particular kind of element in their brain, be it physical, neurological, chemical, or whatever, dies hard. Furthermore, some may feel that more recent research into such matters as the distinction between the two hemispheres of the brain rather weakens Ryle's thesis (e.g., Gardner, 1983).

I do not myself believe that it does. One may well accept (indeed it would be difficult not to do so) that there is a physiological or neurological base to the various mental concepts, such that the state of the brain sets necessary conditions on the display of intelligence, creativity, or imagination, without relinquishing the thesis that the names of mental concepts are not in any way the names of parts of the human brain. Granted that brain damage of various sorts can destroy the possibility of an individual being imaginative, intelligent, and so on and granted that one side of the brain rather than the other is associated with an individual's capacity for, say, visual imagination, it does not follow that to be imaginative is the same thing as to have a certain part of the brain in good working order so that the imagination can be identified with that part of the brain. I am not aware of any research that either does or could claim to establish that, in cases where there is no obvious brain damage or deficiency, the differences between people's imaginative, intellectual, or creative powers are due to the state of their brain, as opposed to such factors as their understanding, experience, and education.

I shall therefore assume in what follows that, notwithstanding the importance of research into the functioning of the brain, the essence of what we call the imagination does not lie there. Whereas ensuring a healthy bodily organ such as the liver demands adopting a certain regimen for the liver, and coping with a malfunctioning liver requires action directed to the liver (in the extreme case replacing it), ensuring a healthy imagination or improving a defective imagination does not involve taking any action in relation to the imagination, for there is no such entity. In the final analysis, we judge a sound, undiseased heart by examining the heart, but we do not judge people's imagination by looking inside their heads, nor could we. For to be imaginative is not to have a brain, or part thereof, constituted in a certain way. As a matter of fact, people generally display imagination to varying degrees in various contexts, and to refer to someone with a well-developed visual imagination or a sharp historical imagination is to talk about the manner of their visualizing or historical understanding rather than about some organ in the brain.

Etymologically, "imagination" derives from the Latin word *imago*, meaning an image or representation. This root meaning is preserved in our use of the verb *to imagine*. "I imagine you now, enjoying yourself in France"; "She imagined having to live with him for the rest of her life"; "Imagine that you are shipwrecked on a desert island." These, and similar examples, imply no more than that the person in question is or should conceive of, visualize, conjure up, or think of some particular set of circumstances. The noun *imagination* is sometimes used in a similar way to refer only to the capacity to conceive of what is not actually happening here and now, as when we say that imagination is one characteristic that distinguishes humans from some other forms of animal life. However, the noun sometimes, and the adjectival form *imaginative* almost always, are normative terms and imply a great deal more than neutral references to the capacity to engage in abstract representations in one way or another. The claim that human beings have imagination while shrimps do not, does not imply that all humans are particularly or equally imaginative in the normative sense. The claim that Smith has imagination or that Jones is imaginative is usually an instance of praise, and clearly refers to the superior quality of the abstract representation engaged in by Smith or Jones. The crucial question is in virtue of what do we regard some people as more imaginative than others in this normative sense? What criteria must my attempts to conceive of what is not immediately present meet, to allow me to earn the honorific label "imaginative"?

Before proceeding to answer that question directly, a possible complication must be considered. That is that there may be a number of quite different meanings of "imagination" currently in vogue. It seems to me quite certain that this is the case. Some people appear to use the word as a synonym for "sensitive," others for "creative," "inventive," "reflective," and so on. This in itself need not be a problem, though for practical purposes of communication it is important that individuals should be explicit about what they mean on any given occasion. In trying to give a more detailed account of a particular sense of a word or a particular conception, which is philosophy's task, we may sometimes be uncertain whether a certain criterion is a necessary part of the conception under analysis, or an indication of a different conception. Such a problem faces us, I think, with the criterion of what I shall term the "whimsical" in respect of imagination.[1]

---

[1] Patrick Keeney has pointed out to me that the term "whimsicality" is at least as obscure as "imagination," and that I have made no direct attempt to explain fully what I mean by it. However, it is, I believe, sufficient for my purposes here to indicate, as I

In one sense, one might reasonably claim that certain writers who are concerned predominantly with depicting realistic emotions, situations, and characters, albeit in a fictional mode, such as, say, Tolstoy, Graham Green, and William Trevor, are not necessarily any more or less imaginative than those writers who create fantasy worlds and characters, such as Tolkein, C. S. Lewis, or A. A. Milne. (Children's literature obviously provides many examples of the latter kind, but novelists such as Iris Murdoch and Vladimir Nabokov also resort to such fantasy, magic, or what I am calling whimsicality.) On the other hand, some might be inclined to argue that whimsicality is a necessary condition of truly imaginative writing, and that Tolkien should be distinguished from Tolstoy as an imaginative writer, precisely because he is not realistic in the way that the latter is; he is a teller of tales, as opposed to a novelist, one might say, and what we mean by an imaginative writer is a teller of tales who meanders into fantasy, just as we might distinguish between imaginative and nonimaginative painters, thinkers, or potters by reference to the fairy-tale quality of their work.

This would seem to me to be a mistake. No doubt many storytellers, in this sense, constitute excellent and obvious examples of imaginative writers, which is to say that whimsicality can be a very obvious sign of imagination. But the display of whimsicality is surely only one form of displaying imagination, and indeed whimsical writers are not necessarily to be judged particularly imaginative. Some children's literature, for example, though certainly whimsical, could be criticized precisely for not being particularly imaginative. Similarly, although science fiction might be classified as an essentially imaginative genre, as contrasted with, say, history, to do so would be to use the word *imaginative* in the neutral sense of imaginary, as opposed to actual or real. But that is not what we mean, when we are concerned with the normative sense of imaginative, referring to the quality of abstract conception. Some science fiction is not very imaginative in this sense, while some history is. I conclude, therefore, that while it is true that to imagine is at bottom simply to conceive of, and while the imaginary is indeed to be contrasted with the real or actual, the essence of being imaginative in the normative sense does not lie either in one's tendency to think the abstract or in one's preoccupation with imaginary beings and worlds, but in the quality of one's conceiving,

---

do in the text, that "whimsicality" broadly refers to the fantasy element in writers such as Tolkien and Nabokov, in contrast to the realism of a Greene or Tolstoy. Certainly, ideas such as realism, fantasy, and whimsicality require further analysis. But here I am concerned only with making it clear that what is loosely referred to as "whimsicality" is not, in my view, a defining characteristic of imaginative writing.

whether about real or imaginary situations. We thus return to the question: What are the qualitative criteria of imaginative conception?

It has already been observed that people may display imagination to different degrees in different contexts. We can distinguish, if we care to, between people's visual imagination, verbal imagination, aural imagination, and so forth. But to do so is, at least on the face of it, only to specify particular areas in which people may display imagination. There is no obvious reason to suppose that the criteria for judging somebody to be visually imaginative will differ from those appropriate to judging somebody to be verbally imaginative, although, of course, the specific form in which the criteria are met will differ, because the nature of visual and verbal representation differs. Similarly, an imaginative poem will display different qualities from an imaginative historical study, because the defining characteristics of poetry and history differ, but this will be a difference in the specific form that certain general criteria take. Those general criteria must be the same in each case, if we mean essentially the same thing in calling them both imaginative. (In exactly the same way, although happy or beautiful people are by no means happy for the same specific reasons or beautiful in the same specific way, if they are happy or beautiful in the same sense as each other, there must be some general criteria of happiness, such as being enmeshed with their situation, or of beauty, such as criteria of form and harmony, that they all meet.)[2]

Although I have referred to imaginative products, such as an imaginative poem, in the previous paragraph, as is commonly enough done, it may be argued that any such ascription is derivative of an ascription of imaginative powers to an agent. A poem is regarded as imaginative, because of qualities displayed by the poet. Since, in general, poems do not appear of their own accord from nowhere, it is safe to judge the poet by the poem. But if a poem were to be produced by a random process, as, for example, by monkeys typing on the keys of a word processor, while it might indisputably display the qualities of good poetry, it would surely not be appropriate to label it an imaginative work. Imaginative works are more than simply good works; they logically presuppose an imaginative creator, for the display of imagination is by definition a conscious activity. Imaginative people con-

---

[2]The view that a concept must consistently meet certain criteria is, of course, disputed by some philosophers. Superficially, for instance, it would seem to be at variance with certain views of Wittgenstein (although I myself am not convinced that it is). I have attempted on a number of occasions to argue for the position that I here take for granted. See, in particular, "Does the question 'what is education?' make sense?" and "Misdescribing a Cow: The Question of Conceptual Correctness" in *Educational Theory,* Vol. 33, Nos. 3 and 4, 1983, and Vol. 35, No. 2, 1985.

sciously conceive in a manner that meets certain general criteria. What those criteria are can perhaps best be seen by considering what is common to a number of different examples of imaginative people.

Suppose that we are faced with an imaginative novelist, an imaginative historian, an imaginative scientist, an imaginative salesperson, an imaginative advertiser, an imaginative police officer, an imaginative husband, and an imaginative soccer player. What is it that we are claiming about each of these individuals, such that they all deserve to be called imaginative, notwithstanding the different nature of the activities they engage in?

The criteria of imagination are, I suggest, unusualness and effectiveness. To be imaginative is to have the inclination and ability consciously to conceive of the unusual and effective in particular contexts. As has been indicated, what constitutes unusualness and effectiveness will differ in different contexts, and can be judged only by those with an understanding of the context. Effective and unusual conceptualization will be different in respect of carrying out scientific research, painting, writing a poem, and policing, because these are quite distinct activities, each, as a consequence, with its own canons of quality against which unusualness and effectiveness have to be judged. Nonetheless, to call a scientist or a police officer imaginative, as opposed to merely good, is precisely to say that he or she conceives of ways to proceed that are unusual and effective. Both criteria must, of course, be met. Merely to generate unusual ideas does not deserve the epithet *imaginative*, for if the ideas are absurd, unworkable, logically incoherent, and so forth, then no normative label is deserved at all. Besides, we have other words to label the mere generation of unusual ideas, such as *bizarre*, *prolific*, or *inventive*, (depending on precisely what we want to imply), which do not suggest anything about their quality. Conversely, the generation of merely effective ideas does not constitute imagination, but is what we would label "competent," "sound," or "good." The imaginative scientist is not simply a capable one; he or she also produces ideas with which we are familiar. Unusualness and effectiveness are, therefore, both necessary and, taken together, sufficient conditions of imaginative conceptualization.

"Unusualness" does not necessarily connote strangeness, extraordinariness, shockingness, outlandishness, or, to use a loose general term, mindbogglingness. After all, we do not regard Shakespeare as an imaginative playwright primarily because he occasionally stuns or amazes us, so much as because he sees beyond the obvious, superficial, and immediately apparent. Similarly, the imaginative activities of the police officer, the historian, or the salesperson will be characterized by their insight, subtlety and farsightedness. They are unusual in that they go beyond the immediately and routinely apparent. It follows that, although there is nothing logically odd about an entire community of very imaginative people, in fact, the recognition of highly imaginative people at a given time and place should be relatively rare. This is because if everybody could see, understand, and think as a Shakespeare, we would not be aware of any unusualness, would not recognize such thinking—if it were the norm—as imaginative. Since what appears obvious to people changes with time and place, it follows also that what is judged to be unusual, and hence imaginative, may change. What we may rightly regard as imaginative in the ancient Egyptians would not necessarily indicate imagination in people today.

By "effective" is meant conducive to a good solution to or resolution of the task or problem at hand. An imaginative salesperson has to come up with techniques that are not merely unusual and ingenious but that also sell products. An imaginative poet has to use meter, rhyme, words, imagery, and so forth, in a way that is not merely more than routine, but that also generates the required effect.

Thus the imaginative novelist, as contrasted with the unimaginative novelist, is so because he or she deals with the material in an effective and unusual way, in point of plot, characterization, use of language, or whatever else we take to be the defining characteristics of the novelist's art. Disagreement about whether a particular novelist is imaginative may therefore come about from at least three distinct sources: (1) differing views of what is meant by "imaginative," (2) differing views as to what constitutes the novelist's art, and (3) differing views as to what actually is effective and unusual in respect of that art. Likewise, the imaginative historian conducts his or her study, whether in terms of approach, procedures, or analysis of data, in an unusual and effective manner. The same may be said of the other examples given, but when we come to the imaginative police officer and even more the imaginative husband, we may be far less clear about what their effectiveness and unusualness might, even in principle, consist of. If that is so, it is surely because we have less clear conceptions of policing and marriage than we do of, say, history and poetry, rather than because of any problem about the meaning of "imagination" or its application in these cases. If we were clear about essentially what marriage involves, and hence about what constitutes a good husband, we could more easily recognize those whose effective and unusual personal skills and strategies entitle them to the label "imaginative." The imaginative soccer player would not necessarily be so called because of his skills, however unusual and effective they might be, because, as we must not forget, imagination is logically bound up with conceptualization. An exceptionally fast and skillful winger who in fact beats opponents and scores goals regularly, would no doubt be classified as a very useful, perhaps good, even gifted player. Why should we call him imaginative? The imaginative soccer player is one who has unusual and effective ideas about the game that he can also put into practice.

The last example raises the question of whether imagination can in principle be displayed in any activity. It also contains a hint that the answer is no. Although, as my list of examples makes clear, there seems no reason to confine imagination to the sphere of the arts, and it may well be displayed in a number of seemingly prosaic pursuits, it can only be displayed in activities that involve thinking. For to have imagination *means* to conceptualize in a particular kind of way. Consequently, to the extent that an activity is characterized in terms of the routine performance of noncognitive skills, it cannot have scope for imaginative performance. An imaginative road sweeper, for example, or an imaginative auto mechanic seems an incongruous idea. Of course, an imaginative person could be a road sweeper or auto mechanic, and no doubt from time to time the opportunity may arise to reconceive the practice of road sweeping or engine repair in an imaginative way. But in general it is hard to see how the daily performance of sweeping roads and repairing engines contains much scope for imagination. In any case, the important point remains that imagination, being a species of cognitive activity, can come to the fore only insofar as activities involve opportunities for thinking about their execution.

So far all my examples have been of an imaginative something (e.g., poet, scientist). Yet we frequently refer to people as imaginative without specifying in respect of what, as when we say that the Athenians were more imaginative than the Spartans or that Nancy is a particularly imaginative person. It is clear that the notion of being imaginative without reference to any context does not make sense. Imagination involves effective and unusual conceptualization, and what is unusual and effective can be determined only in some context. ("This is an unusual and effective implement" makes no sense if there is no answer to the question "for what?") If Jones is an imaginative person, he must be able to be imaginative about some thing (or things). That being so, the question arises as to what context is implicit when we use the label "imaginative" without explicit reference to a context.

The simple answer is to presume that people who are labeled

"imaginative" without qualification are supposed to be so in respect of everything, or at least in respect of whatever are regarded as important aspects of life. An alternative possibility is that we are supposed to infer a particular context (or set of contexts) from our knowledge of the speaker, the person spoken about, or both. For example, Geoff is a husband, a poet, and a gardener, so, when told that he is imaginative, we assume that he is imaginative in these areas. Or, since we know the speaker is interested only in the visual arts, we assume that when she calls somebody imaginative she means in respect of them. (The idea of somebody being imaginative in most important contexts is obviously not logically absurd; but it is likely to be a rare occurrence in practice, since this would necessitate the thorough understanding of all such areas, without which one logically could not consciously conceive of the unusual and effective.)

However, although the word *imaginative* is undoubtedly used without qualification in both these ways, I suggest that very often the unqualified use of the label implies a specific context—namely, what may be broadly referred to as the field of interpersonal relations. This is to say that it seems that some people are dubbed "imaginative" because of their insights into, and dealings with, other people. For example, unimaginative people, faced with the breakup of a friend's marriage, react in various predictable ways, in line with received opinion and obvious and superficial appearances. Imaginative people, by contrast, conceive of a variety of possible explanations and suggestions that are unusual but have cogency; as a consequence they display deeper and more subtle understanding. (It is no accident that the word *unimaginative* is often coupled with words, such as *dull* and *stupid*, that imply a lack of perception.) There is no particular problem with this usage in terms of the account of imagination given, provided that one does not slip into associating imagination exclusively with this species of it. This is indeed a form of imagination, the effectiveness and unusualness criteria being met by the way in which the situation is conceptualized, but there is no obvious warrant for assuming that a truly imaginative person must display it in this area. As we have seen, imagination may be displayed in most areas of life, and all that the ascription of the label "imaginative" implies is that a person should display it in some context(s). (One might, of course, argue that this species of imagination is more important than certain others, but not that it more truly constitutes imagination.)

In my view, the greatest problem in discussing imagination comes when we turn to children. I doubt very much whether, in general, when people refer to young children as "imaginative" they are using the word in the way I have outlined. Here we encounter one of many similarities between "imagination" and "creativity." Standard analyses of creativity would suggest that creative adults have to meet the two criteria of quality and originality in what they produce (for example, White, 1975; Barrow & Woods, 1975). Yet the paintings, writing, and other products of young children rarely meet these criteria; nonetheless, they are very often labeled "creative." Some would argue that the child's work, though perhaps not original and of high quality in any objective sense, may nonetheless represent originality and quality in terms of the child's own progress. However, this, though true, hardly clarifies the conceptual confusion, since that is not what we mean when we refer to creative adults such as Beethoven, Einstein, or Michelangelo. Others might argue that we call the child "creative" because there is an empirical connection between the production of what is original and of quality from the child's point of view, and the subsequent production of work that is original and of quality by publicly accepted criteria. But there is no satisfactory evidence to support this empirical claim, and, in any case, it still involves two different senses of "creative," one for the child and one for the adult. A study of creativity tests and exercises and the use of the word by teachers and textbooks forces one to the conclusions that creativity as applied to children usually means something quite different from its application among adults, and that, as applied to children, it has several distinct meanings. (For example, sometimes it is used as a synonym for "self-expression," or "productivity," or "inventiveness," or "good problem-solving ability.") In just the same way, it seems to me that sometimes, in calling children imaginative, people do not mean that the children consciously conceptualize effectively and unusually in particular contexts, but rather that they are, for example, inclined to daydreaming, inclined to fantasizing, introspective, good storytellers, sensitive, or even creative. Insofar as this claim is true, there is very little we can do about it. Philosophers are not empowered to police language. But we can point out that each of these is a distinct conception of imagination (that is, a different use of the word), most of which, incidentally, would themselves benefit from more detailed analysis, and that in making claims about imagination, it is of obvious but crucial importance to know what sense of the word we are dealing with. If there is an argument for confining the use of the word to the sense that I have outlined, it would be that there is no other obvious word to describe the business of consciously conceptualizing effectively and unusually in particular contexts, whereas we do not need synonyms for fantasizing, displaying sensitivity, and so forth.

Whatever value there may be in so-called imagination in these and other senses, there is a very clear and strong reason for wanting to develop imagination in the sense outlined in this chapter. Imaginative people in this sense are by definition equipped to come up with effective and novel insights, solutions, and suggestions in various contexts. Indeed, I would argue that an educated person, as distinct from a well-trained person or an indoctrinated person, must necessarily possess imagination. For education, implying understanding and a critical spirit, as opposed to the mere acquisition of information and skills, could scarcely take place where an emphasis on the effective and unusual was not at a premium (Barrow, 1980). My final question is, therefore, what conclusions we can draw from the above about desirable ways in which to develop imagination in people?

First, the important negative point is that developing imagination is not a matter of getting hold of "it" and training it, exercising it, or otherwise giving it room to roam. For "it" does not exist until we are some way along the path of developing it, and even then "it" exists only figuratively. Second, the first positive point is that if we want people to develop imagination, we have to develop their understanding, for people logically cannot show imagination if they have poor understanding. (One may hit upon suggestions at random that others presume to be imaginative, but one would not then in fact be imaginative.) Third, the understanding and embryonic imagination have to be developed in particular contexts. We have to get people to be imaginative about something, since the notion of having imagination that takes no specific form is incoherent. We therefore have to develop it by means of developing understanding of particular matters. Fourth, it is evidently not the business of the arts alone. An imaginative scientist is as plausible as an imaginative musician, and, on the face of it, no less important. Fifth, it would seem reasonable to believe in the importance of widening the experience of the child, both actually and vicariously, and of stimulating the child to attempt an imaginative treatment of material.

The last point cannot be said to rest on logical necessity, as the previous ones do. Nor is it shown that it is empirically necessary. There are people who are very imaginative in various particular areas, who have had little or no formal schooling and whose experience is relatively limited. Nonetheless, since imagination involves conceiving of the unusual and effective, and since to be imaginative involves being both able and inclined to engage in such conceptualization, common sense suggests that opening the mind to the myriad customs, explanations, theories, problems, practices, values, and beliefs of human beings throughout history may serve to encourage both that inclination and ability. Similarly, it is hard to see how calling on people to use their developing imaginative powers and drawing attention to the imaginative quality of the achievements of others could not be preferable to not doing so. It is surely with implicit, and no doubt often subconscious, reference to such strategies that phrases such as "feeding," "fostering," or "nurturing" the imagination have become clichés. The imagination has to be cultivated indirectly: It grows, if it grows at all, as a consequence of our efforts in imparting understanding in this kind of way. Concern for the imagination therefore requires a curriculum that (1) introduces students to much that is unfamiliar, thereby both teaching them that there is enormous variety in the world and, ideally, exciting or stimulating them to explore, understand, and draw intellectual nourishment from the multiplicity of human experience, (2) is itself taught in an imaginative way, so that much that cannot be taught may be caught, and (3) more specifically, calls for and places value on the display of imagination, as much as the logically necessarily prior need for understanding.

Thus, the development of imagination has to be seen as a curriculum-wide matter. We can best approach the task of promoting it by encouraging it and displaying it ourselves as teachers in all fields. It cannot be seen as the business of special courses or exercises in such things as problem solving, critical thinking, or creativity, because imagination also presupposes understanding of and competence within the specific contexts in which it is displayed.

REFERENCES

Barrow, R., and Woods, R. (1975). *Introduction to philosophy of education*. London: Methuen.

Barrow, R. (1980). *The philosophy of schooling*. Brighton: Wheatsheaf.

Gardner, H. (1983). *Frames of mind*. New York: Basic Books.

Ryle, G. (1949). *The concept of mind*. London: Hutchinson.

White, J. P. (1975). Creativity and education. In R. F. Dearden, P. H. Hirst, and R. S. Peters (Eds.), *Education and the development of reason*. London: Routledge & Kegan Paul.

6 ◇ The Origins of Imagination and the Curriculum

KIERAN EGAN
Simon Fraser University, Canada

INTRODUCTION

In educational discourse, imagination is generally considered desirable, but its nature is far from clear. Also, what stimulates its development—what causes it—is, although crucial for education, perhaps even vaguer. The "arts" are seen as particularly useful in its stimulation, though their stimulating effects are clearly felt very differently by different children. While the arts are considered important for the stimulation of imagination, we want to see its action in mathematics and the sciences no less than in painting and composing. There seems, however, room for imaginative play more at the refined research end of mathematics and the sciences than in their foundations. In educationalists' rhetoric, imagination is represented commonly as in conflict with the conventional, the stereotypical, and the learning-by-heart. A difficulty in the way of getting a clearer grasp on its nature and causes in education is due to the way it tends to be entrameled in the conflict between the rational and irrational. To which does imagination owe its proper allegiance? Because we have inherited a powerful tradition of educational thought that sees education as the process of inculcating rationality in children and because imagination has been tied in various ways with "irrational" forms of thought, the place of imagination within the traditional conception of education has been rather vague and a topic of some discomfort. It has been somewhat of an anomaly, and so it has commonly been ignored.

Recent research on oral cultures and the development of literacy has generated some ideas that might allow us to get a better grasp on the nature, function, and development of imagination. This remains somewhat provisional, but it allows us to focus on the development of

91

imagination in children, using some additional conceptual tools. This chapter is an exploration of some implications of this research. I will begin by trying to situate it in rather general terms.

We have inherited from the classical Greeks a deep-cutting distinction between rational and irrational thinking. Nineteenth- and early-twentieth-century anthropologists, themselves assuming the distinction, elaborated it in their descriptions of the myths and lore of "primitive" people. A puzzle created by this distinction is why irrational forms of thought should have persisted, given that rationality is so obvious and so effective.

The mental life of children has commonly been represented in terms influenced by this distinction. Children are assumed to begin in confusion and ignorance, and education is the process of inculcating rationality and knowledge. In Plato's enormously influential theory of education, the process of educating is seen as analogous to unchaining helpless prisoners in a dark cave, able to see only flittering, meaningless shadows, and leading them outside to behold the source of light and truth. Christian ideas of education blended quite well with this, representing the child as beginning in sin and ignorance and being able to progress only gradually and with great difficulty to virtue and knowledge.

Children and "savages" have been assumed to lack certain forms of thought that are the marks of rational adults. Attempts have been made to capture the perceived differences in distinctions such as primitive/developed, irrational or prerational/rational, mythical/historical, simple/complex, mythopoeic/logico-empirical, "cold"/"hot," traditional/modern, and so on. Relatively recently, attempts have been made to break down these distinctions when applied to different kinds of cultures. Goody, for example, has argued that any distinction that suggests "two different modes of thought, approaches to knowledge, or forms of science" is inadequate, not least because, as he points out, "both are present not only in the same societies but in the same individuals" (1977, p. 148). That is, whenever we try to define precisely some distinctive feature of "our" thinking, we can always find examples of it in "their" cultures, and whenever we identify a distinctive feature of "their" thinking, we can find cases of it in "our" culture. "We" and "they" constantly exhibit features of thinking that are both rational and irrational, complex and simple, logico-mathematical and mythopoeic, and so on. We are them and they are us.

What about the evident differences then? One can hardly claim they do not exist. How do we account for them if we give up explanations involving "primitiveness" or deficiencies of mind or of language? And how do we characterize the "Greek miracle," in which evident changes took place in forms of mental activity and expression? Goody's argument is that the evident differences are best accounted for as due to technology, especially the technology of writing. His argument builds on, and extends, a growing body of work that is clarifying how literacy affects strategies of thinking. The economy of the mind inclines us towards particular strategies in an oral culture, where what one knows is what one remembers, and to different strategies in a literate culture, where various mental operations can be enormously enhanced by visual access to organized bodies of knowledge.

The path from orality to literacy is one we want all children to take in our educational systems. Becoming clearer about what this move entails seems likely to result in some enlightenment of our practical educational problems. Considering oral cultures might also help us to get a better understanding of some aspects of young children's thinking. This is not to posit some mysterious recapitulation based on biology or psychological development, but more graspably to see a recapitulation of certain technical aids that can influence forms of thinking. By making children literate, we recapitulate in each individual's case the internalizing of a technology that can have profound and quite precise effects on cognitive processes and modes of communication. As Walter Ong notes, "Technologies are not mere exterior aids but also interior transformations of consciousness" (1982, p. 82). Oral cultures do not lack reflective thinking, Goody emphasizes; what they do not have are "tools for constructive rumination" (1977, p. 44).

"Technology" is a slightly aggressive term to use for writing, and "tools" for thinking is a handy but tendentious metaphor. One is led to assume that spades and computers have similar transforming powers over our manual and cognitive functions. That they have transforming powers is without doubt, but that these are the same as or akin to what internalizing literacy produces needs further arguments and evidence, not metaphorical glossing over. I would prefer to use a less aggressive and less tendentious term than "technology" for writing—not on etymological grounds but simply because of its modern associations—but am hard put to come up with a good alternative. My preferred term suffers the disabilities of being "foreign" and perhaps a bit pretentious. It is a coinage of Levi-Strauss, as far as I'm aware: In discussing the structural categories underlying totemic classification, he debunks the notion that totemic species are chosen because of their economic or culinary value. He argues that totemic species are not so much "bonnes à manger" (good things to eat) but are rather "bonnes à penser" (good things to think with) (Levi-Strauss, 1962).

Literacy is a set of *bonnes à penser*, as well as having the utilitarian values that are so obvious.

A main purpose of this chapter is to explore oral *bonnes à penser*. Orality, we shall see, is not a condition of deficit—to be defined simply as the lack of literacy. Thinking about orality only in terms of literacy is like, in Walter Ong's neat simile, thinking of horses as automobiles without wheels (1982, p. 12). Orality entails a set of powerful and effective mental strategies, some of which, to our cost, have become attenuated and undervalued in significant parts of our culture and educational systems. I will explore some of the effective strategies of thinking used in oral cultures, and will then note some similarities between these and common features of young children's thinking. I will consider Albert B. Lord's argument that orality and literacy are "contradictory and mutually exclusive" (1964, p. 129), and will argue in reply that they are so only in particular regards, that some of the *bonnes à penser* of orality are unnecessarily lost for many children in our educational systems or are suppressed to an unnecessary degree, and that with some small ingenuity we might find ways of conserving a number of them. Some indeed, I will argue, should be conserved as foundations for more sophisticated forms of understanding. The set I will consider seems centrally concerned with the development of the imagination.

A word of caution is required, more for me perhaps than for the reader. Any simple assumption about equating the thinking of adults in oral cultures with that of children in ours will be undermined in two ways. First, adults have the accumulated experience and development that children necessarily lack. Second, most children in Western cultures live in an environment that presupposes literacy and its associated forms of thought; adult interactions with young children constantly assume conventions that depend on literacy, and preliterate children are constantly encouraged to adopt forms of thinking and expression that are more easily achieved as a product of literacy.

A related caution: I will not try to establish an exhaustive inventory of the intellectual strategies common in oral cultures. Nor do I see the purpose of education in Western cultures as uncritically preserving and developing such strategies. We are not in the business of preparing children to live in an oral culture—though it may be worth reiterating that we are preparing them for a literate and oral culture. Indeed, we see fast developing around us features of what Ong has called "secondary orality." The electronic media are its most energetic promotors, but even newspapers and journals are explicitly, and somewhat paradoxically, relying more and more on strategies of communication that draw increasingly little on the skills of "high literacy" and their associated forms of thought (Ong, 1977). Even so, we need to remember that orality is not the end of our educational development, but it is a constituent of it, and its study might provide some *bonnes à penser* for constructing a richer primary school curriculum and a richer sense of how children might effectively learn its contents.

A central theme of this chapter might be summed up in Levi-Strauss' observation:

> I think there are some things we have lost, and we should perhaps try to regain them, but I am not sure that in the kind of world in which we are living and with the kind of scientific thinking we are bound to follow, we can regain these things exactly as if they had never been lost; but we can try to become aware of their existence and their importance. (1978, p. 5)

I will begin, then, with a brief account of some of the fruitfully overlapping branches of research in classical studies and anthropology that have helped to clarify the kinds of thinking that have proven effective in cultures that do not have writing. As a way into this I will sketch what may be a familiar story to some readers—the relatively recent rediscovery of orality. I will gather together prominent features of orality under three subheadings—the poetics of memory, participation and conservation, and classification and explanation—and then I will explore how far and in what ways these are evident in young children's thinking. One purpose of this exploration is to attempt to recover a view of early childhood thinking unencumbered by the lingering influence of the distinctions mentioned above. A related purpose is to reconsider the general character of the foundations of education when literacy and rationality are conceived of as growing out of, rather than displacing, the oral culture of early childhood.

THE REDISCOVERY OF ORALITY

The relatively recent rediscovery of orality is connected with some problems presented by Homer's epic poems. The influential evolutionary paradigm of late Victorian times seemed to work fine if one focused on the development of science: From myth to rationality to empirical science was an entirely plausible progressive story. The more general applicability of this paradigm to human culture, however, ran up against the anomaly of Homer. The classically educated Victorians were more familiar with those far battles on the windy plains of Troy, with the wooden horse and how the topless towers of Ilium were finally brought down, than with much of the society around them. How could such vividly powerful epics and their richness of human insight, their technical sophistication and emotional force, their overwhelming, engaging reality be composed by and for what were in all other regards considered primitive people. "Primitive" mentality—that mess of confusion—must, it would seem, have the resources to create some of the greatest cultural achievements.

Two other complications were added. First, the story of the *Iliad*, taken as straightforward fiction, began to be seen as about actual events that occurred in the thirteenth century B.C.E. This historicity began to be established by Heinrich Schliemann's excavations at Troy and Mycaenae, and has become, bit by bit, fuller and clearer, allowing Michael Wood to gather the pieces together in the persuasive if not compelling picture presented in the popular television series and book, *In Search of the Trojan War* (1985).

The second further complication was the growing evidence that Homer and the other poets in the tradition of which he was a part were illiterate. As Berkley Peabody puts it, "Despite the implications of its name, literature does not seem to have been the invention of literate people" (1975, p. 1). Homer, the master poet, lived about 500 years after the events of which he sang, at a time when the kingdoms whose ships sailed for Troy were themselves long destroyed. Growing knowledge of the spread of literacy in Greece made it increasingly difficult to see Homer, traditionally blind, sitting at a desk composing his poems.

But how could such enormously long and technically complex poems have been composed without writing? Surely no one could make up those supple hexameters as he sang, and then recall them word for word? Virgil, the other great epic poet of the ancient world, labored for years over his *Aeneid*. We know that he constantly revised it and on his deathbed asked that it be destroyed. Surely no illiterate bard could toss off a book an hour on the hoof, as it were, of a power, vividness, and quality that the great Virgil struggled for years to match and couldn't.

The story of the rediscovery of the Homeric methods of composition is itself an epic of scholarly ingenuity, and one that I will sketch only most briefly. This story begins with an American in Paris. Having completed an M.A. degree at the University of California, Berkeley, Milman Parry wrote his Ph.D. thesis in Paris. He argued that the structure of the Homeric poems and their every distinctive feature are due to the requirements of oral methods of composition. Parry supplemented his arguments during the early 1930s by studying the methods of oral composition still being used by Yugoslavian singers of heroic tales. After Parry's early death his work was continued by Alfred B. Lord.

Parry's analyses of the *Iliad* and *Odyssey* showed that they were largely made up of formulae—repeated morphemic clusters—whose composition was dictated by the metrical requirements of the hexameter line. For example, Homer has a large number of adjectival epithets for most of the recurring nouns in the poem—for wine, the sea, ships, the major characters, and so on. The epithet chosen at any point is not necessarily the most apposite for the meaning of the line, but is dictated rather by its fit into the meter of the line. In many cases the epithet is almost meaningless, but it allows the hexameter to ride along. One-fifth of Homer's lines are repeated more or less entirely elsewhere in his epic poems, and in about 28,000 lines there are about 25,000 repeated phrases (Parry, 1928).

The oral poet did not memorize the poems he performed, as we would have to do. The singer learned through a long apprenticeship— a long illiterate apprenticeship—the particular metrical form of his tradition, until it was like a somatic rhythm, in which he could think. The content of the song was held together first by a clear grasp of the overall story, and within that the meter determined the patterns of sounds. As Albert B. Lord puts it, "Man without writing thinks in terms of sound groups and not in words" (1964, p. 25). The oral performance, then, does not involve repetition of a memorized poem or recitation as we know it—the idea of a fixed text is a product of literacy—but rather each performance is a new composition. It may be very like others, and certain patterns will recur from performance to performance, but the singer is composing, not repeating something fixed in memory. We see, in Lord's words, "the preservation of tradition by the constant re-creation of it" (1964, p. 29). Or, as Jack Goody puts it, referring to modern performances of myths in oral cultures, what we see is not repetition of a fixed model but a "continuous creation" of the basic story at each telling.

Chunks of sound, then, are arranged metrically in the Homeric poems, and agglomerate line by line to repeat the heroic story. The poet "stiches" the chunks together as he goes, the formulae to fit the metrical line, and the episodes to fit the story. The Greeks called such trained singers "rhapsodes," literally, "song-stitchers"—though the rhapsodes of the classical period were trained rather like modern ac-

tors, literate learners and repeaters of a fixed text. Homer and his illiterate fellows were composing stitchers. The oral singer had in mind
a story, an absolutely overwhelming metrical pattern in which the story
was to be told, and a wide array of formulae that made the fitting of
the elements of the story to the meter of the line *relatively* easy. Clearly
there are always greater and lesser talents for stitching a story together, and clearly Homer was one of the greatest. It seems likely that
he came as a culmination of his tradition and recited his poems to
trained scribes.

Parry's insight has been supported and extended by Albert B.
Lord's extensive studies of contemporary singers of heroic tales in the
Balkans. He has described in some detail the conditions of their intensive and extensive, and almost invariably illiterate, training, which
cannot be very dissimilar from Homer's. Their work has been further
elaborated by Berkley Peabody's ingenious analysis of Hesiod's *Works
and Days* (1975). He shows in further detail the way the oral singer
does not "tell" a story to an audience but uses the techniques developed over unknowable generations to catch the audience up and realize for them an "unchallengeable" world.

This process of catching up the audience, of enthralling them, and
impressing the reality of the story on them is a central feature of education in an oral culture. The social institutions of oral cultures are
sustained in large part by sound, by the spoken or sung word, and
whatever it can achieve in the way of committing individuals to particular beliefs, expectations, roles, and behaviors. In sustaining social
institutions, the techniques of fixing the crucial patterns of beliefs in
the memory—rhyme, rhythm, formula, story, and so on—are vitally
important. Education in such cultures is largely a matter of constantly
immersing the young into the enchanting patterns of sound until they
resound to the patterns, until they become "musically" in tune with,
harmonious with, the institutions of their culture.

The Homeric poems were called the educators of the Greeks because they performed this social role. It was not because of their aesthetic value that they were learned by every Greek; that was
instrumental to their general social value as "a massive repository of
useful knowledge, a sort of encyclopedia of ethics, politics, history,
and technology which the effective citizen was required to learn as the
core of his educational equipment" (Havelock, 1963, p. 29). In such
an education a very large proportion of mental energy has to go into
ensuring memorization of the main messages of the culture, because
they can exist and survive only in people's memories. Little mental
energy is left for reflection on those messages, or analysis of them,

because such activity would interfere with the need to sink them un-questioningly into every mind.

A further extension of Parry's and Lord's work was undertaken by Eric Havelock. His *Preface to Plato* (1963) and *Origins of Western Literacy* (1976) show that the principles of poetic composition that Parry and Lord rediscovered help to make clearer the achievements of early Greek philosophy, and in particular to clarify why Plato wished to exclude poets from his ideal state. Plato's *Republic* is re-read, so to speak, as a program for educating people out of the residues of oral culture and into the forms of thinking that full literacy makes possi-ble. The mind need no longer be immersed into the oral tradition, memorizing and copying the paradigmatic structures and patterns of the Homeric poems, but is to be freed to engage its proper objects— which we might call abstract concepts and Plato called Forms or Ideas. This mode of thinking Plato saw as opposed to the Homeric tradition; Plato's scheme of education brought the mind to reality, whereas Ho-mer's crippled the intellect by its seductive illusions and distortions of reality. So the new forms of thinking made possible by literacy, near their beginning in educational discourse, were represented as enemies of the oral *bonnes à penser*: "Plato's target was indeed an educational procedure and a whole way of life" (Havelock, 1963, p. 45). There are clear ambivalences in Plato's reflections on the oral tradition (see the *Phaedrus* and the possibly apocryphal *VIIth Letter*) and on Homer, but in the end those forms of thinking, education, and society that were geared "to retain tenaciously a precious hoard of exemplars" (Have-lock, 1963, p. 199) had to be destroyed to make place for the new ab-stract forms of thought and whatever world they brought with them. Plato conceived of his educational scheme not as building on the oral tradition, but as a replacement for it. His work, in Havelock's words, "announced the arrival of a completely new level of discourse which as it became perfected was to create in turn a new kind of experience of the world —the reflective, the scientific, the technological, the the-ological, the analytic. We can give it a dozen names" (1963, p. 267). Plato's success was such that it is extremely difficult for us now to imagine the kind of consciousness created in the oral tradition and the kind of experience listening to a singer of tales or teller of myths gen-erated.

Havelock's description of the techniques of oral recitation by singers of heroic tales, such as Homer, helps us to see their reception by a typical audience as rather different from the way we read the text of those poems today. The accumulated purpose of those techniques was to ensure "a state of total personal involvement and therefore of emotional identification with the substance of the poetized statement that you are required to retain" (Havelock, 1963, p. 44). A Greek, or Australian Aborigine, youth needed to expend considerable mental resources to learn the oral foundations of his or her cultural institutions. The professional singer—in whom the rhythms and stories of the culture profoundly indwell—are central figures in such cultures, but the messages are repeated constantly and everywhere. Proverbs, maxims, clichés, and formulae uttered at the table, on rising or going to sleep, in the market or the field, are constantly repeated bits and pieces of the great myths or epic poems of the culture.

Learning the sustaining messages of one's oral culture is different from the constant effort to accumulate knowledge which we are familiar with. In an oral culture, memorization is central, but it is not performed in the way that we might try to learn something by heart. For us, memorizing is usually an attempt to copy a text in such a manner that we can repeat it on command—our techniques are typically impoverished, involving largely repetition, some mnemonics perhaps, reciting aloud with our eyes closed, and so on, rather ineffectually. In an oral culture, learning proceeds more at a somatic level, using the whole body to support the memorizing process. The Homeric singer, and singers throughout the world, usually use a simple stringed instrument, or sometimes a drum, whose beat reinforces the rhythm of the telling and draws the hearer into the enchantment of the song. The audience does not so much listen to it as we might listen to a play, but they are invited to live it. The acoustical rhythm created by the singer and instrument is supported by the repetitive meter, by rhythmic movements of the body, by the pattern of formulae and the story, to set up conditions of enchantment that impress the message into the minds of the hearers. "The entire nervous system, in short, is geared to the task of memorization" (Havelock, 1963, p. 151). The techniques of the skilled performer generate a relaxed, half-hypnotized pleasure in the audience: "rhythmic patterns, vocal, verbal, instrumental, and physical, all set in motion together and all consonant in their effect" (Havelock, 1963, p. 152). (For a fuller account, see Havelock, 1963, Ch. IX, "The Psychology of the Poetic Performance.")

This semi-hypnotized state is similar to that described often by anthropologists as the condition in which audiences receive the foundational messages of their culture. Levi-Strauss rather dramatically claims that his study of mythology aims "to show, not how men think in myths, but how myths operate in men's minds without their being aware of the fact" (1969, p. 12), by a process that he prefers to compare with music than with linguistic forms or texts: "Thus the myth and the musical work are like conductors of an orchestra, whose audience becomes the silent performers" (Levi-Strauss, 1969, p. 17). Similarly, Edmund Leach argues that the structural patterns of myths and their underlying messages are communicated powerfully and unambiguously despite considerable variations in the surface stories and performances.

> Whenever a corpus of mythology is recited in its religious setting, such structures are "felt" to be present, and convey meaning much as poetry conveys meaning. Even though the ordinary listener is not fully conscious of what has been communicated, the "message" is there in a quite objective sense. (1967, p. 12)

In Levy-Bruhl's words, when a sacred myth is recited in ritual or other settings of heightened emotion, "what they hear in it awakens a whole gamut of harmonics which do not exist for us" (1985, p. 369). The written form of the myth, which we can study," is but the inanimate corpse which remains after the vital spark has fled" (Levy-Bruhl, 1985, p. 369).

    I have already mentioned Jack Goody's further rediscoveries of orality in undermining traditional notions of the move from "primitive" to rational thought, and in showing that the differences typically educed as evidence for such a shift are better understood as epiphenomena of the move from orality to literacy. In addition, he has clarified some particular steps that accompanied the move from orality to literacy and has detailed, with Ian Watt, various consequences of literacy against the background of orality (Goody & Watt, 1968).[1]

    I want to turn now from the story of the rediscovery of orality to simply listing some of the main *bonnes à penser* common in oral cultures. This will not be a systematic survey, but one motivated by my educational interests. I will begin with those features of orality exposed by the foregoing brief discussion of Parry, Lord, Havelock, Goody, and Ong, and try to elaborate these by drawing on some other works.

---

[1]For an excellent survey of this field, the best source presently available is Walter Ong's *Orality and Literacy* (1982). Ong's numerous further contributions to the rediscovery of orality—in medieval contexts, Romanticism, African talking drums, and so on—are referred to in that book.

ORAL BONNES A PENSER

By listing certain features of oral cultures, I am not trying to imply that such cultures are all alike, or that they all use much the same set of techniques for preserving their cultural institutions. While anyone can recognize enormous differences between the oral cultures of pre-classical Greeks and early-twentieth-century Trobriand islanders, between Australian aborigines and west coast British Columbians, I will not be concerned with those differences here. Clearly, oral cultures throughout the world have invented different *bonnes à penser* effectively to give form to and preserve their particular institutions. Myth comprises a range of techniques that differ significantly from place to place. And myth itself, according to Levy-Bruhl, is a cultural invention designed in part to recreate or recapture the sense of participation in nature from which the great neolithic inventions of animal taming, agriculture, tool and pottery making, weaving, and who knows what linguistic inventions (tenses? the subjunctive?!) had long alienated their developers. So it is not at all to deny the ungraspable diversity of oral cultural institutions that I will gather here under four subheadings an "ensemble of characteristics" of orality—to use Levy-Bruhl's translators's term (Levy-Bruhl, 1985, p. 29).

However hard we try, it is perhaps impossible for us to think of orality simply as a positive set of *bonnes à penser*. What intrudes on our attempts to understand orally sustained forms of thought is the intellectual capacities and forms of communication that have been stimulated by literacy. But we need to make the effort to see orality as an energetic and somewhat distinct set of *bonnes à penser*, not simply as an incomplete and imperfect use of the mind waiting only for the invention of literacy. Orality, then, is not at all the same as what we usually mean by illiteracy. Illiteracy is perhaps best understood as a condition in which one has not acquired the positive capacities that orality can provide without gaining those of literacy either. Let us then consider what goods these oral *bonnes à penser* seem to serve, so that we might more explicitly be "aware of their existence and their importance," and then consider which among them might be good also for us and which worth our efforts to preserve or to stimulate.

Poetics of Memory

Let us begin this ensemble with those techniques discussed in the previous section. If the institutions of one's culture rely on the living memories of its members, then the techniques that seem best able to impress the appropriate messages into their minds and maintain them there in as stable a form as possible are vitally important. The common Victorian sense of the "mental incapacity" of people in oral cultures, as assessed by their distaste for or inability to perform mental functions that were commonplace in literate Western cultures, kept running into odd anomalies. Levy-Bruhl, in 1910, summed up one of them. He described various prodigious, but to the natives commonplace, feats of memory.

> This extraordinary development of memory, and a memory which faithfully reproduces the minutest details of sense-impressions in the correct order of their appearance, is shown moreover by the wealth of vocabulary and the grammatical complexity of the languages. Now the very men who speak these languages and possess this power of memory are (in Australia or Northern Brazil, for instance) incapable of counting beyond two and three. The slightest mental effort involving abstract reasoning, however rudimentary it may be, is so distasteful to them that they immediately declare themselves tired and give it up. (1985, p. 115)

There are some difficulties in Levy-Bruhl's way of putting this, due in part to his assumptions about the "prelogical" and "mystic" nature of "primitive mentality." It is not, for example, a matter of his subjects having a "power of memory" so much as a highly developed set of techniques for learning and remembering. In addition, I will argue below that the problem for his subjects does not lie in "abstraction" as such—a common assumption also applied to children's thinking—but rather in the dissociation of thought from matters embedded in one's life world. Goody, for example, describes his innocent request of some LoDagaa to count for him. "Count what?" was their (to them) obvious question. They had a number of sophisticated forms of counting, and an abstract numerical system, but their methods of counting cows and cowrie shells differed. Nor, as we shall see, is "abstract reasoning" beyond anyone with a human mind; it is just that certain mental capacities involving abstraction that are very heavily dependent on writing are not available to people who do not write or read.

Nevertheless, Levy-Bruhl describes the apparent anomaly of mental prodigies in the supposedly mentally deficient. He perceived that there were no differences on any simple scale of mental superiority/inferiority, but that the conditions of life in oral cultures stimulated different mental developments to deal with those conditions. He was precise in locating a wide range of these differences. The uses of memory in oral cultures, he concluded, "are quite different because its contents are of a different character. It is both very accurate and very emotional" (Levy-Bruhl, 1985, p. 110).

The emotions are engaged by making the culturally important messages event-laden, by involving characters and their emotions in conflict in developing narratives, in short, by building the messages into stories. "All myths tell a story," Levi-Strauss points out (1962, p. 26), and we have already seen Albert B. Lord's conclusion about the role of the story in providing the firm structure for the constant reconstruction of heroic songs. The formulae and groupings and meter, in the end, "serve only one purpose. They provide a means for telling a story . . . . The tale's the thing" (Lord, 1964, p. 68). The story form is one of the few cultural universals—everyone, everywhere has told and enjoyed stories. They are one of the greatest cultural inventions for catching and fixing meaning. Perhaps my use of "invention" here is a bit tendentious, in the way in which I criticized "technology" above. Perhaps "discovery" is more appropriate; some enormously creative person or people discovered that messages shaped into the distinctive form of the story were better remembered and carried a charge of emotional identification that greatly enhanced social cohesion and control.

Myth stories also, of course, have what we would consider aesthetic values. But while we distinguish aesthetic from utilitarian values, for members of oral cultures these are bound up together. The aesthetic force of myths or heroic tales is a part of what makes them memorable. The story form through most of human experience has been one of the most powerful and effective sustainers of cultures across the world. Its great power lies in its ability to fix affective responses to the messages it contains and to tie what is to be remembered into emotional associations. Our emotions, to put it very crudely, are much better things to remember with than are our intellects (though literate memory-training can also produce prodigies, as Matteo Ricci demonstrated [Spence, 1984]). Most of the world's cultures and its great religions have at their sacred core a story, and we indeed have difficulty keeping our rational history from being constantly shaped into stories. Certainly the simplified histories sanctioned in the schools of most nation states have at least as much in common with the origin myths of oral cultures as they do with the austere ideals of rational historiography.

So one of the techniques developed in oral cultures long ago whose importance for education we have of late tended to forget or neglect or perhaps even repress is the story form. I think there are a number of ways we might use this most powerful of communicative media in education today, especially in the primary school (Egan, 1987).

In the previous section I noted some of the other techniques that are used in oral cultures to create conditions for effective reception and memorization of the most important cultural messages. The condition of emotional enchantment that Havelock describes owes much to the story form, but also owes a lot to those other techniques with which the story is embellished—we have seen the functions of rhyme, rhythm, meter, repetition of formulae, and redundancy, and we should add the constant use of highly vivid or visual images conveyed through their sensory qualities. These techniques are used in oral cultures throughout the world to establish faith in various social institutions. The techniques Havelock describes as enchanting archaic Greeks are much the same as E. E. Evans-Pritchard shows being wielded among contemporary Azende to instil faith in the witch doctor (1936).

These have been, of course, prominent among the techniques of Western poetry, and the condition of mind that Havelock describes is close to what we would readily describe as poetic. As with the singers of heroic tales or the reciters of myths, the poet is the shaper of sound to create particular emotional effects and fix particular meanings. The shaping of sound finds one outlet in poetry and another in rhetoric. These two, along with music, are perhaps the most evident and direct cultural survivors from the oral tradition into the literate world.

Prominent among the *bonnes à penser* of poetic thinking is metaphor and its subset of poetic tropes. Thinking in oral cultures moves fluidly according to the complex logic of metaphor more readily than it follows the systematic logics of rational inquiry. This metaphoric power should be easily appreciated and easily accessible to us, as it suffuses our language at every turn. The words *every turn*, *accessible*, *power*, and so on, all involve casual uses of metaphor. Metaphor is clearly one of the foundations of all our mental activity, a foundation upon which our systematic logics of rational inquiry also rest, or —a better metaphor—a ground out of which they grow. Myth and our everyday language, then, are permeated with metaphor. Ernst Cassirer's study of myth and language also reached this conclusion: "The same form of mental conception is operative in both. It is the form which one may denote as *metaphorical thinking*" (1946, p. 84). Or, as Levi-Strauss observes, "metaphor . . . is not a later embellishment of language but is one of its fundamental modes—a primary form of discursive thought" (1962, p. 102).

These, then, are a few characteristics of orality for our ensemble, generated by the need to memorize and be committed to one's cultural institutions. We find these techniques, these *bonnes à penser*, in greater or lesser degree in all oral cultures: "At different periods and in different cultures there are close links between the techniques for mental recall, the inner organization of the faculty (of memory), the place it occupies in the system of the ego, and the ways that men picture memory to themselves'' (Vernant, 1983, p. 75).

We are familiar with these *bonnes à penser* still, but usually with a much attenuated or altered form. Rhyme, for example, is little more than fun for us now, a part of children's games, anachronistic and so ironic in modern poetry; we would hardly consider its systematic use a matter of vital social importance. We can write, so we do not need rhyme to sustain the memory of our institutions. These survivors of orality serve largely—I am tempted to write ''merely''—aesthetic purposes for us. Among this set we would perhaps feel uneasy describing only metaphor and the story form as casual cultural survivors, hangovers able to find a precarious new purpose entertaining the literate—like the lords and ladies of a defeated civilization made into clowns and dancers and worse, to while away the idle hours of the conquerors. But art has a utilitarian purpose when it supports faith—whether in gods, in the validity of one's cultural institutions, in one's society, or in one's sense of oneself. So as we go on we might stir up a bit of unease in thinking about any of the *bonnes à penser* invented to create and sustain memory as casually dismissable as mere entertainments. Their origins lie in the remarkable human ambition ''to liberate the soul from time and open up a path to immortality'' (Vernant, 1983, p. 95). All the amazing cultural and technological achievements throughout history have been built on their efficaciousness and the intellectual space they once generated and can still generate. So we would do well to give their place in early childhood education more careful inspection.

Participation and Conservation

Jenness records an Ojibwa Indian: ''The white man writes everything down in a book so that it will not be forgotten; but our ancestors married the animals, learned their ways, and passed on the knowledge from one generation to another'' (Levi-Strauss, 1966, p. 37). This expresses a sense of participation in the natural world, a sense of having knowledge that is different from the kinds of propositions that are a staple of rational inquiries. It reflects a mental condition anthropologists have tried often to describe as a kind of oneness with nature, compared with which our normal relationship with the natural world seems alienated. ''The mainspring of the acts, thoughts, and feelings of early man was the conviction that the divine was immanent in nature, and nature intimately connected with society" (Frankfort, et al., 1949, p. 237). There is from all the attempts to pinpoint the causes and character of this sense of participation in nature a conviction that, despite their inadequacies when it comes to pragmatic control *over* the world, myths and oral consciousness somehow do an admirable job of enabling people to feel that they are comfortable participants *in* their life world. But it is not a simple condition, obviously, nor is it one we can feel unequivocally regretful of having largely lost. Ong describes it this way:

> The psyche of a culture innocent of writing knows by a kind of empathetic identification of knower and known, in which the object of knowledge and the total being of the knower enter into a kind of fusion, in a way which literate cultures would typically find unsatisfyingly vague and garbled and somehow too intense and participatory. (1977, p. 18)

One of the cornerstones of rationality is knowing, as it were, where we end and the world begins, and distinguishing the world from our feelings, hopes, fears, and so on. This form of thinking seems to be very largely a product of literacy. As Ong puts it, "Writing fosters abstractions that disengage knowledge from the arena where human beings struggle with one another" (1982, pp. 43, 44), or, in Peabody's words: "The shift in medium from utterance to record affects the way such an institution works and tends to change what was an immediate, living, active agent into an increasingly distant, timeless, passive, authority" (1975, pp. 1, 2). In an oral culture, the ear is most highly attuned to picking up cultural messages, supplemented by the eye. In our case, it is usually the other way around.

Sound is alive and participatory. It is effective within only a short physical range. The hearer must be in the presence of the speaker— no carefully crafted memos from the president or manager. "The living word," as Socrates put it, " . . . has a soul . . . , of which the written word is properly no more than an image" (Plato, *Phaedrus*, ed. Jowett, p. 279). The living word is the word in the arena of human interactions and conflicts; it is not the distanced and "cooled" word of the written text. Language use in an oral culture, then, tends to be, in Ong's phrase, "agonistically toned"; it is charged with the direct energy of the speaker's body and so the speaker's hopes, fears, wants, needs, intentions, and so on. Oral heroic tales are full of bragging, elaborate abuse of adversaries, and, to us, grotesquely exuberant praise of leaders or those from whom the speaker wants a favor. The tensions of daily struggles are face-to-face in an oral culture. These facts of oral life lead to a highly polarized world, of good and evil, friends and enemies, fear and security, and so on. In such societies the forms of verbal play also tend to be "agonistically toned"—riddles, tricks, and jokes tend to involve challenging material.

In an oral culture, "the meaning of each word is ratified in a succession of concrete situations, accompanied by vocal inflections and physical gestures, all of which combine to particularize both its specific denotation and its accepted connative uses" (Goody & Watt, 1968, p. 306). This embeddedness in the life world means that words are not themselves objects of reflection in any systematic way, and consequently oral cultures have no epistemology in our sense. As long as words are tied into their context of reference, philosophical problems do not arise. In oral cultures people do not dissociate words from things to the point where they might wonder how short the legs of a small table have to be for it to be considered a tray. This, again, has nothing to do with "defects" or "inadequacies of the primitive mind," but is rather a function of the uselessness in the conditions of most oral cultures of many of our forms of thought and techniques of thinking. In nearly all oral cultures, for example, time is reckoned in terms of the significant daily activities of the social group. An "abstract" or, better, a dissociated or disembedded system for measuring time, such as we employ, is useful only when it is necessary to coordinate a number of quite diverse kinds of activities. Such diversity does not exist in most oral cultures, where time measurement is contained in the sequence of activities that constitute the rhythms of daily life.

Luria (1976) describes studies he performed with illiterate peasants in remote areas of the Soviet Union. He posed to them apparently simple problems, such as: In the far north, where there is snow, all bears are white. Novaya Zembla is in the far north and there is always snow there. What colors are the bears around Novaya Zembla? His subjects would, no doubt politely wishing to play their part in the conversation, reply that they had never been to Novaya Zembla so didn't know, or that they had seen a black bear but never a white one, and so on. That is, the kind of conversation in which Luria tried to engage these peasants was a kind whose rules and underlying forms of thought are familiar to us, but that could only appear bizarre to illiterate peasants. Pragmatic thought in oral cultures participates more intimately in the life world; it does not have any need to treat the world and experience as objects distanced from their emotional, aesthetic, and utilitarian needs—it needs and makes "no clear-cut distinction between subjective states and the properties of the cosmos" (Levi-Strauss, 1969, p. 240).

Oral cultures have been described as homeostatic, conservative, and stable in ways that our modern literate cultures are not. One striking difference between oral and literate cultures is their somewhat different attitudes to the past; we have and value accurate historical accounts, whereas oral societies cultivate what J. A. Barnes has called "structural amnesia" (cf. Goody & Watt, 1968, p. 309). While oral cultures seem to preserve particular historical events in stories or often preserve genealogies of leading families, it usually turns out that the record kept does not accurately reflect past reality but is faithful rather to present social conditions and statuses. As conditions and status change, so do the accounts or genealogy. Malinowski shows this process at work among the Trobriand islanders. As changes occurred in the structure and power relationships of the society, so the myths of origin changed to reflect the current social structure. The historical changes, that is, were gradually effaced, or, as Malinowski puts it, "myths serve to cover certain inconsistencies created by historical events" (1954, p. 125). The record of the past, then, does not make sense of the present; rather "the individual has little perception of the past except in terms of the present" (Goody & Watt, 1968, p. 310).

We find it hard to think of this structural amnesia as anything other than a lack of history, another incapacity of the lack of literacy. It is hard to see its positive side; it seems simply a matter of making the best of a bad job, or the only thing one can manage if one cannot keep written records. But we might focus rather on its positive value of preserving a sense of stability and clarity. The social structure and its prevailing institutions are constantly supported by divine sanction and constantly renewed; "time is recorded only biologically without being allowed to become 'history'—that is, without its corrosive action being able to exert itself upon consciousness by revealing the irreversibility of events" (Eliade, 1959, pp. 74, 75). One constant technique used to achieve this end is the assertion of constant rebirth—rebeginning as the first beginning. We preserve a vague shadow of this in our New Year festivals. While Malinowski's notion of myth as simply a pragmatic charter that determines for its users what their social roles and tasks are, discounts other functions of myth, the sense of intellectual security it seems commonly to give is not to be casually depreciated. This is indeed another of those *bonnes à penser*— sloughing off the memory of events that are no longer relevant or useful to present life.

This stress on preserving stability and so only what is relevant to present social conditions leads to what is often characterized as a conservative frame of mind. It is conservative in a much more radical sense than that in which the term is used in our political spectra. The pressure to preserve in memory the institutions of one's culture does not invite playful innovation or experimentation. While no doubt some oral cultures are more resilient in this regard than are others, on the whole anthropologists attest to the powerful sanctions against change. "The most apparently trifling innovation may lead to danger, liberate hostile forces, and finally bring about the ruin of its instigator and all dependent upon him" (Levy-Bruhl, 1910/1985, p. 42). The cultural institutions support a limited stock of archetypal forms of appropriate behavior for each member of the society, and the repetition of these alone is sanctioned and validated by the myths. These are the behaviors of sacred ancestors or gods, which it is the human task to copy: "The inhibition against new invention, to avoid placing any possible strain on the memory, continually encouraged contemporary decisions to be framed as though they were the acts and words of the ancestors" or, we might add, gods (Havelock, 1963, p. 121). Or, as Eliade puts it, the individual in oral cultures "acknowledges no act which has not been previously posited and lived by someone else, some other being who was not a man. What he does has been done before. His life is a ceaseless repetition of gestures initiated by others" (1959, p. 15). In such a culture, "only the changeless is ultimately significant" (Frankfort, 1961, p. viii).

While no doubt there are oral cultures for which these generalizations are somewhat less appropriate than for others, they do point to further common *bonnes à penser* of such societies. The pressures against change and innovation serve stability, order, and intellectual security. One's familiar territory is intellectually mapped out, categorized, and under secure control—its dangers are known. Alien territory, outsiders, and the new threaten one's categories; the taboos are casually broken by those with different beliefs and habits (Douglas, 1966).

CLASSIFICATION AND EXPLANATION

Inhabitants of oral cultures often have remarkably detailed knowledge of the flora and fauna of their environments, but their systems of classification often look very odd compared with ours. One oddity much commented on by earlier anthropologists were cases where natives could give remarkably detailed inventories of kinds of plants, trees, or weather conditions, but had no words for "plant," "tree," or "weather." This further supported conclusions about such people's inability to "abstract"—a defect they were supposed to share with children, and which children are supposed to be still deficient in, according to many educationalists. Yet we find in many oral cultures, and in children, the constant use of enormously abstract concepts—such as "good" and "bad." Indeed there are some purely oral languages that use abstractions where we would prefer concrete terms (see Boas, 1911). It is not, to repeat it yet again, abstraction that is the problem, but dissociation from the life world. Literacy enables and encourages this kind of dissociation; it is a product of the techniques of writing, not some property that some human minds have and others lack.

Common among the basic techniques of classification in oral cultures is the use of what Levi-Strauss calls "binary opposites." These are not necessarily opposites in any precise logical or empirical sense, but become used as such by serving as the basis for further discriminations: "The substance of contradictions is much less important than the fact that they exist" (Levi-Strauss, 1966, p. 95).

It is notorious that Levi-Strauss' analyses of myths turn on his first identifying sets of binary opposites on which the myths are built. To many of his critics, this has often seemed a rather arbitrary business, but after the volumes of his *Introduction to a Science of Mythology*, even the most skeptical reader has to concede, at least, the surprising prevalence of such oppositions giving structure to the contents of myths. "All classification," he claims, "proceeds by pairs of contrasts" (Levi-Strauss, 1966, p. 139).

The more simple and general observation about classification in oral cultures is that any attempt at classifying is clearly basic to rational thought. It makes little sense to consider people who develop sophisticated classificatory schemes "irrational." Similarly, of course, children constantly classify too. The differences between classificatory schemes in oral cultures and those in our scientific culture commonly rest on the qualities of phenomena used as the basis for classification.

It is the kinds of explanations offered in oral cultures about natural phenomena that have been taken as clear evidence of those cultures infirmities of mind. Weird medical practices could be put down to simple ignorance of how the body works, but cosmological and natural explanations often have seemed perversely crazy; simple ignorance cannot account for the dogmatic grotesqueness. Levi-Strauss points out, in a neat phrase, that the mistake of earlier interpreters of such explanations "was to think that natural phenomena are *what* myths seek to explain, when they are rather the *medium through which* myths try to explain facts which are themselves not of a natural but a logical order" (1966, p. 95). We must, he says, attend to the form as well as the content of such explanations if we want to understand them.

For us explanation is a central part of our project to understand and control nature, to have practical effects. But its main purpose in oral cultures "is not a practical one. It meets intellectual requirements rather than or instead of satisfying needs" (Levi-Strauss, 1966, p. 9). In serving such intellectual purposes it does not, like our logics, tie itself to the ways the world in fact works; indeed the *sauvage* mind, "does not bind itself down, as our thought does, to avoiding contradictions" (Levi-Bruhl, 1910/1985, p. 78). This perhaps overstates the matter—certainly casual self-contradiction is not a typical feature of the daily conversation of inhabitants of oral cultures any more, nor probably any less, than of an average gaggle of professors. But in the myths of various oral cultures and in their medical lore, our concern with noncontradiction is not a prominent structuring feature. Underlying the surface bizarreness, however, is a quest for order in diversity, whose motive should be familiar to us from the similar motive that drives our science (Horton, 1970, pp. 131–71).

To tie this point in with that discussed above, we might note Malinowski's argument: "They [Trobriand islanders] never explain in any sense of the word; they always state a precedent which constitutes an ideal and a warrant for its continuance, and sometimes practical directions for the procedure" (1954, p. 110). And to tie it in with the earlier discussion of poetics, we might note that what seem like explanations in oral cultures do not focus only on the relevant relationships among content features, but mix in the whole equipment of the psyche, leading to what Goody calls the "personalization of theory" (Goody, 1977, p. 42).

Such explanations tend to look more like, and commonly take the form of, stories. They are stories wrapped up in, or gathering up, the psychic life, the emotions, hopes, and fears, and the prominent contents of their life world. This world of story-shaped explanations echoes Bacon's observation: "For as hieroglyphics came before letters, so parables came before arguments" (Bacon, 1609/1905, p. 824).

From our point of view, this kind of thinking is ineffective. What we mean by "effective," however, is caught up in our conception of a diverse, ever-changing, and, we hope, improving society. Thought in oral societies is and has been generally effective in preserving stability and order in their cultural institutions.

CHILDREN'S BONNES A PENSER

These conclusions about Homeric poets and oral cultures may seem a little brittle as generalizations that might be stretched to modern children. But of course we need not rely only on these generalizations. While they may serve as *bonnes à penser* for our inquiry, we do have the empirical resource of modern children as stubborn checks to our theorizing. And, given that we were all children at one time, we have our memories as well as our observation to help us. We have also our ability to reflect on our everyday forms of thought. It is easy to make superficial connections between a number of the oral *bonnes à penser* considered above and features of modern thought, and some caution is needed to avoid collapsing features of "oral" and "literate" thinking that are in fact profoundly different. At the same time we need to be cautious of perpetuating in some subtle form the "different minds" thesis of nineteenth-century imperialism. We might feel somewhat uncomfortable with Nilsson's robust assertion that "primitive mentality is a fairly good description of the mental behavior of most people today except in their technical or consciously intellectual activities" (Dodds, 1951, p. viii). Since young children rarely engage in technical or consciously intellectual activity, we might wonder whether our characterization of oral *bonnes à penser* also is a good description of their mental behavior.

I have noted above some ways in which the environment and the developmental status of young children today make easy comparisons improper. But we can explore the echoes we find in children's mental behavior with that we see in oral cultures. In this section, then, I will explore children's oral culture and the forms of thought and expression that it contains. One of our tools of exploration of our own past cultural lives is our memory. But, oddly perhaps, for most people that early form of consciousness is inaccessible: Either it has been suppressed by an Augustinian disdain and reluctance to consider the enjoyments of childhood—the happy hours with multicolored snails climbing up our arms and legs, gazing dreamily into the mysterious core of glass marbles—as any meaningful part of our experience, or it has just been forgotten as a kind of irrelevant prelude to the formation of our rational consciousness. Some people, almost invariably poets, seem to have access to their early, that is, oral, consciousness, so I will draw on their writings as well as observations of children.

My general point is that the *bonnes à penser* available to people who do not read and write, and who consequently lack the capacities that literacy provides, condition the mental life and the forms of expression of such people, whether they are modern children or members of oral cultures. What such people think *about* is no doubt endlessly varied, and conditioned by all kinds of other social, environmental, and developmental facts. What *resources* they have to think with, however, and the effects of these resources on how they learn and make sense of their world and experience, is the focus of concern here. I will leave aside entirely any question of the historical continuity of these *bonnes à penser* from immeasurably ancient oral cultures to present day inner city streets and school yards. While apparent absurdity, such a thesis needs serious attention in light of the work of Iona and Peter Opie (1959, 1985). What is clear from their work is that wherever numbers of children of various ages can spontaneously interact, as in school yards or in town and city streets, there is a continuing oral culture of childhood, parts of which are more ancient and persistent than anyone thought possible. It was known that certain nursery rhymes and folktales, usually read by parents, went back for centuries. But even where the content betrays a seventeenth-century origin, the rhyme or tale or singing game or verbal trick may be much older, having simply been refashioned in the seventeenth century by a process the Opies chart as operating constantly. Rather like the reshaping of myth stories to modern conditions, so the Opies record old rhymes and games incorporating the names of modern cartoon characters or film stars, and spreading with astonishing rapidity across their widespread field of research in Britain. The singing games played today in city streets and school yards are passed from generation to generation of children, with barely any contact with the cultural life of adults. The Opies identify games similar to some of today's in pre-Renaissance times, and it seems not unlikely that a child from a modern city might well recognize the chants of a circle song game that referred not to the grand old Duke of York or London Bridge falling down, but perhaps to grand old Hector and those topless towers of Ilium tumbling long ago.

So, while we ignore for now the historical transmission of oral *bonnes à penser*, clearly children respond spontaneously to particular long-persisting oral cultural institutions of their own, such as the singing games. This has something to do with fundamental structures of the human mind, which will also remain ineffable as far as this inquiry is concerned, but also, and more accessibly, it has something to do with learning some of the *bonnes à penser* of orality.

One purpose for exploring these here is to try to offer a somewhat different way of viewing young children's intellectual capacities than is common at present. In the same way that anthropologists have exposed that "primitive thinking" is not necessarily any less sophisticated or less complex than scientific thinking, but merely deals with different things for different social and intellectual purposes and in particular uses techniques that allow "accumulation," so we might develop an equivalent sense of the intellectual sophistication of young children, if we stop considering their mentality and ability to learn almost exclusively in terms of the mastery of the techniques of rationality. The influence of I.Q. testing (Gould, 1981) and even of Piaget's otherwise liberating theories has been to focus on those aspects of young children's thinking that are least developed—particularly on their mastery of those very recently developed *bonnes à penser* of literacy and rationality.

If our focus is on the *bonnes à penser* of orality, and on the imagination that they stimulate, then we can see plainly that these reach an advanced state very rapidly in human beings who are exposed to them. The profile of "oral intellectual development," or of the development of imagination, clearly does not resemble the gradually progressive scales of I.Q., height, weight, and so on, to maturity. Rather, imagination and mastery of oral *bonnes à penser* seem to reach a peak with remarkable speed and then, with appropriate stimulation, be maintained on a plateau (if my geoclasmic metaphors may be forgiven) until maturity, when, ideally, they coalesce with the developing *bonnes à penser* of rationality. In the too frequent cases when rationality is seen as all that matters and can be measured, the profile may be represented as reaching a peak at about age five and then declining to near extinction in adulthood. Perhaps this overstates it, but overstatement may be justified to help make clearer the restriction of the presently dominant view of what is to be stimulated and developed in the educational process and, more importantly, what children have available to learn with. The commonest primary curriculum today is designed as though by those who are aware only of young children's primitive literacy-generated *bonnes à penser* and who are almost entirely unaware of the highly developed, rich and agile oral capacities and *bonnes à penser* children bring with them to school. Well, enough of the sermonizing; let us consider under the same subheadings used in the previous section some oral *bonnes à penser* available to young children.

Poetics of Memory

No doubt due to the influence of computers and to models of thinking in artificial intelligence research and cognitive science that build on analogies with computer functions, we tend to think of the memory as a kind of static store that has been put in place by learning and can be accessed by a process of recall. This way of conceiving of the human memory is hardly intuitively obvious. Indeed, without literacy and the ability to store coded information outside of the mind, one could hardly think of the memory as a storehouse. In early Greek psychology, as expressed in myths, Mnemosyne is the goddess of memory and also the mother of the Muses. In the oral tradition in particular, the memory is an *active* force, and in the long tradition of rhetoric, "reason" and "memory" are considered nearly synonymous (Ong, 1958). The active memory is not confined to oral cultures, of course. The computer storage called "memory" is clearly unlike the human memory in all kinds of significant ways. The analogy holds only because of the element of factual recall. But what is "recalled" from the human memory is rarely the same as what went in. In focusing, as we have, on the importance of emotional coloring and affective impressing of cultural messages, analogies with computers become hopelessly inappropriate. The human memory is an ever-active, emotionally charged, organizing, classifying, reorganizing, and reclassifying faculty, whose separation from "reason" or, indeed, "emotion" makes only limited sense for limited purposes. If our concern is with young children learning the bases of their cultural lives, then our concern with emotion and the active "poetic" memory is more appropriate than a concern with lodging discrete information and skills for later recall. Our memory is more like a place of creative ferment that transforms the character of its contents than like a set of library shelves where things can be looked up and taken out on call.

The set of *bonnes à penser* discussed under this subheading in the previous section are all, in a superficial form, evident in the games, songs, and expressions common among children today. They are exhaustively documented by the Opies and remembered by those of us who have attended schools or lived in heavily populated areas where children spontaneously play together. The poetics of memorization observed in oral cultures are also evident in the oral culture of children—the uses of rhyme and rhythm, of hypnotic repetitions, of chanting while dancing in circles or skipping, of clapping, of getting the words exactly right, and so on. We find also the ubiquitous enchantment by stories. Children pass on in varying forms sets of ghost stories and amazing adventures, many of which remain outside the adult collections of folktales. Stories, as noted above, are the verbal form that can evoke and shape emotional responses to their contents. Their persisting appeal to children indicates their importance in providing children with an affective grasp on the world and on experience.

The techniques used to impress the institutions of oral cultures into the minds of their members were successful because they create powerful images. These were not simply imagined events or characters, but events or characters charged with binding ties of emotional attachment. These techniques stimulated—in a sense brought into being—the imagination, that ability to be moved by, to behave as though one perceives and is affected by, what is actually not present or real. We live in a world of nature, but have invented techniques, developed over uncounted millennia, for stimulating a vivid mental life that draws members of a society together by strong affective bonds. For children in our society, too, these techniques create mental worlds distinct from the natural world around us, mental worlds charged with vividness and emotional intensity. It is a world that generally gives delight and hurts not, and that can enrich our interactions with the world of nature. In their spontaneous play and their games, children use these techniques to create what Huizinga has called "a second, poetic world alongside the world of nature" (1949, p. 23).

So the techniques for memorization stimulate and develop the imagination and the emotions. They create a poetic world that is parasitic on the world of nature but that is also distinct from it, in that things impossible in nature can be imagined to happen. This emotional, imaginative world, generated by the need to remember, is the location from which our culture starts. Influenced by psychoanalysis, Ruth Griffiths concluded her studies of imagination in early childhood with the observation: "It appears evident that phantasy or imagination provides the normal means for the solution of problems of development in early childhood" (1935, p. 187). She saw clearly that "imagination may be called the reflection of the emotional life . . ." in the sense that the conceptual fluidity and flexibility of the imagination allow expression, and development, of the emotional life in ways that action or behavior could not, but she added that "the function of imagination in childhood involves much more than a mere expression of emotion, and may be shown indeed to be necessary to intellectual as well as to emotional development" (Griffiths, 1935, p. 119).

This is a point I think should be emphasized; as rationality is rooted in and emerged gradually from myth in our cultural history, so its development in individuals today can be better understood if seen as rooted in the developed from the *bonnes à penser* that are the main intellectual resources of our first oral culture of childhood. The superficial similarities between the *bonnes à penser* of oral cultures and children's spontaneous play and fantasizing, then, are more profoundly similar in their main intellectual function—they create, stimulate, and develop the imagination. The imagination is the general concept we use for the *bonnes à penser* that generate the poetic world apart from nature. In developing a rich and flexible poetic or imaginative world, we elaborate the *bonnes à penser* that enable us to deal more adequately with the world of nature and to establish meaning in our experience. This is the foundation of education. It is not something to be replaced by logico-mathematical, more rational, more realistic forms of thinking. These forms grow out of imagination and, ideally, grow along with it; imagination is what gives rationality life, color, and meaning. Those who can most fully recall their consciousness as young children identify it as grasping the world emotionally and imaginatively (Coe, 1984).

The *bonnes à penser* of the culture of young children, then, strikingly resemble those common in preserving the institutions of oral cultures. The lore and language, play and games, fantasy and stories, of young children constitute an oral culture that persists from generation to generation, sustained by techniques now familiar to us, and changing gradually in response to present needs. That culture is largely invisible to most adults, as we tend to focus on our interactions with children as determiners of their cultural lives. In those interactions, of course, it is the *bonnes à penser* of rationality that predominate. But, even so, we should not underestimate the amount of support we give to the development of oral *bonnes à penser*. We supply a reliable source of memory storage for children and so remove that pressure to master the techniques of orality that in oral cultures come from the adult world—though the need to "know the words" before they can enter certain games provides some of this pressure in their own oral culture. But we also use endless formulae to impress an array of behavior patterns on children, for road safety, cutlery and utensil use, care of toys and furniture, and so on. We recite proverbs, tell stories, teach rhymes, play verbal games, and tell jokes—all of which help to build the mental structures that systematize memory and poeticize the prosaic world, creating imaginative space and the power to be enchanted by magic and ecstasy. If we begin to think of the objectives of our early childhood curriculum as tied up with magic and ecstasy, with imagination and the *bonnes à penser* of oral cultures, we might see our way to making literacy, numeracy, and rationality richer and more meaningful attainments.

Participation and Conservation

Autobiographers of childhood all describe the mysterious sense of participation in nature that characterizes earliest experience, ach-ingly unrecapturable once the prosaic demands of the pragmatic world carry us away from our first world. The powerful image used again and again in our culture for leaving that early participatory consciousness is the loss of Eden (S. Egan, 1984, esp. Ch. 2). Catching the flavor of that early consciousness requires the powers of the poet because the "experience of childhood . . . is something vastly, *qualitatively* different from adult experience, and therefore cannot be reconstituted simply by accurate narration" (Coe, 1984, p. 1).

It is no wonder that the Garden of Eden is placed at the beginning of human experience. That place of security in nature is an image, an echo, of our early childhood: "Few childhoods, even among the most sordid and the most degrading, are entirely without *some* experience of paradise" (Coe, 1984, p. 67). The—one would like to write "invariable," but so many children have to deal with so much horror —ideal for normal childhood is a sense of being at home in the world, of experiencing a oneness, an immersion, and a participation that absolutely take the world for granted, about which there may be endless questions but no doubts.

This indwelling in our first world is characterized also by a sense of the luminosity, vividness, and brightness of those particulars that catch children's attention. This magical wonder can be engaged by the mysterious heart of a glass marble or the perfection of a soap bubble, or, more commonly, by parts of the natural world. (Oddly perhaps, almost all autobiographies of childhood are silent about toys; they seem to make no lodgment in the mind.) Panstovsky reminds us that "everything was different. Everything was more vivid—the sun brighter, the smell of the fields sharper, the thunder was louder, the rain more abundant and the grass taller" (Coe, 1984, p. 285). This sense of abundance and brightness suffuses the autobiographies of childhood. Thomas Traherne, whose memory of earliest childhood seems more vivid and powerful than most, summed it up long ago: "Then did I dwell within a world of light" (*Divine Reflections in the Native Objects of an Infant-Ey*, c. 1670, in Coe, 1984, p. 255).

In part no doubt, some of this memory of vividness is purely a physiological matter, supported by research that indicates the decay of our senses of taste and smell in particular. But again and again, so many sensations and perceptions in early childhood are remembered as having a particularly powerful and vivid source. In the middle of a Liberian jungle, Graham Greene plays the same note:

> . . . I had got somewhere new, by way of memories I hadn't known I possessed. I had taken up the thread of life from very far back, from so far back as innocence . . . . One doesn't believe, of course in "the vi-

sionary gleam'', in the trailing glory, but there was something in that
early terror and the bareness of one's needs . . . . The sense of taste was
finer, the sense of pleasure keener, the sense of terror deeper and purer.
(1936, pp. 120, 127)

The sense of participation in nature seems to owe something to
a consciousness that, to put it clumsily, is not yet conscious that it is
conscious. One of the distinctive features of thought in oral cultures is
a general lack of systematic reflection on thought itself. When we develop the *bonnes à penser* that enable us to be conscious of our consciousness, we bite the apple of the tree of knowledge and leave Eden.
Our educational purpose is not to preserve this sense of participation
in nature that relies on being unreflective about one's thinking, but we
will want to explore whether some of its vividness, its intellectual security, and its sense of wonder cannot be in significant part taken with
us when we leave Eden.

The ''agonistic tone'' that Ong described as characteristic of
much daily interaction in oral cultures finds echoes in the culture of
childhood today. Before age seven or eight, there seems little difference between boys and girls in this regard, though the particular forms
might differ somewhat. Bragging, exaggerating the extent of one's own
or one's friends' or parents' achievements, are common, as is the polarized world of good and bad, friends and enemies, love and hate, fear
and security. The high pitch of vocal force is characteristic, too.

A significant feature of living in Eden is that things do not change.
Children are notoriously conservative with regard to pragmatic elements of their lives. They become immersed in the particulars of their
life world and cannot weigh the possible benefits of change against the
fixed supports of their known world. As Coe puts it: '' 'Whatever is,
is right'—necessarily so, since there is no known alternative'' (Coe,
1984, p. 239). Children have not yet developed the conceptual capacities that are our agents of dealing with change—the set of *bonnes à
penser* we may sum up as historical consciousness. Thomas Traherne
catches the sense of immortality and permanence that is a feature of
Eden and of early childhood in describing a view over a field of ''im-
mortal wheat which never should be reaped nor ever was sown'' (Coe,
1984, p. 25).

Childhood is the secure haven from which we start our journeys
through the vicissitudes of life. It is the source of our sense of home
and our sense of our true selves, and much of our wandering journey
is made up of trying to recapture that security, that true self that is always with us somewhere within but so hard to keep contact with.
Matthew Arnold writes of the ''unspeakable desire After the knowl-

edge of our buried life" and the struggle to keep to "our true, original course," and to act and speak true to "Our hidden self" (Matthew Arnold, "The Buried Life" 1965, pp. 271–77). Our consciousness begins in a unique, isolated identity, then through language and the shared *bonnes à penser* with which we communicate we gradually become socio-political members of a culture, but within each socio-political being there remains the memory of that isolated, unique self from very far back. An ideal education will not be happy to allow our buried selves to remain lost, providing no access to our true selves as we negotiate our ways through life. We will want to conserve and secure our sense of self and cultivate ways of being true to it.

Classification and Explanation

Coe suggests that "the first intellectual preoccupation of the child is to establish its inventory" (1984, p. 239). One prominent part of the inventory will usually be collections of small, easily obtained, cheap, brightly colored items. These are often classified, but typically in schemes that make little sense or are not satisfactory from an adult point of view. The properties of the objects that form the basis for classification will often vary, so no overall logical scheme is commonly apparent (Inhelder & Piaget, 1969). This is perhaps a somewhat negative way of looking at it. If we focus only on the degrees of progress towards logical classificatory schemes, we are likely to see young children's classification not as a positive thing in itself, but merely as an immature form of something that is to develop later. It is hard sometimes to suppress a sense of irony when reading a researcher's report of a young child's inability to coordinate more than a single feature of some object in a classification task; it sometimes seems that the researcher has precisely the same difficulty coordinating more than a single feature of what the child is about. The intellectual focus in the one case we call science, in the other, a mental incapacity. This returns us to the difficulties anthropologists have had with the classificatory schemes of various oral cultures. The discoveries of the sophistication and underlying similarities with scientific forms of thought of some of these "primitive" forms of classification (Horton, 1970) might alert us to be more circumspect in dealing with young children's classification schemes. Our rational schemes are determined by their effectiveness for some purpose; children's schemes are not primarily concerned with pragmatic effects but with intellectual order and satisfactions.

The point made previously about the use of "abstract thought" in oral cultures might be repeated here with regard to young children.

Children clearly have no difficulty in dealing with all kinds of abstractions and in classifying according to abstract principles: Simply listing "My best friends" or "My favorite pastimes" entails dealing with abstractions. The problem, again, is not with abstraction but with dissociation from the life world of the child. Any use of language entails dealing with "abstraction."

Prominent among all classification systems is the forming of binary opposites, elaborating the poles, and mediating between the poles. Any classificatory system requires first the binary discrimination between what is to be included and what excluded. Again, these binary discriminations will commonly not be opposites in any precise logical or empirical sense, but they will serve as conceptual poles for the purposes of organization and classification. Temperature is grasped intellectually by first discriminating "hot" and "cold"; these are not empirical or logical opposites, but they function as conceptual opposites between which one can begin organizing temperature concepts like "cool," "warm," and so on.

Young children's explanations also reflect a number of features noted in oral cultures. Our logical rule of noncontradiction seems not to bind them so tightly, and their search for explanations seems more for a satisfying story into which to fit the *explanans* than for a logical account. Parents know only too well the experience of being in the midst of a carefully crafted scientific account of something a child wants explained and having it dismissed as clearly irrelevant to what was being asked. As is the case for the diviner or witch doctor in an oral culture, or the scientist in ours, the child is looking for a wider causal context with unifying principles that helps to account for the endless, and so intellectually uncontrollable, diversity of the world (Horton, 1970, pp. 131–71). But for the child and for the witch doctor, that wider context can be made up of a story that can meaningfully encompass the event or phenomenon to be explained. Empirical generalizations, theories, and covering laws are the forms that lead to effective control over events and nature; stories can give us intellectual control and emotional satisfaction. Children also, of course, want common sense pragmatic explanations, but we need to be aware in our desire to provide scientific explanations that story-shaped intellectual control and emotional satisfaction have their values too. In an ideal educational scheme, we will not have to sacrifice any of these.

CONCLUSION

I have tried to pull together, and stitch together, a number of topics not usually dealt with in studying early childhood learning and curriculum. I hope readers will agree that the connections made between the *bonnes à penser* of oral cultures and those common in young children's thinking are genuine, not some straining of terms to support a fanciful hypothesis. I think some of the connections are fairly clear, though in some areas I have moved more hesitantly. One cause of the hesitancy is that the features of children's thinking that I have been most concerned with are those that have in general been least enlightened by research so far. This kind of exploration, however, might provide some notches for research to get a grip on children's fantasy and imagination, and the various *bonnes à penser* of children's minds.

Making connections between the thinking of Australian aborigines, Homer, and modern children invites skepticism, especially if one overdoes the comparisons, as is hard to avoid—or at least to seem to avoid—when drawing attention to the similarities of things usually seen in terms of their contrasts. The divide between orality and literacy, between mythopoeia and logic, between prerational and rational, between mythical and historical, and so on, has usually been seen as two forms of thought struggling for the human mind, and if one wins the other loses. The oral *bonnes à penser*, if this is the case, are thus rendered redundant by literacy. Even some of those scholars who have exposed the workings of certain crucial features of orality conclude that orality and literacy are "contradictory and mutually exclusive" (Lord, 1964, p. 129). This perpetuates Plato's view, as Havelock interprets it. Plato's distinction between the *philodoxoi*, who were caught up with appearances and personal meaning, and the *philosophoi*, who were able to transcend these and see exactly what was the case in reality, set up an opposition we have generally accepted absolutely, where we might be a bit more discriminating. No doubt we have to lose some of the *bonnes à penser* of orality with the onset of literacy, but the educational task is to ensure that enabling people to see exactly what is the case, insofar as we can, does not dissociate whatever is the case from its personal meaning for us.

In oral *bonnes à penser* we have seen the roots, and the continued life, of the imagination. We will not sensibly pass this up for a dessicated literacy: We want literacy to flower with the imagination and children to discover that the shared forms and socializing conventions of language and literacy do not prevent us from retaining contact with our unique isolated consciousnesses, but provide a means of reaching out to others similar but never the same.

Children in their first few years recapitulate the acquisition of language and then of literacy. Language is the first disrupter of the infant's intimate participation in the natural world: "Language creates distance between the self and the object; language generalizes, transforming a unique perception into a common one; language transmutes realities into abstractions" (Coe, 1984, p. 253). That unique consciousness of reality, which is the birthright of each of us, can seem hopelessly lost if language becomes a purely conventionalizing instrument, which persuades the child that its uniqueness was merely an illusion and that one is simply a socialized unit among others who are the same. Between the development of language and the development of literacy, children live in an oral culture. Perfection, fulfillment, and ripeness of this stage of development require two educational achievements. The first is the discovery that language can be fluid and flexible, and does not need to obliterate the original unique consciousness, but can become the agency of its expression; this is one of poetry's functions. It can, with the success of this achievement, provide the child with the ecstatic sense of power that words have given humankind. Naming the natural world and experience correctly, so that every word is at home, taking its place to support the others, is the beginning of our dissociation from nature and also of our power over it. Many mythologies, particularly African ones, describe Creation as taking place bit by bit as God names the parts of the world. Adam in Eden is given the power and ecstasy of naming the animals (a *New Yorker* cartoon showed a delighted Adam gazing up at a giraffe saying "I call you groundhog"). Again, Thomas Traherne, with his preternatural poetic memory of very early childhood, conveys this sense of power:

> The city seemed to stand in Eden, or to be built in Heaven. The streets were mine, the temple was mine, the people were mine, their clothes and gold and silver were mine, as much as their sparkling eyes, fair skins and ruddy faces. The skies were mine, and so were the sun and moon and stars, and all the World was mine; and I the only spectator and enjoyer of it. (S. Egan, 1984, p. 73)

(If his parents, walking along by his side, were to wonder "What's going through the little fellow's head?" the answer would not of course be these polished phrases, but the feeling and the sparkle and the brightness would surely be there.)

The second educational achievement in mastering language is to enable the child to discover that language can have a distinct, dynamic life of its own. It is not merely something into which or through which our experience can be expressed, but it is itself an extension of our experience. It can initially be the means of a new kind of aesthetic delight: Its sounds can be shaped into patterns; it can allow puns, jokes, stories, malapropisms; it can pour magical meaning into voids, and spark meaning out of its combinations.

The same problems and possibilities recur with the achievement of literacy. It can become a mass of conventional forms and clichés that stamp the individual consciousness far back into the recesses of the mind, or it too can become a liberator and amplifier for each unique consciousness. The educational task is to ensure that the socializing, conventionalizing skills of literacy are mastered, but in a way that does not cut off or undermine its individualizing powers. In addition, it can become a further amplifier of our experience.

The implication of this discussion, then, is that the foundations of education are poetic. We begin as poets. The *logographoi* in our cultural history, the wielders of rational prose, came long after and built upon a heritage of poetic insight, organization of consciousness, and techniques for thinking. To become subtle wielders of rational prose and the mathematical language that accompanied its development—in history, science, mathematics, social studies, and so on—we must first develop the poet in each child. "Poet" is perhaps a dangerous word to use because of its varied modern associations to different people; I mean what Vico saw and what other scholars whose work I have drawn on in this chapter have tried to describe. Perhaps it might be better to settle for "imagination." By this I mean the *bonnes à penser* explored above. The sermonizing here has been to stress that in early childhood we are concerned with the foundations of education. To build them properly, we need to be clear about the top floors, of course, but we also need to build proper foundations out of appropriate material and not to be so enamored of the decorations and embellishments of the penthouse suites of rationality that we skimp on the foundations or try to build them out of the delicate material of the pinacles of the building.

The *bonnes à penser* of orality that we will seek to develop must be influenced by the literacy and rational modes of inquiry and consciousness that are to succeed them, but also our conception of that literacy and rationality must be shaped by the orality from which they emerge.

REFERENCES

Allott, Kenneth (Ed.). (1979). *The poems of Matthew Arnold*. New York: Longman.

Bacon, Francis. (1609/1905). *De sapientiae veterum (Wisdom of the ancients)*.

In John M. Robertson (Ed.), *The philosophical works of Francis Bacon*. London: Routledge.

Boas, Franz (1911). *The mind of primitive man*. New York: The Macmillan Co.

Cassirer, Ernst. (1946). *Language and mind*. (Trans. Susanne K. Langer). New York: Harper.

Coe, Richard. (1984). *When the grass was taller*. New Haven: Yale University Press.

Dodds, E. R. (1951). *The Greeks and the irrational*. Berkeley and Los Angeles: University of California Press.

Douglas, Mary. (1966). *Purity and danger*. London: Routledge and Kegan Paul.

Egan, Kieran. (1985). *Teaching as story-telling*. London, Ontario: The Althouse Press.

Egan, Kieran. (1987). *Primary understanding*. New York: Routledge and Kegan Paul.

Egan, Susanna. (1984). *Patterns of experience in autobiography*. Chapel Hill: University of North Carolina Press.

Eliade, Mircea. (1959). *Cosmos and history*. New York: Harper & Row.

Evans-Pritchard, E. E. (1936). *Witchcraft, oracles and magic among the Azande*. Oxford: Oxford University Press.

Frankfort, Henri. (1961). *Ancient Egyptian religion*. New York: Harper.

Frankfort, Henri, et al. (1949). *Before philosophy*. Harmondsworth, Middlesex: Pelican.

Goody, Jack. (1977). *The domestication of the savage mind*. Cambridge: Cambridge University Press.

Goody, Jack, & Watt, Ian. (1968). "The consequences of literacy." In Jack Goody (Ed.), *Literacy in traditional societies*. Cambridge: Cambridge University Press.

Gould, Stephen Jay. (1981). *The mismeasure of man*. New York: Norton.

Greene, Graham. (1936). *Journey without maps*. New York: Viking.

Griffiths, Ruth. (1935). *A study of imagination in early childhood*. London: Kegan Paul, Trench, Trubner.

Havelock, Eric A. (1963). *Preface to Plato*. Cambridge, MA.: Harvard University Press.

Havelock, Eric A. (1976). *Origins of Western literacy*. Toronto: Ontario Institute for Studies in Education.

Horton, Robert. (1970). "African traditional thought and Western science." In Bryan Wilson (Ed.), *Rationality*. Oxford: Blackwell.

Huizinga, Johan. (1949). *Homo ludens*. London.

Inhelder, B., & Piaget, Jean. (1969). *The early growth of logic in the child*. New York: Norton.

Jowett, B. (1956). *The works of Plato*. New York: Modern Library.

Leach, Edmund. (1967). "Genesis as myth." In John Middleton (Ed.), *Myth and cosmos*. New York: Natural History Press.

Levi-Strauss, Claude. (1962). *Totemism*. London: Merlin.

Levi-Strauss, Claude (1966). *The savage mind*. Chicago: Univ. of Chicago Press.

Levi-Strauss, Claude. (1969). *The raw and the cooked*. New York: Harper & Row.

Levi-Strauss, Claude. (1978). *Myth and meaning*. Toronto: University of Toronto Press.

Levy-Bruhl, Lucien. (1985). *How natives think*. Princeton, NJ: Princeton Univ. Press.

Lord, Albert B. (1964). *The singer of tales*. Cambridge, MA.: Harvard University Press.

Luria, A. R. (1976). *Cognitive development: Its cultural and social foundations*. Cambridge, MA.: Harvard University Press.

Malinowski, Bronislaw. (1954). *Magic, science and religion*. New York: Anchor.

Ong, Walter J. (1958). *Ramus and talon inventory*. Darby, PA: Folcroft Library Editions.

Ong, Walter J. (1977). *Interfaces of the world*. Ithaca, N.Y.: Cornell University Press.

Ong, Walter J. (1982). *Orality and literacy*. London and New York: Methuen.

Ong, Walter J. (1983). *Ramus, method, and the decay of dialogue: From the art of discourse to the art of reason*. Cambridge, MA: Harvard Univ. Press.

Opie, Iona, and Opie, Peter. (1959). *The lore and language of schoolchildren*. Oxford: Oxford University Press.

Opie, Iona, and Opie, Peter. (1985). *The singing game*. Oxford: Oxford University Press.

Parry, Milman. (1928). *L'epithète traditionelle dans Homere*. Paris: Société d'Editions "Les Belles Lettres."

Peabody, Berkley. (1975). *The winged word*. Albany: State University of New York Press.

Spence, Jonathan, D. (1984). *The memory palace of Matteo Ricci*. New York: Viking Penguin.

Vernant, Jean Pierre. (1983). *Myth and thought among the Greeks*. London: Routledge & Kegan Paul.

Wood, Michael. (1985). *In search of the Trojan War*. London: BBC.

7 ◇ Prospects for the Good Life: Education and Perceptive Imagination

KAREN HANSON
Indiana University

The means and ends of education are, as Dewey argues, not completely separable. Questions about methods demand answers about goals, and well-defined aims require clarity about possible paths toward their achievement. Nevertheless, full conscientiousness, as well as all hope for progress, depends upon finding some initial point of entry into the tangle of questions about theory and practice, objectives and instruments.

In her 1977 book on education, *Schools of Thought*, Mary Warnock avows and tries to justify her conviction that the most important question about education is "What should be taught?"—that the most crucial issue in education is the determination of the curriculum. She also tries to answer this question, to speak to this issue, and her remarks on this topic are grounded on the supposition that an individual is improved and life enhanced by education. Education would be pointless, she reasons, if it did not lead to, or contribute to, a better life. Thus, problems of educational practice are tied to practical and theoretical questions about the nature of the good life.

Warnock's own conception of the good life requires the development in the child of imagination, virtue, and a capacity for work, and she would base all curricular decisions on the prospect of such development. She recognizes that there is controversy about two of her desiderata. Whether or how the schools should engage in moral education and to what extent, or in what ways, the schools should serve as or be related to vocational preparation are, she acknowledges, questions that excite dispute. But about the third of her goals there is, she claims, no argument.

> Being more imaginative, is, I believe, like being more healthy. There is no need to raise the question "Why do you want it?" or "How does it

benefit you?'' If you know what ''being healthy'' means, you know that it is desirable, and desirable both for its own sake and for its consequences . . . . Analogously, while everyone exercises imagination in some degree, the desirability of exercising it more is not to be defended on the grounds that it leads to anything good, though it may well do so, but simply on the grounds that, if understood, it will be seen to *be* good. Thus it becomes clear that if a particular study can be shown to increase the imaginative powers of a child, then it is a strong candidate for inclusion in the educational curriculum, granted that the point of the curriculum is to offer to the child the possibility of a better life than he could have without it. (Warnock, 1977, p. 153)

But Warnock's confidence that she has here at last isolated one educational goal that is beyond dispute is, it seems to me, unwarranted. It is not at all obvious that ''being more imaginative is . . . like being more healthy''; indeed, if the analogy is as appropriate as Warnock believes it to be, then the idea of an ''excessive imagination'' should strike us as impossible and the phrase ''a morbid imagination'' should seem to us oxymoronic. But the fact is that these notions are not self-contradictory, and this fact should alert us to the possibility that being more imaginative is not in itself always and necessarily good or desirable. This possibility of morbidity, in particular, may remind us that we can care about the *bent* of a child's, an individual's, imagination and, perhaps, that we can worry about significant connections between an individual's imagination and his or her behavior.

Yet Warnock holds that, if imagination is properly understood, the exercise of it will always ''simply . . . be seen to *be* good.'' The form of her insistence suggests that the depth of any disagreement we may feel on this point can be measured only by a direct examination of the notion of imagination. I should like to explore briefly Warnock's remarks on this topic, to assess her understanding of imagination, and then to relate that assessment to the specific educational recommendations she proffers. In the course of this discussion, I hope also to prepare a setting for some of my own thoughts on the cultivation of imagination, and so to work toward my own point of entry to the knotty problems of education.

Warnock claims that

Imagination . . . is involved in all perception of the world, in that it is that element in perception which makes what we see and hear meaningful to us. It is . . . the image-making capacity, [and so] also involved in memory of the past and the envisaging of the future, as well as in dreaming and daydreaming, [in] fantasy. (1977, p. 152)

In taking the view she does, Warnock seems to be standing on the shoulders of giants. She says that her concept of imagination "is related to the concept as analysed by philosophers such as Hume and Kant and Wittgenstein" and is close to the sense of the word as it was employed by Shelley, Coleridge, and Wordsworth (Warnock, 1977, p. 152). But *is* there a philosophically defensible and an educationally useful concept of imagination that was held in common by all these great and diverse philosophers and poets, or is there such a concept to be distilled from their various writings? Warnock argues that there is; however, the primary locus of her arguments is not *Schools of Thought*, but her 1976 book, *Imagination*. We must attend to that earlier work, then, if we are to do justice to her remarks in the later.

I think that there is one particular thesis set out in the earlier work, and reiterated in the later—the assertion that imagination is involved in all perception—that we should scrutinize most carefully; for it is from her conviction that imagination is involved in all perception that Warnock derives her sense of the profound importance of educating the child's imagination. Such education then "may or may not lead to 'creativity,' " she says, "but it will certainly lead to [the child's] inhabiting a world more interesting, better loved and understood, less boring, than if he [or she] had not been so educated" (Warnock, 1977, p. 153). We might agree that if the role of imagination is so vast, its education will have the pervasive consequences Warnock envisions. But is its role so vast? Is imagination involved in all perception?

Warnock is certainly correct in enlisting Hume and Kant in defense of her position, although each of these philosophers supports the central claim for rather different reasons. A short rehearsal of their relevant remarks will highlight the critical differences.

Hume divides what he calls "all the perceptions of the human mind" into "two distinct kinds, . . . *Impressions* and *Ideas*."

> Those perceptions which enter with most force and violence we may name *impressions*; and under this name I comprehend all our sensations, passions and emotions, as they make their first appearance in the soul. By *ideas* I mean the faint images of these in thinking and reasoning. (Hume, 1888, p. 1; Book I, Part I, section I)

We might be tempted to understand Hume's distinction in the following way: By "ideas" he means images, and images are used, are what we are aware of, in thought. He labels "impressions" whatever we are aware of in sensory perception, as well as in internal sensation and in unrecollected, original feelings and emotions.

But there is an ambiguity in this interpretation of his distinction, and that ambiguity could lead us to misconceive his position. Most of us think that what we are aware of in most ordinary sense perception is an external world, that we see and touch, for example, tables and chairs and trees and flowers, and that these objects have a continued existence independent of our perception of them. But Hume famously says that "all impressions are internal and perishing existences, and appear as such" (Hume, p. 194; Book I, Part IV, section II), that what we are aware of in sense perception is not felt as external to us (Hume, 1888, p. 191–2; Book I, Part IV, section II). That we think there *is* an external world, that we think some of our impressions are impressions *of* external objects, objects that have a continued existence independent of our perception of them, is then, to Hume, a feature of our psychology that wants an account.

He offers such an account, in which imagination is given a central role. It cannot be, Hume says, the *senses* that produce this belief in the continued existence of external objects. How, he asks, could the senses be responsible for our idea that objects continue to exist even when those objects do not appear to the senses? That, he says, would be "a contradiction in terms" and would involve the idea "that the senses continue to operate, even after they have ceas'd all manner of operation" (Hume, 1888, p. 188; Book I, Part IV, section II). And it cannot be *reason* that grounds our belief in the objects of the external world: "Whatever convincing arguments philosophers may fancy they can produce to establish the belief of objects independent of the mind, 'tis obvious these arguments are known to very few, and that 'tis not by them, that children, peasants, and the greatest part of mankind are induced to attribute objects to some impressions" (Hume, 1888, p. 193; Book I, Part IV, section II).

It is, Hume concludes, the *imagination* that supports our notions of the objects of the external world. Our impressions are discontinuous and ever-changing, yet we can make coherent or roughly uniform collections of some of them, and, when we do, the imagination helps us posit the notion that there are independent objects that, in having these coherent impressions, we are perceiving.

> The imagination, when set into any train of thinking, is apt to continue, even when its object fails it, and like a galley put in motion by the oars, carries on its course without any new impulse. (Hume, 1888, p. 198; Book I, Part II, section II)

Although the objects of our sense impressions do sometimes have a certain coherence and uniformity, this coherence would be much greater if only we posited the idea of the continued existence of these objects. So the imagination does this, continuing on its own "till it renders the uniformity as complete as possible" (Hume, 1888, p. 198; Book I, Part I, section II). And, what is more, imagination supports the supposition of each external object by supplying to the mind, from memory, an appropriate image, so there will seem to be no gaps or discontinuities in the sense impressions.

> When the . . . resemblance of our perceptions makes us ascribe to them and identity, we may remove the seeming interruption by feigning a continued being, which may fill those intervals, and preserve a perfect and entire identity to our perceptions. (Hume, 1888, p. 208; Book I, Part IV, section II)

Thus it is, in Hume's view, imagination that is primarily responsible for our conviction that there is an external world, a world of objects having continued existence independent of our perception of them. Since we *do* take ourselves to inhabit a world of tables and chairs, trees and flowers, a world of independent objects, if Hume's account is correct, then imagination does indeed play a huge role in our lives. If Hume's view is right, then Warnock is right: Imagination *is* involved in all perception of the world.

There are, of course, good reasons to reject Hume's account. The components out of which it is constructed are questionable: What counts as a single impression? How are impressions differentiated and enumerated and how do we judge the similarities and differences between them? How do we tell the difference between an impression and an idea? (Hume says that the only experiential difference between the two is their relative "force and vivacity" (Hume, 1888, p. 2 [Book I, Part I, section I]). But if we overlook the vagueness of this measure, either we shall feel this claim to be untrue to our experience or we shall find ourselves facing further theoretical problems as we try to understand Hume's accounts of memory and thinking.) But we need not here pursue a detailed criticism of Hume's theory of perception. It is the use of Hume's theory to support educational recommendations that is our present concern.

Warnock, in particular, argues from the importance of the imagination to the idea of the importance of a curriculum that develops this faculty. She seems confident that once we grant that imagination plays a pervasive role in perception, once we see that it is the faculty that makes what we see and hear meaningful to us, we will admit the propriety of making the development of imagination one of our fundamental educational goals. But it seems to me that Warnock's enlistment of Hume's account severely weakens the connection she is trying to make between theory, or analysis, and recommended practice. She pledges some allegiance to Hume because she wants her concept of imagination to be recognized as fitting within the boundaries of the Western philosophical tradition's understanding of that notion. But this tradition seems hostile to the conclusion that the imagination needs education and development.

For Hume, the role that imagination plays in perception is that of a magician: It makes us believe we see (hear, and so on) what we do not. And while it is true that Hume's account might warrant the claim that imagination makes our experience meaningful, or significant, this significance is literally mundane and distinctly banal: We really have a series of fleeting, ephemeral impressions, but imagination lets us take those impressions to signify one continuously existing independent object—a tree, for example, a table, a chair. Do we need education to "enrich" our lives thus, to help us to this sort of meaningfulness in our experience? Not even Hume would think so. Indeed, we should remember that his theory assigns this task of going beyond mere impressions to imagination, and not to reason, just because of his recognition that "children, peasants, and the greatest part of mankind"—in short, for Hume, the uneducated—automatically see a world full of external, independent objects. We must conclude that Warnock's alliance with Hume, though firmly grounded on some claims about the nature of imagination, cannot be of any help to her in the matter of curriculum planning.

A similar judgment would, I think, be the consequence of a study of the connection between Warnock's claims—and aims—and Kant's analyses. Again, Kant certainly does hold that imagination is involved in all perception, so Warnock is surely correct to cite him as an authoritative antecedent. Kant explicitly says that "imagination is a necessary ingredient of perception itself."

> What is first given to us is appearance. When combined with consciousness, it is called perception. (Save through its relation to a consciousness . . . , appearance could never be for us an object of knowledge, and so would be nothing to us; and since it has in itself no objective reality, but exists only in being known, it would be nothing at all.) Now, since every appearance contains a manifold, and since different perceptions therefore occur in the mind separately and singly, a combination of them, such as they cannot have in sense itself, is demanded. There must therefore exist in us an active faculty for the synthesis of this manifold. To this faculty I give the title, imagination. (Kant, 1965, p. 143–4; A120)

But again, the way in which Kant describes the role of imagination, his insistence that there would be no perception *at all* without the proper functioning of this faculty of the mind, suggests that there is no need to *develop* imagination through education.

Kant in fact goes beyond Hume at this point; Hume implies that, were we as circumspect as we ought to be, if we did not "disguise" our experience, we would be aware of sense impressions in their purity. But Kant claims that, without imagination, there would be no human experience; not even appearances would exist. So Hume's account might, after all, be taken to suggest the idea that education could deal with imagination—but the suggestion would have to be that education might *eliminate* the mediation of imagination in perception, in order to bring us closer to metaphysical truth. Kant's account does not admit the possibility of pristine appearance, appearance uncombined with consciousness, or the manifold of appearance unworked by imagination. Since Kant holds that the faculty of imagination is a precondition of *all* experience, it is, again, hard to sustain, in conjunction with his account, the idea that specific educative experience is necessary to develop this faculty.

In sum, it is not clear that Warnock's citation of these great historical sources, and of this portion of the tradition of discussion on imagination, can provide a firm foundation for the educational recommendation she offers. It even seems there might be something peculiarly unhelpful to the educational project in the specific assertion that all perception involves imagination. There is a variant of that assertion—namely, the claim that perception involves *interpretation*—that might be all that Warnock really wants or needs to argue, for this latter claim would not so easily vitiate the idea that education should be directed toward the imagination.

William James presents elegant expositions of the thesis that we interpret reality in perceiving it; see, for example, Chapter IX ("The Stream of Thought") of Volume One of *The Principles of Psychology* (1890), and Lecture VII ("Pragmatism and Humanism") of *Pragmatism* (1976). A version of this claim is most strongly advanced today by Nelson Goodman, one of the inheritors of pragmatism's legacy. (See, for example, "The Way the World Is" in *Problems and Projects* [1972] and Chapters V–VII of *Ways of Worldmaking* [1978].) I shall not argue here either for or against this thesis. I will only note that interpretations can be novel or standard, fresh or familiar; and we might think that a particular educational curriculum could foster the ability to perceive the world in fresh and original ways. We might say that such a curriculum would help develop the imagination. But it is thus clear that, even if all perception does involve interpretation, we should not conclude that all perception involves imagination. The standard or familiar interpretation should hardly be called "imaginative."

I would take historical support for this position from section xi of Part II of Wittgenstein's *Philosophical Investigations* (1963). I would, in fact, want to draw heavily on those remarks of Wittgenstein's in order to suggest what I would take to be an adequate account of imagination. But, oddly enough, so would Warnock, and she implies, in *Schools of Thought* (1977), that her contrary view of imagination would be endorsed by, or at least that it is derived from, Wittgenstein. I think she is clearly wrong here, and if I can show that she is, I shall also be preparing the ground for my own claims about education and imagination.

In the relevant section of the *Investigations*, Wittgenstein comments on perception and interpretation and speaks about seeing an object as we interpret it, seeing according to an interpretation, seeing an aspect of an object. We can use the famous duck–rabbit example to make plain what it is to "see . . . as . . . ." That figure can be seen, by most of us, as either a duck's head (i.e., a pictured duck's head) or a rabbit's head. Most of us can shift at will from seeing one aspect of the picture to seeing the other. We can also think here of the well-known Necker cube. If we focus on one of its squares, the square can be seen either as an outer surface or as an inner surface of a transparent box. This picture can seem spontaneously to reverse in depth. Wittgenstein says that "the flashing of an aspect on us seems half visual experience, half thought" (1963, p. 197).

It is because of such comments that Warnock takes Wittgenstein to support her contention that imagination is involved in all perception. Wittgenstein does say that

> The concept of an aspect is akin to the concept of an image. In other words: the concept "I am now seeing it as . . ." is akin to "I am now having *this* image."
>
> Doesn't it take imagination to hear something as a variation on a particular theme? And yet one is perceiving something in so hearing it. (1963, p. 213)

But all that Wittgenstein here remarks is a *kinship* between aspects and images, and he implies only that imagination *can* be involved in perception. In fact, he explicitly claims that " 'seeing as . . .' is not part of perception. And for that reason it is like seeing and again not like"

(Wittgenstein, 1963, p. 197). And he explicitly denies that the concept of "seeing . . . as" is appropriately applied to all perception. One can't say, at the sight of the knife and fork beside one's dinner plate, "Now I am seeing this as a knife and fork."

> One doesn't "take" what one knows as the cutlery at a meal *for* cutlery; any more than one ordinarily tries to move one's mouth as one eats, or aims at moving it. (Wittgenstein, 1963, p. 195)

But, of course, one knows these objects to be cutlery only because one has had a certain upbringing, because one lives in a certain social setting. We might note that in a world without rabbits, or pictures or descriptions of rabbits, none of us would see the rabbit aspect of the duck–rabbit. The possibility of particular interpretations is bound, in various ways, by social circumstances and physical environment. And, thus, the possibility of that subset of interpretations that we might properly call "imaginative" is likewise constrained. Again, we shouldn't call the common or the conventional, "imaginative."

What counts as going beyond the obvious or conventional, what may require the engagement of imagination, will vary. Picture a duck rancher, a man who lives isolated in a marsh devoid of rabbits. For him, seeing the rabbit in the duck–rabbit may be quite a task. *His* seeing of the rabbit *might* be thought to require imagination. It is worth remarking, too, that this person could be helped to the achievement of this sight, guided in his use of imagination. If we enrich his experience in appropriate ways, if we give him, say, a copy of Dürer's picture of a rabbit or, perhaps, a volume of Beatrix Potter, we might provide the springboard for his leap beyond the perception that is a product of his everyday existence. He can now see more in the picture than the familiar duck.

I am thus approaching a point of agreement with Warnock. She recommends exposure to art and literature in the schooling of imagination, and I would certainly concur. The fact of this particular agreement should not, however, obscure the differences in the bases and implications of our respective views. I have rejected Warnock's contention that imagination is involved in all perception, and I have tried to show that her reliance on some historically important accounts of imagination is either inappropriate or misguided. Finally, though I am ready to endorse some of her specific recommendations for the curriculum, I am dubious about her ultimate test of whether or not a course of studies enhances the imagination. "The test," she says, "is whether or not the educational curriculum is boring" (Warnock, 1977, p. 153).

Warnock offers interesting speculations on the topic of boredom and on the kinds and arrangement of studies that might keep pupils interested. The connection she tries to draw between the engagement of imagination and *absorption*—which is incompatible with boredom—is initially plausible; and, if there is this connection, she has that as a good reason for proposing the curricular criterion she does.

Of course, the claimed connection deserves further scrutiny. We have seen reason to doubt Warnock's insistence on the omnipresence of imaginative functioning and so might well suppose that some activities can be absorbing without thereby necessarily engaging the imagination. (Think of a child practicing adding by working his or her way through a page of exercises. The child might be absorbed in this work, though trying for standard, not imaginative, answers.) Moreover, it may be that the imagination can be engaged and the individual yet remain bored. (Think of the plausibility of some of Anton Chekov's characters, individuals absorbed in fantasy and daydreams who yet remain enervated, weary, and excruciatingly bored.)

Beyond these theoretical uncertainties about the relationship between imagination and boredom there is also the larger question of whether or not it is in fact important to avoid all boredom in school. Against Warnock's contention we might find ourselves siding with William James, who brusquely asserts that "it is nonsense to suppose that every step in education *can* be interesting" (1958, p. 51). If we think again of a child learning addition, or practicing the multiplication tables, or mastering some rules of grammar, we must realize that, though the child might be absorbed in this work, he or she might not be; nonetheless, we might feel that this material should be learned. We want the child not just to be imaginative, but also to be, in some sense, conventional, to learn and to some extent participate in our shared thoughts, our shared form of life. This shared social foundation may be, in fact, what supports the vault of imagination.

I indicated that I am prepared to accept some of Warnock's specific curricular recommendations, though on the grounds of my own conflicting view of imagination. I mentioned, in particular, the claim that great art and literature exercise or fuel the imagination and so should be studied. I should like to conclude by spelling out the terms of my agreement with Warnock on this point and then indicating what I take to be the justification for any appropriate reference, in educational planning, to the cultivation of imagination.

We might all grant that exposure to art and literature allows us a broader range of experience and can provide us with actual access to others' imaginative conceptions. And, of course, natural and social science, too, can both inform and be informed by imagination and a knowledge of these spheres, of the motivations for and implications of these sorts of theories, can also enrich the student's imagination. It may then seem that the appeal to the cultivation of imagination simply restores the traditional curriculum, and quite possibly sanctions as well some voguish variety of new studies, or currently fashionable school activities that promise new ranges of intellectual and emotional development.

But, in fact, not all new contenders for a place in the curriculum can be justified by the claim that they build imagination; and not all approaches to the traditional curriculum contribute equally to the growth of imagination. Moreover, the enhancement of this capacity is not, and should not be, our only desideratum in education; and so our concern for this enhancement is not our only tool for curricular design. Still, the improvement of the imagination should be one central educational goal; and if the reasons for this are better understood, we shall increase our chances of understanding and hence achieving the goal itself. We can take more direct guidance in both educational planning and practice from a keener sense of what is crucial about the promotion of the student's imagination. What does finally constitute the importance, for education, of a concern with imagination? Why should we aim to develop it?

Our answer must begin with a recognition of the peculiar powers of the imagination, and the first feature of imagination at which we should look is one that is also studied by Warnock. If proprietary rights to the philosophical version of this insight are being sustained, however, the work of Jean-Paul Sartre must be acknowledged, as Warnock herself notes in *Imagination*. In Sartre's *Being and Nothingness* (1956), as well as in his two small books focused on the topic of imagination. *L'Imagination* (1981) and *L'Imaginaire* (1971), the claim is prominent: Imagination is a key to freedom. I have tried to emphasize the way in which the exercise of imagination moves us away from the conventional, the common, and the familiar. Imagination is what allows us to envision possibilities in or beyond the actualities in which we are immersed. We do not thus merely escape in thought the bounds of reality; we know that something other than this immediate temporary reality is possible—and we may then be excited to effect changes in the world. Imagination may be a form of escape, but insofar as that escape is to the sight of possibilities beyond the immediate, it can be a path to personal and social freedom.

It can also, however, picture new forms of degradation and subjection. Not all of its free designs are happy or virtuous. Theorists such as Warnock may have faith in the inherent goodness of imagination, and others may suppose it neither good nor bad unless and until it impels action that requires evaluation. But imaginings are not always beautiful and just, and we ignore their true character if we approach them with a moral or aesthetic sieve so coarse as to catch only action. A fine, worthy imagination involves accuracy of perception and intellection and delicacy and decency of affective response. Both the activity and the passivity of imagination must be developed and shaped together, for if these phases or aspects are either out of balance or improperly turned, imagination may offer not freedom but new forms of captivity.

The morbid imagination is on its face unpleasant; beyond that, it is wearing, bent on eroding clear sight of wholesome possibilities. Thus a problem of feeling may become a problem of perception and, perhaps ultimately, a problem of behavior. The vigorous and well-educated imagination, on the other hand, should enlarge opportunities. It will do this in part by recognizing the extent to which the world is subject to interpretation and acting on that recognition. Added significance will then spread over the world, through the deepened experience of an individual. Such experiences need never, in and of themselves, be rejected as excessive.

But imagination *can* wretchedly wander, and there is a mode of imagining that may sometimes be denounced as faulty. Fancies detached from real circumstances, for example, while they can sometimes offer needed relief, can also obstruct useful vision, as the soothing compress upon the tired eyes is also sometimes a blindfold. If the world is to be imaginatively interpreted, then *it* must be interpreted. There must be a strong focus upon the world and its relevant actual circumstances, physical or mental, formal or emotional, present or historical, social or private. The excessive imagination neglects this task of focus. Excesses of imagination may then be enthralling, but for imagination to contribute finally to liberation, reality must be carefully surveyed, the actual world must be allowed to impinge on both intellect and feeling. Only from this point can new possibilities that *are* genuinely new possibilities be discerned. Imagination is, then, to be prized and nurtured because of its link to freedom; but, as is often the case, this exercise of freedom will be most productive if it is disciplined.

A kind of sober ecstasy is also at the heart of another special power of imagination, a power that suggests yet another fundamental reason why the proper cultivation of imagination must be a concern of education: It is imagination that gives us whatever capacity we have to move toward better, more harmonious, and more finely tuned relations with others. I have stressed the link between the imaginative view and the uncommon view. There is at least one object in this world that none of us can ever behold from exactly the same real perspective as any other's. That object is oneself. If we are to match others' perceptions of us, of ourselves and our behavior, we must reach out imaginatively and identify with those others, try—in and through imagination—to take their perspectives.[1] If we can do this, if we can imaginatively identify with others, we can at once achieve both a better sense of ourselves and of those others. And when we do this for as long as we sustain this sympathetic imagination, we live with those others on truly common ground. We move from isolation to a kind of communion, and this, in itself, may amount to a better life. And a better life is, I think, after all the central goal of a good education.

REFERENCES

Goodman, N. (1972). *Problems and projects*. Indianapolis, IL: Bobbs-Merrill.

Goodman, N. (1978). *Ways of worldmaking*. Indianapolis, IL: Hackett.

Hume, D. (1888; originally published in 1739). *A treatise of human nature*. (Ed. L. A. Selby-Bigge). Oxford: Oxford Univ. Press.

James, W. (1890). *The Principles of psychology*. London: Macmillan.

James, W. (1958; originally published in 1899). *Talks to teachers*. New York: Norton.

James, W. (1976). *Pragmatism*. Cambridge, MA: Harvard Univ. Press.

Kant, I. (1965; originally published in 1781, second edition 1787). *Critique of pure reason*. (Trans. Norman Kemp Smith). New York: St. Martin's Press.

Sartre, J.P. (1956). *Being and nothingness*. New York: Philosophical Society.

Sartre, J.P. (1971). *L'imaginaire*. Paris: Gallimard.

Sartre, J.P. (1981). *L'imagination*. Paris: Presses Universitaires de France.

Warnock, M. (1976). *Imagination*. Berkeley, CA.: Univ. of California Press.

Warnock, M. (1977). *Schools of thought*. London: Faber & Faber.

Wittgenstein, L. (1963). *Philosophical investigations*. (Trans. G. E. M. Anscombe). Oxford: Blackwell.

---

[1]This is a claim I argue for and develop in more detail in *The Self Imagined* (London: Routledge and Kegan Paul, 1986).

8 ◇ "What If" and "As If": Imagination and Pretend Play in Early Childhood

OTTO WEININGER

Ontario Institute for Studies in Education, Canada

Patrick, just three, decided one day that he was going to use "imagination" to bake a cake. He announced that to do this he would need flour, eggs, baking powder, sugar, salt, marshmallows, and chocolate chips, and that the cake would have to go into the microwave oven to cook. Smiling, his mother agreed, assuming that he intended to pretend all these ingredients and play at baking a cake. But after listing these ingredients for her, he went into the kitchen, sat himself up at the counter, and began to ask her to get the ingredients that he would need. He decided he needed the biggest bowl and a stirrer, and would need the flour first. His mother asked how much he needed, and Patrick responded, "About one cup." After receiving this, he poured it into the mixing bowl and asked for the baking powder, but seemed a bit puzzled. So his mother said, "We usually use only a little bit of baking powder," and Patrick said, "I need only a little bit too." His mother suggested a teaspoon, and he agreed this was about right. The rest of the ingredients followed, in much the same fashion, until he stopped and said that he would have to use his imagination again. After a few seconds of reflection, Patrick announced that all he needed was an egg and some water. After he added these and stirred everything up, he put the mixture into a baking pan and placed it in the microwave with his mother's help. He wanted to know how long it should stay there, and his mother replied, "It looks as if it needs about five minutes." Patrick agreed that was just the right amount of time. When the cake came out, Patrick was obviously delighted, and set it on the windowsill to cool while he watched it, smiling.

Patrick was using his imagination, and to him, as well as to many other young children with whom I have worked, there is a great difference between "imagination" and "pretend." When a young child uses imagination, he is thinking about solutions to various problems he has perceived around him; so when Patrick announced he would use "imagination" to make a cake, he was thinking, silently and out loud, about what he would need and what the process would be in order to do this.

Imagination is different from pretend, although the two are intimately connected in the ongoing interactive process of thoughts and actions in a child's intellectual development. *Imagination* is to the young child what problem solving is to the adult. *Pretend* is another activity altogether; it is play, the kind of play that usually has a theme that often involves other people, either children, dolls, or "pretend people" (Weininger, 1982).

The following episode should make clear the difference between these two activities, imagining and pretending. Three-year-old Hillary went to the housekeeping center to play "a tea party." She talked aloud as she set the table and the teacups and spoons, saying, "We are going to have milk and cookies," as she placed two empty plates on the table; then she set the chairs at the table, saying, "These are for the mommy, the daddy, and the baby brother." Off she went to gather two other children to come and play "tea party" with her. When the threesome came together at the table, Hillary announced, "I'm the girl and you are the mommy and you are the baby brother." The two other three-year-olds accepted their roles, sat down according to her instructions, and all three began to play:

> HILLARY: You have milk in your tea, Mommy.
> MOTHER: Yes, but we need to have cookies.
> HILLARY: They are on the table. Don't you see them in the brown plate?
> MOTHER: Oh yes, but I like big fat cookies.
> HILLARY: Well then, they are big fat cookies.
> BROTHER: I want chocolate cookies.
> MOTHER: You are allergic to chocolate cookies, and you must not eat any.
> HILLARY: Why is he allergic?
> MOTHER: Because chocolate cookies are no good to eat, he gets sick.
> BROTHER: I want to eat chocolate and I'm not sick.
> HILLARY: We will pretend you are sick.
> MOTHER: Yes.
> BROTHER: I don't want to be sick.

HILLARY: Well, you have to.

BROTHER: I won't play with you then.

HILLARY: OK—you be the daddy and he is not sick.

MOTHER: I want to be the daddy.

HILLARY: Well, we can only have one daddy.

BROTHER: I'm not hungry.

And off baby brother goes, leaving Hillary and the other little girl to continue to play tea party, which they did in a very loud and aggressive fashion. Teacups were thrown around, cookies were spilled on the floor, and the tea party broke up when Hillary took all the dishes and put them into the pretend sink and said they all needed to be washed.

In this sequence of pretend play, the action follows as a consequence of the statements made by one child, and the other children's acceptance of these directions. At no time did the children set out to think about how the play would proceed. Instead, roles were given, directions accepted or rejected, and the interaction proceeded from one seemingly planned episode to another with little or no apparent thinking through of sequences. It appears that Hillary wanted the play to proceed, and even offered alternatives for the baby brother. In this way, she seemed to be thinking about ways to prolong the pretend play, but there was no evidence of an organized, well-developed cognitive structure within which these children were playing. Unlike Patrick's thought-through cake mixing, theirs was a spontaneous episode. Imagination is usually described as a way in which the young child will play out roles and discover for himself or herself what is involved in these roles. Often the definition of imagination includes the idea of exploring, for example, what mothers and fathers do, what teachers do, what the nurse or the plumber does. While it has been said that imagination imitates observed behavior, this would seem to me to be a rather limiting definition, as often the play, artwork, or stories that we see as being most "imaginative" bear little resemblance to anything a young child has really seen.

I do not conceptualize imagination as finding out what a role *is*, but rather as thinking through what one *might do* in a particular role or situation. In this sense, when a child plays out a role, he or she utilizes pretend play, which forms the foundation from which the child will find out about what others do and what their role identities are. Perhaps as important to the child as finding out the activity content of roles is the discovery of how he or she *feels* when placed within such a role. The pretend play gives the child the ingredients that he or she can then "think with," so to speak. Patrick, for example, has no doubt pretended before to make a cake; he has probably watched and helped one of his parents to actually do so. In this way, he has added the sequences and the materials necessary for the cake-making process to his thinking repertoire. It is then possible for him to imagine the cake-making process in his mind, verbalize parts of it, and, finally, to play it out in reality.

Imagination, I suggest, can best be described as the *thinking function* of pretend play; the imaginative thinking, which is the "what if" function, sets the stage for the actual activity of play, which is the "as if" activity. In other words, the thinking process is a higher order activity than the pretend play itself, although obviously the play is necessary in itself and facilitates further thinking and imagining processes. As a six-year-old told me while maneuvering his toy robot transformers, "You imagine in your head, and that tells you how to play"; imagining continues as the playing proceeds, and becomes planning for further play action. It follows then that if the child does not have the opportunity of being involved in pretend play, then imaginative thinking and the processes involved in that sort of thinking will be limited.

Pretend play, it seems to me, is a special category of play that involves a child's understanding and representation of reality. It is, in effect, a "what if/as if" situation. For example, the child thinks, "What if I were a fire fighter? What would I do?" The child thinks about this for a while, assembling the bits of reality known about fire fighters derived from story-books, the comments of adults, observations of real life, and television. The child first imagines what being a fire fighter would be like and how it would feel to be one, and then plays it out "as if" he or she were one. To the best of his or her ability, given the factual knowledge of the reality and the availability of props that can be used in the "as if" situation, the child says and does what he or she has imagined a fire fighter does. A group of three-year-olds that I observed played out fire fighter roles with little variation. They made such comments as: the fire fighter "puts out fires," "saves people from high buildings," and "makes alot of noise when riding in the fire engine." But as they played these pretend roles, it became obvious that they stopped at times and seemed to be in the process of thinking. When I asked what they were thinking about, one of the three-year-olds said, "Fireman can save a cat when it's high up in a tree."

       ME: What do you mean "high up in a tree"?
   TERRY: Well, if a cat is so high up it can't get down. The fireman could climb his ladder and get the cat.

ME: I think so. Why were you thinking about that?
TERRY: Because cats climb up and fireman climb up.
ME: So since they both climb, then maybe firemen could get a cat that's high up in a tree"?
TERRY: Yeah.
ME: Did you ever see a cat high up in a tree and it couldn't get down?
TERRY: No, but I just thought of it.

I think that Terry was able to use his imaginative thinking processes to evolve the idea of a cat that climbs and might need to be rescued by a fire fighter who also climbs. Perhaps the ladders that these children were using in their fire fighter pretend play gave Terry the concept of climbing, and in his imagination he could visualize a cat climbing up and needing help to get down again. Thus, pretend play provided the basis for the child's further use of imaginative thinking. Although he did not go on to play out this new possibility, we might reasonably expect to see an episode with a cat at some time in the future when Terry plays fire fighter or draws pictures of fire fighters and burning houses, which is the activity with which he finished the morning's events here described.

The artwork with which children often begin or end play sessions seems also to be part of the "as if" process. They draw activities that mirror those that they imagined as they played, and sometimes a new element is added, one that the observing adult did not see in the play. When questioned, they may not seem to have any particular reason for adding this figure or activity to their drawing of their pretend play. I suspect that it may be a new idea that crept into their imagining as they were pretending, being recorded for possible further use!

The beginning of pretend play is visible in the actions of children as young as one year, who put a comb to their hair, for example, and pull it along the side of their face, imitating the activity that has been performed on them with the same "prop." Given the right prop, the baby will imitate the behavior associated with that prop. For example, if offered a cup, the baby drinks; a hat, the baby puts it on his or her head; a sleeping pillow, the baby puts his or her head on it. Adults often describe this as pretend play, but it is more accurately pre-pretend play, because it involves only actions that are known to the child. If a new prop is introduced while one action is going on, then that action usually stops and the new prop is taken up and a new action follows.

Actual pretend play begins when a child uses a prop for something *other* than the activity for which he or she has seen it used by a care giver. Thus, a hairbrush becomes a sailing boat; a wooden block, a hairbrush; or a stick, a bridge. This usually happens when the child is about two years old; that is when children seem to be capable of making an "as if" transformation of an object, a necessary prerequisite to pretend play involving objects, others, and themselves "as if."

This recognition of the connection between imagining and pretending, then imagining and pretending some more, has a special meaning for adults who work with children who are ready to be involved in "what if/as if." I suggest that it is very important for teachers of preschool children to be very good observers and listeners, to see what children play with, to watch what they do with the materials, and to listen to what they say about the props and materials provided to them. It is equally important that the teacher becomes part of the play of the child, but—and this is essential—at the developmental level that the child is showing. We all remember the relative who insisted that the Fisher Price garage could *only* be a garage, not a part of the fortress wall, and the legendary behavior of the father who gives the young child a gift of an electric train or racing car set and proceeds to insist that it be played with in terms of adult reality—it must represent the Grand Prix, we must stay with the same color car, there can be no cheating by having one car fly over the other to win. He ends up playing by himself as the child returns to the blocks where he or she is allowed to pretend without adult guidance and limitations.

The teacher should not be the leader or the organizer of the pretend play, and must try not to form premature conclusions or make assumptions for the child. The teacher observes and asks questions about what the child says, and helps to draw out information from the child, maintaining the conversation on the theme provided by the child, but at a pace that allows the child to feel comfortable and pleased with the conversation. The teacher also encourages children's play by providing props that extend the play but do not change the theme. In doing so, teachers provide for further pretend play and thereby a more effective basis from which thought processes and imagination can develop. Teachers help children with their thinking by making statements about their work—not evaluative statements, like "I like your cake," or assumptive ones, like "What a naughty horse, eating up all the flowers!"—but statements of the obvious on which the child can expand, like "It's a high cake."

The following interlude is an example of how a teacher can encourage and facilitate without arranging or managing children's play. Two four-year-old girls wanted to play "pretending to go to the zoo," and had made pictures of the animals that they were going to see. The teacher suggested that they "might be able to use the blocks to make a special place for each of the animals in the zoo." The girls proceeded to make a rather elaborate setting for their picture animals, giving each one of them a separate space. When they had completed this work, the teacher asked if they needed some pieces of paper to make signs for the zoo. The girls readily used this, and to me it seemed like a very natural extension of their zoo play. They made pictures of the zoo animals on the small pieces of white cardboard and then pretended to write the names of the animals beside their pictures. They proudly showed their zoo to the teacher and any member of the class willing to come and visit. Then it occurred to one of the girls that they could charge admission when a child came to see the zoo, this led to making money, making a map of the zoo, and, for one of them, acting as a guide for the visitors. The pretend play spawned other pretend play activities, but all within the same "zoo theme"—and the teacher encouraged the children by suggesting ways only to extend it, not to change it; she recognized the richness of the play and helped them to develop it.

In pretend play, the children test out concepts, which are then added to their thinking repertoire and are available for a much higher level of reality testing, the testing out of concepts through interpersonal interactions and relationships. They begin to recognize that other children also behave according to their own "as if" constructions during pretend play; they start to see the need to be flexible, adaptable, and to be able to incorporate and integrate others' thinking and feeling into the play along with their own.

Another point of importance for the teacher of the young child is to recognize that the props and materials provided in the play area for children will be used in different ways, which give meaning and content to the pretend play the children are currently involved in. Once a child is capable of "as if," the actual prop may seldom be used as it was intended. Thus, a two-year-old may play with a spoon only as a utensil for eating, while a three-year-old may use it as a shovel or a bridge. Indeed, one three-and-a-half-year-old I observed stated that it was "really an elevator" as he lifted the spoon from the floor to the chair, while a small stuffed dog sat on it! The materials might suggest to the child ideas for play, or imaginative connections that do not conform to the teacher's ideas for their use. This is the beginning of an important part of the problem-solving process—the idea that the use for an object is contextual and not fixed for all time.

As children grow older, their capacity to make use of materials in relation to their fantasy increases. They begin to harness their fantasy in ways to help them understand their growing perception of the world about them. As they use materials to represent fantasy rather than reality objects and situations, they gradually begin to understand the concept of symbolism, which is really only the adult version of the two-year-old's "as if" with a block for a boat. The five-year-old can say, and still believe in the pretend play, "This paper cup is a magic cup which helps you fly when you're holding onto it." An understanding of symbolism would seem to underlie the development of thinking and understanding. If the child is not given the freedom and permission to use his or her imagination, then we may expect certain undesirable results. Exploration of symbolism may emerge much later than is expected—that is, after about four years of age—or worse, the child may remain at a concrete thinking level (Weininger, 1979).

Gradually the idea that "whatever I think will work" changes, as the child finds out that the play hypothesis at which he or she is working has flaws or is not agreeable to the others involved. However, by this time the child is nearly ready to change the almost totally egocentric nature of his or her behavior in the preschool years. The child has found out through pretend play that he or she doesn't know everything and may have to ask others for advice or information. But the child has also discovered that some of what he or she knows and imagines about the world is correct, and so has the confidence to ask questions without feeling like a "dummy."

Young children need adult interaction, not adult control; when children are permitted to control their play, to give it their own structure, and to pace it at their own energy levels, then play is productive and fulfilling, and forms the basis for cognitive learning. However, this doesn't mean license; in addition to freedom to explore, create, and imagine with materials and props set out by the teacher, young children also require the safety provided by the teacher's understanding of the young child's need for age-appropriate limits. Letting children play with clay doesn't mean the teacher has to be willing to let a four-year-old attach clay to the hair of every other child in the room, without interference!

Imagining—"what if"—is a solitary activity within the child's mind, and is only sometimes overheard in actual words. Pretending—"as if"—is usually done with other children, or, for the child who has no one with whom to play, with imaginary people or dolls. The teacher is not there to force the process, or to try to do the imagining or the pretending for children, although he or she has a vital function in the facilitation of both. The teacher guides, but does not control; questions, but does not judge; answers, but does not criticize. By so doing, the teacher fosters in the best possible ways the process of imagination, pretend play, and intellectual development in the children with whom he or she works.

REFERENCES

Weininger, O. (1979). *Play and education: The basic tool for early childhood learning*. Springfield, IL.: Charles C. Thomas.
Weininger, O. (1982). *Out of the minds of babes: The strength of children's feelings*. Springfield, IL.: Charles C. Thomas.

PART III

Imagination across the Curriculum

9 ◇ The Imagination of the Scientist

ROGER SHEPARD
Stanford University

Beginning in 1968, I embarked, with several students (initially, Jacqueline Metzler and Lynn Cooper) on a study of the mental processes of imagining the transformations of objects in space—particularly the process that we came to call "mental rotation" (Cooper & Shepard, 1973; Shepard & Metzler, 1971). Previously, such processes of imagining, when they had been investigated at all, had been investigated primarily by obtaining introspective reports of individuals about their mental processes, for example, during recollection or problem solving. Because the mental processes described were never otherwise available for comparison with the descriptions given by the individuals and because the descriptions themselves were both vague and various, most psychologists were understandably skeptical about the prospects for a solidly scientific study of such inherently mental processes.

However, by devising tasks in which an individual had to choose on each trial between two responses, one of which was objectively correct and one of which was objectively incorrect, we succeeded in converting what had seemed to be a subjective phenomenon into an objective one. And, by measuring the latency of each response, we succeeded in turning what had seemed to be a hopelessly qualitative phenomenon into a quantitative one. The scientific results have been reviewed elsewhere (most extensively in Shepard & Cooper, 1982; also see Cooper & Shepard, 1984; Shepard, 1978b, 1984). For present purposes, two aspects of these results are of principal relevance—because they led me to take a new interest in the previously problematic introspective reports concerning imagery.

Preparation of parts of this article was supported by National Science Foundation Research Grant No. BNS 85–11685 to Stanford University. For bringing to my attention some of the scientists' self-reports, I am indebted to several colleagues, including, particularly, Benton Jamison, Steven Pinker, and Omar Snyder.

First, the extraordinarily lawful character of our chronometric data indicated that processes of imagining objects transformed in space, despite the vagueness of the subjects' verbalizations about those processes, were extremely orderly and therefore susceptible to scientific study. Second, now that we had solid evidence concerning the nature and time course of such processes, we could verify that the subjects' introspective reports about such processes, though crude and qualitative, did generally correspond to the underlying processes implicated by our more quantitative measurements.

I soon found myself wondering whether a more deliberate consideration of the previously neglected introspective reports about nonverbal mental processes might not be warranted. Particularly, I was motivated to undertake a more thoroughgoing examination of what scientists, inventors, and mathematicians had had to say about their processes of creative thought. Individuals who have revolutionized our understanding of the universe as well as our way of life in it are not, of course, experimental subjects in our psychological laboratory every day and certainly not while they are achieving major conceptual breakthroughs. We therefore do not have the benefit of precise chronometric measurements of their creative mental acts. Nevertheless, if introspective reports generally bear a discernible correspondence to the kinds of processes implicated by our laboratory measurements, we might hope to obtain some valid information about the processes underlying some of the highest achievements of the human mind by examining the reports given by the individuals responsible for those achievements.

Accordingly, about ten years ago, after our laboratory findings appeared reasonably secure, I began to look into what scientists themselves had said about the mental processes that led to their major achievements. I summarized what I had found in the way of illuminating self-reports in the first half of a chapter entitled "Externalization of Mental Images and the Act of Creation" (Shepard, 1978a), which appeared in the volume *Visual Learning, Thinking, and Communication* (Randhawa & Coffman, 1978). The first section of this chapter reproduces the most relevant portions of that material.

In the following section, I try to articulate some of the implications and challenges that this material seems to present to anyone concerned with promoting imaginative thinking in young people and, especially, imaginative approaches to science. To me, the challenges are rendered both more urgent and more difficult by two circumstances. First, young people in school are faced with the necessity of mastering an ever-increasing body of established conventions and knowledge. Second, the world, while becoming increasingly techno-logical, is also becoming increasingly dominated by large organizations in which the individual typically has less scope for freewheeling exploration.

SCIENTISTS' REPORTS ON THE ROLE OF IMAGINATION IN THEIR OWN MAJOR ACHIEVEMENTS[1]

Imagery and Nonverbal Processes in Some Creative Thinkers

Albert Einstein

On several different occasions Einstein reported that verbal processes did "not seem to play any role" in his processes of creative thought. Rather, he claimed to achieve his insights into the fundamental nature of space and time by means of Gedanken experiments on mentally visualized systems of light waves and idealized physical bodies (including clocks and measuring rods) in states of relative motion (Hadamard, 1945, Appendix II; Holton, 1972; Wertheimer, 1945, p. 184). Indeed, the paradox that eventually led him to the development of the special theory of relativity first came to him when, at age 16, he imagined himself traveling along beside a beam of light (at the velocity of some 186,000 miles per second). It then struck him that the stationary spatial oscillation that he mentally "saw" corresponded neither to anything that could be perceptually experienced as light nor to anything described by Maxwell's equations for the propagation of electromagnetic waves (Holton, 1972, p. 98). The elimination of the paradox required a revolutionary restructuring of the spatiotemporal configuration visualized in this thought experiment. However, the translation of this restructuring into the verbal and mathematical symbols necessary for communication to others was, for Einstein, a very uncongenial and difficult business, which he could undertake only when he had worked out his conceptualization of the physical situation by means of "more or less clear images which can be 'voluntarily' reproduced and combined" (Einstein, in Hadamard, 1945, p. 142).

---

[1]The material in this section is excerpted, with minor changes, from pages 134–58 and 181–2 of B. S. Randhawa and W. E. Coffman (Eds.), *Visual Learning, Thinking, and Communication*. Copyright 1978 by Academic Press, Inc., New York. All rights of reproduction in any form reserved.

As a child, Einstein, like a number of other eminent people—including, among many others, Thomas Edison, Harvey Cushing, Charles Darwin, Auguste Rodin, and Woodrow Wilson (see Lombroso, 1901, pp. 13, 357; Thompson, 1971)—manifested language disabilities suggestive of dyslexia (Patten, 1973). Einstein did not speak until age three and spoke with difficulty for some years thereafter (Holton, 1972). He was so unsuccessful at the verbal and even the arithmetic tasks emphasized in his early schooling that his teacher predicted that "nothing good" would come of the boy (Sullivan, 1972). By contrast, Einstein demonstrated an early fascination with the behavior of physical devices (particularly, a magnetic compass and a model steam engine) and an unusual skill in dealing with spatial structures. He erected houses of cards as many as 14 stories high and devised an original, purely geometrical proof of the Pythagorean theorem before the age of 10 (Holton, 1972; Patten, 1973; Sullivan, 1972). It is tempting to conjecture that Einstein's early and often solitary preoccupation within a relatively private visual-spatial domain, in preference to the socially and institutionally controlled verbal domain, set the stage for his later roles in the developments that have transformed twentieth-century physics, namely, those of quantum theory and the special and general theories of relativity.

Throughout, Einstein's work in theoretical physics was marked by an interplay between concrete perceptual visualization on the one hand, and a relentless drive toward abstract, aesthetic principles of symmetry or invariance on the other. This interplay seems to have been mediated not by verbal deductions, "logical bridges," or mathematical formalisms, but by soaring leaps of spatial and physical intuition. "There is no logical way to the discovery of these elemental laws. There is only the way of intuition, which is helped by a feeling for the order lying behind the appearance" (Einstein's prologue in Planck, 1933, p. 10). Max Planck, incidentally, who was shortly followed by Einstein in taking the first steps toward the development of quantum theory, expressed what appears to be a consonant view: "Again and again the imaginary plan on which one attempts to build up that order breaks down and then we must try another. This imaginative vision and faith in the ultimate success are indispensable. The pure rationalist has no place here" (Planck, 1933, p. 215). I am inclined to agree with Holton that, in Einstein's case, the abstract principle of symmetry, which emerged time and again—in his insistence on a symmetrical relation between rest and motion, charge and current, electric field and magnetic field, space and time, matter and energy, and gravitation and inertia—was itself rooted in an aesthetic appreciation of a more concretely visual kind of symmetry.

James Clerk Maxwell

There are some suggestive parallels between Einstein and the theoretical physicist James Clerk Maxwell, who was Einstein's greatest immediate predecessor. In his crowning achievement, Maxwell was able to crystalize, in a symmetrical set of four simple equations, the fundamental relationships governing electric fields, magnetic fields, and the propagation of electromagnetic waves—namely, light. These are precisely the "Maxwell's equations" that Einstein had in mind when he later performed his epochal thought experiment on pursuing a light wave through space.

In an instructive discussion of Maxwell's development, James R. Newman (1955) points out that the usual view of Maxwell as an abstract theoretician overlooks the route, rich with concrete geometrical and mechanical imagery, by which he reached the final pinnacle of abstract formalism. As a child, Maxwell was fascinated with mechanical devices; in this, he resembled not only Einstein but two other great physicists, Ernst Mach and Isaac Newton (Holton, 1972, p. 109). Just as Newton in his early youth made drawings, mechanical toys, clocks, and sundials (though he was by no means a prodigy in his school subjects), Maxwell devised a scientific toy in which a set of figures on a turning wheel produced the illusion of continuous movement; constructed (as he wrote his father) a "tetra hedron, a dodeca hedron, and two more hedrons that I don't know the wright (sic) names for"; and discovered (as had the young Descartes before him) a method for generating a perfect ellipse using two pins and a loop of thread. Later in life Maxwell devised elaborate mechanical models to demonstrate, for example, that the stability of Saturn's rings implied that they must be neither liquid nor rigidly solid but composed of separate particles (see Newman, 1955, p. 61). And Maxwell is said to have "developed the habit of making a mental picture of every problem" (Beveridge, 1957, p. 76).

Indeed, Maxwell arrived at his celebrated electromagnetic equations, not by a chain of logical steps, but by a series of increasingly abstract hydrodynamic and mechanical models of the medium or "ether" presumed to underlie electromagnetic fields and waves. At first Maxwell visualized Faraday's lines of electrostatic force as tubes in which electric flow was represented by the flow of an incompressible fluid such as water. Later he devised a more elaborate mechanical model to account for magnetic attraction and electromagnetic induction as well as the electrostatic effects explained by the earlier hydrodynamic model. He now envisioned the lines of magnetic force as parallel rotating cylinders separated by ball bearings rotating in the opposite direction. Changes in the rotation of a local set of cylinders, corresponding to changes in the magnetic field, induced a movement at right angles in the bounding layer of ball bearings, corresponding to changes in the electric flow, and vice versa. Then, in a particularly brilliant stroke, he went on to show that the rate of propagation of what would be interpreted as an electromagnetic disturbance in such a system corresponded to the velocity of light. Finally, when the abstract structure of this system was sufficiently formalized, Maxwell was able to dispense with the concrete mechanical model and, with it, the last vestiges of asymmetry between the electric and magnetic fields. As remarked by Sir Edmund Whittaker, he now displayed the underlying elegantly symmetrical structure of electromagnetism "stripped of the scaffolding by aid of which it had first been erected" (Newman, 1955, p. 67).

Michael Faraday

Having traced electromagnetic theory backward from Einstein through Maxwell, I will pursue it one step further back to where the modern conception of magnetic and electric fields might be said to have originated—in the mind of another of Einstein's towering predecessors, Michael Faraday. Interestingly, as Koestler has noted, Faraday was a visionary in a quite literal sense. He not only had an aversion to writing and later, seemingly, to "language itself," he also "lacked any mathematical education or gift [beyond] the merest elements of arithmetic." Yet the invisible "lines of force," which he visualized as narrow tubes curving in the space around magnets and electric currents and, indeed, pervading the universe, "rose up before him like things" (see Koestler, 1964, p. 170; Tyndall, 1868).

The great nineteenth-century scientist Helmholtz later remarked in his Faraday memorial lecture: "It is in the highest degree astonishing to see what a large number of general theorems, the methodological deduction of which requires the highest powers of mathematical analysis, he found by a kind of intuition, with the security of instinct, without the help of a single mathematical formula" (Kendall, 1955).

Hermann von Helmholtz

In addition to his role in guiding his student, Heinrich Hertz, toward the conclusive experimental proof of Maxwell's theoretically derived equivalence between light and electromagnetic oscillation, Helmholtz himself made contributions to physics of the most fundamental sort. He is, in fact, regarded as a prime architect of one of the most basic pre-Einsteinian invariance principles, namely, the principle of conservation of energy. A scientist of extraordinary breadth as well as depth, Helmholtz also made the first measurements of the speed of neural conduction, invented the ophthalmoscope, and forged unprecedented advances in the understanding of visual and auditory perception. It is of some interest, therefore, that Helmholtz, while kept at home during the earliest school years by poor health, reportedly took a particular interest in playing with a set of wooden blocks, with the result that when he finally began school at age 8, he "astonished" his teachers with the knowledge of geometry that he had already acquired on his own (Koenigsberger, 1965, p. 6).

Also of interest is the similarity between a passage that Helmholtz wrote later in life and Einstein's statements concerning the role of sensory experience and of reproducible mental operations on objects in space. According to Helmholtz, "Memory images of purely sensory impressions may . . . be used as elements of thought combinations without it being necessary, or even possible, to describe these in words . . . . For, equipped with an awareness of the physical form of an object, we can clearly imagine all of the perspective images which we may expect upon viewing from this or that side" (Warren & Warren, 1968, pp. 252–4).

Helmholtz reported another aspect of many of his own "happiest" scientific ideas: namely, their tendency to come to him, sometimes virtually full-blown, immediately upon awakening or while hiking in the green hills near Heidelberg, no longer actively thinking about the problem to which they represented the solution (e.g., Warren & Warren, 1968, p. 11). This phenomenon of sudden "illumination" has, of course, been described by many of the most creative thinkers—including two of the greatest mathematicians of all time, Gauss and Poincaré (Hadamard, 1945, pp. 12–15); the prolific philosopher and logician, Bertrand Russell (Hutchinson, 1949, p. 112); the two originators of the theory of evolution, Darwin and Wallace (Beveridge, 1957, p. 93); the neurophysiologists, Loewi and Cannon (Cannon, 1945); the physicist, Ampère (Koestler, 1964, p. 117); and the inventors, Watt and Tesla (shortly to be considered more fully). Some interesting descriptions of this phenomenon are also quoted in an early survey of chemists by Platt and Baker (1931). And a contemporary physicist has gone so far as to assert that "every new discovery originates in such a sudden non-verbal flash" (Capra, 1975, p. 39).

The unexpected eruption into consciousness of a creative solution to a previously intractable problem seems to imply the preceding occurrence of unconscious and, presumably, unverbalized thinking on a very high order—as when Henri Poincaré, in the act of stepping on a bus leaving for a geological excursion and in the middle of an unrelated conversation, was suddenly struck with the startling and profound realization that his "fuchsian functions" were in fact "identical to those of non-Euclidean geometry" (Poincaré, in Ghiselin, 1952, p. 37). Moreover, the striking consistency with which the various scientists just mentioned have used the phrase "flashed before my mind" in describing these sudden insights (as well as the seeming appropriateness of the word "illumination") points to a strong visual component.

Sir Francis Galton

Many thinkers in fields other than physics would agree with the Eastern philosophers who assert that "the instant you speak about a thing you miss the mark" (Capra, 1975, p. 34) or that "all things in their fundamental nature . . . cannot be adequately expressed in any form of language" (Ashvaghosha, 1900, p. 56), or with the Western philosopher, Schopenhauer, who wrote that "thoughts die the moment they are embodied by words" (Hadamard, 1945, p. 75). Shifting, for example, to the quite different fields of anthropology and genetics, we encounter Charles Darwin's renowned cousin, Francis Galton, who asserted that, when he was working on a scientific problem, as much as when he was planning a shot in billiards, his thought was never conducted by means of words. Very much as did Einstein, Galton complained that "it often happens that after being hard at work, and having arrived at results that are perfectly clear and satisfactory to myself, when I try to express them in language I . . . waste a vast deal of time in seeking for appropriate words and phrases" (Hadamard, 1945, p. 69).

Galton, incidentally, was apparently the first to undertake a large-scale empirical investigation of the many forms and degrees in which mental imagery and related phenomena occur in children and in adults—including writers, artists, and scientists (Galton, 1883, pp. 83–114; 155–77). In the same work, moreover, Galton described a metaphorical "antechamber of consciousness" (pp. 203–7) that, along with Poincaré's mechanical analogy of thoughts as "hooked atoms" moving about in space (Poincaré, in Ghiselin, 1952, p. 41), provided a promising, if sketchy, early indication of a possible mechanism for the phenomenon of illumination.

Jacques Hadamard

A noted mathematician, who like Galton was moved to undertake his own study of the processes of creative thought, Hadamard (1945) aligned himself explicitly with Galton: "I insist that words are totally absent from my mind when I really think" (p. 75), and "they remain absolutely absent from my mind until I come to the moment of communicating the results in written or oral form" (p. 82). With difficult mathematical problems, Hadamard claimed, even algebraic signs became "too heavy a baggage" for him, and he had to rely on "concrete representations, but of a quite different nature—cloudy imagery" that indicated relations of inclusion, exclusion, or order, or that held the structure of the whole problem together in such a way as to preserve its "physiognomy."

I suspect that those who have written computer programs of any complexity know exactly the difficulty to which Hadamard alluded when, after stating that "every mathematical research compels me to build such a schema," he added that if he was interrupted in the course of his calculations, the concrete symbols that he had written on paper became "dead" for him so that he often could "do nothing else than throw the sheet away and begin everything anew" (p. 82). (One is reminded, here, of the famous dictum by Gauss to the effect that notation is nothing, conception everything.)

Fortunately, Hadamard's labors were not always so trying. Much as in the case of Helmholtz, Hadamard reported, with "absolute certainty," the following event:

> On being very abruptly awakened by an external noise, a solution long searched for (involving the valuation of a determinant) appeared to me at once without the slightest instant of reflection on my part—and in a quite different direction from any of those which I had previously tried to follow. (p. 8)

I turn now to descriptions of some inventors in whom such sudden illuminations, perhaps because they provided solutions to less abstract problems, were more explicitly of a concrete visual or spatial character.

James Watt

The revolutionary effects of the steam engine, on industry, transportation, and society, came about as a direct consequence of Watt's inventions—including the centrifugal or "fly-ball" governor (often presented as the purest early example of a negative-feedback servomechanism), the pressure-volume "indicator diagram" (which played a central role in the later development of thermodynamic theory), and, most particularly, the steam condenser. Watt's own account of the origin of this last invention is most interesting. After finding, by calculation, that the primitive Newcomen engine wasted three-fourths of the heat supplied to it, Watt worked for two years trying to overcome this debilitating inefficiency, but without success. Then, during the enforced idleness of "a fine Sabbath afternoon," the solution suddenly presented itself.

As Watt himself described the incident:

> I had entered the green and . . . had gone as far as the herd's house when the idea came into my mind that as steam was an elastic body, . . . if a connection were made between the cylinder and an exhausting vessel it would rush into it and might then be condensed without cooling the cylinder . . . I had not walked further than the Golf house when the whole thing was arranged in my mind. (Thurston, 1878, pp. 87–8)

I do not doubt that his mental "arranging" as well as the preconscious processes preceding the moment of illumination were not so much logical as "analogical" (cf. Myers, 1903, p. 226; Sloman, 1971). The incident is not unlike that in which Oliver Evans invented the automatic flour mill by putting the whole system, including bucket elevators and screw conveyors, together in his mind while lying in bed (Ferguson, 1977, p. 834). A much more recent case in which a novel, highly complex machine took form as a visual image is provided by Seymour Cray, the "genius at compaction" who designed the world's fastest supercomputer, the cylindrical $8 million Cray–1. Cray is said to proceed by building a "visual concept" of the whole machine in his head. "There are no intermediate steps. He simply conceives it and then draws it" (Metz, 1978, p. 406).

It is perhaps worth noting that Watt's childhood was parallel in some suggestive respects to the childhoods of Newton, Maxwell, Helmholtz, and Einstein. Owing to poor health, Watt received little formal schooling as a child, and was relatively isolated from his peers. At the same time, he was said, by the age of 6, to have occupied himself with the solution of geometrical problems and, later, to have done much drawing and carving, and to have constructed many beautiful models and ingenious mechanisms, including "a very fine barrel-organ" (Thurston, 1878, p. 81).

Nikola Tesla

Some of the most striking illustrations of concrete visual imagery in problem solving are to be found in accounts of the eccentric and reclusive inventor Tesla, to whom we are indebted for such ubiquitous supports to our modern way of life as fluorescent lighting, the three-phase electrical distribution system, and the self-starting induction motor. One should perhaps be cautious about accepting literally some of the more enthusiastic reports, such as that Tesla, before actually constructing a physical machine, would first determine what parts were most subject to wear by "inspecting" an imaginary model that he had "run for weeks" purely mentally (O'Neill, 1944, p. 51). But there is little doubt that Tesla's creativity owed much to mental imagery of an extraordinarily concrete, three-dimensional, and vivid character, and may have been in some way connected with his susceptibility to spontaneous visual sensations and phantasms from childhood onward (Hunt & Draper, 1964, p. 184).

The conception of the self-starting, reversible induction motor reportedly came to Telsa, with dramatic suddenness, in the form of a kinetic visual image of hallucinatory intensity. While walking toward the sunset with a former classmate, Szigety, Tesla's recitation of a poem by Goethe was suddenly interrupted by a vision of a magnetic field, such as Faraday and Maxwell had so beautifully depicted as a family of curving lines (see Maxwell, 1873), brought into rapid vortical rotation within a circle of electromagnets energized by sinusoideally alternating currents of the same frequency but relatively shifted in phase. He saw, further, that a simple iron armature placed within this field was dragged around by the field and, in fact, could be caused to start, to stop, or to reverse rotation merely by switching connections to the coils of the magnets (Tesla, 1956, p. A-198; see Hunt & Draper, 1964, p. 34). In short, this one vision led him simultaneously to the invention of the self-starting alternating current motor and to the inspiration for constructing the polyphase system of electrical generation and distribution now used throughout the world.

Creative thinkers in whom visions have figured are, in fact, both numerous and illustrious (see Lombroso, 1901, pp. 56–7; 73–7; 96). Among those already mentioned, they include Descartes, Goethe, and Schopenhauer. There is also the notorious Girolamo Cardan, whose multifarious medical, mechanical, and mathematical contributions may well be connected with his proclivity to exceptionally intense imagery. Certainly it is suggestive that, for the highly theoretical invention of imaginary numbers, which "has illuminated the whole mathematical science" (Hadamard, 1945, p. 135) and hence, incidentally, the theories of electromagnetism, quantum mechanics, and (via Minkowski's geometrization) relativity, and also for the very practical inventions of a Braille-like system for teaching the deaf to read and write and a mechanical linkage (the Cardan joint) that is an essential part of every automobile, we are indebted to an individual who, by his own account, was from childhood subject to "hypno-fantastic hallucinations" and for whom "whatever he imagined, he could see before him as a real object" (Lombroso, 1901, p. 74).

Sir John Herschel

In a published lecture "On Sensorial Vision," the nineteenth-century British astronomer, chemist, and philosopher John Herschel provided us with an illuminating report of several distinct types of highly structured, subjective visual phenomena that he had spontaneously experienced at various times. The son of Sir William Herschel, who was the discoverer of Uranus, Sir John had his own most significant influences as the compiler of the enormously important General Catalogue of Nebulae and as one of the independent inventors of photography. In the last connection, Herschel was in fact the first to speak of "positive" and "negative" photographic images; he also made some of the earliest explicit comparisons between the photochemical processes on the photographic plate and in the retina—including those giving rise to afterimages, which persist following the removal of the external stimulus (see, e.g., Herschel, 1867, p. 402). The high esteem in which Herschel was held by his compatriots is indicated by his interment next to Isaac Newton in Westminster Abbey.

One of the phenomena that Herschel reported provides a remarkable illustration of a virtually hallucinatory and involuntary counterpart of the voluntary ability of the mind, noted by Helmholtz, to "imagine all of the perspective images" of an object. It also appears related to the more recent claim that, following a brief flash of illumination in a totally dark room, the residual image of the room may appear to undergo appropriate perspective changes as the observer then moves through the darkness with fixed regard (Gregory, Wallace, & Campbell, 1959; Richardson, 1969, p. 25). According to Herschel, while passing by the place where he had recently witnessed the demolition of a structure that had been familiar to him since childhood, he was astonished "to see it as if still standing—projected against the dull sky. Being perfectly aware that it was a mere nervous impression," he says, "I walked on, keeping my eyes directed to it, and the perspective of the form and disposition of the parts appeared to change with the change in the point of view as they would have done if real" (Herschel, 1867, p. 405).

Herschel also provides us with detailed descriptions of spontaneous visual phenomena of a quite different nature, which he repeatedly experienced. These, he says, consisted in "the involuntary production of visual impressions, into which geometrical regularity of form enters as the leading character . . . under circumstances which altogether preclude any explanation drawn from a possible regularity of structure in the retina or the optic nerve" (Herschel, 1867, p. 406). These geometrical visions, which typically appeared in darkness while Herschel was still awake but which also arose with particular vividness on two occasions when he had been given chloroform as a general anesthetic, tended to be of rhombic or rectangular lattice works, sometimes containing repeating complex or even colored "close patterns" or "fillagree work," or else they were of a "very beautiful and perfectly regular and symmetrical 'Turkscap' pattern, formed by the mutual intersection of a great number of circles outside of, and tangent to, a central one" consisting of "exceedingly delicate . . . assemblages of coloured lines (and sometimes containing lozenge-shaped forms) in the intersections of the circles with each other" (pp. 409–10). From Herschel's descriptions, these highly symmetrical and regular images appear to bear a striking resemblance to drawings that I made of some of my own hypnagogic images well before I knew of Herschel's lecture on the subject (see Shepard, 1978a). Herschel raises an interesting question concerning such images.

> Now the question at once presents itself—what are these Geometrical Spectres? and how, and in what department of the bodily or mental economy do they originate? . . . If it be true that the conception of a regular geometrical pattern implies the exercise of thought and intelligence, it would almost seem that in such cases as those above adduced we have evidence of a thought, an intelligence, working within our own organisation distinct from that of our own personality [—or "working," as we might now tend to say, within a system inaccessible to our own conscious introspection. Herschel went on to suggest that] in a matter so entirely abstract, so completely devoid of any moral or emotional bearing, as the production of a geometrical figure, we, as it were, seize upon [a creative and directive] principle in the very act, and in the performance of its office. (Herschel, 1867, p. 418)

Perhaps, then, it is no accident that a number of creative insights in science have taken the form of a regular, repeating, or symmetrical pattern in space. Suggestive examples include Tesla's image of the circular rotation of Faraday's symmetrical magnetic field and, most clearly of all, Maxwell's space-filling cylinder-and-ball model of the electromagnetic field (illustrated in Newman, 1955, p. 63).

In any case, if the visual-spatial regions of the brain have an inherent tendency toward what Herschel (1867, p. 412) aptly called the "kaleidoscopic power" of the brain, it is not entirely surprising that so many thinkers have remarked on the tendency of creative ideas or long-sought solutions to emerge when the verbal-analytical regions are relatively quiet—just upon awakening or during reveries, hypnagogic states, or dreams. Certainly many of the more original of my own ideas have taken sudden and essentially complete, though unverbalized, form in a hypnopompic state preceding full awakening (see Shepard, 1978a).

Omar Snyder

A previously unpublished case, though of a more recent and less widely known scientist, is also of particular interest to me, both because the solution to a difficult problem suddenly appeared in a visual-spatial form seemingly resembling that indicated by Watt and Tesla and because in this case I myself was able to interview the scientist, Omar Synder, to whom the solution occurred. This incident took place in 1943 while Snyder was working on the "Manhattan Project" for the development of the atomic bomb (a device whose possibility was prefigured, of course, in Einstein's fundamental equation relating matter and energy, $E = mc^2$). Before describing the particular incident, however, I should mention that according to Snyder his experience was not unlike others that occurred to the great twentieth-century physicists with whom he had contact on the project—notably Fermi, von Neumann, and Wheeler. All three, he said, reported that the answer to a difficult problem would sometimes "just come."

Snyder's own answer came after he had been struggling for some time with what, in the words of the official report on the Manhattan Project (Smyth, 1945), "turned out to be one of the most difficult problems encountered" (p. 117) in the design and construction of the atomic reactor; namely, the "canning problem" of sealing the uranium slugs in metallic sheaths or jackets that "would protect uranium from water corrosion, would keep fission products out of the water, would transmit heat from the uranium to the water, and would not absorb too many neutrons" (p. 117). The problem of achieving a uniform, heat-conducting bond between the uranium and the enclosing can while at the same time ensuring a gas-tight seal proved so troublesome that "even up to a few weeks before it was time to load the uranium slugs into the pile there was no certainty that any of the processes under development would be satisfactory" (Smyth, 1945, p. 147). Then, one day, during lunch hour, Snyder achieved the solution in a manner that was sudden, unexpected, and remains vividly in his memory. He was walking down the hall of one of the laboratories and, in his words, "I had gone one pace past the water cooler when sud-

denly the entire process for the manufacture of the three-metal composite for the fuel elements flashed in my mind instantaneously." Much
as in Watt's invention of the steam condenser, Snyder immediately set
to work constructing a physical realization of his idea. ("I didn't need
any drawings; the whole plan was perfectly clear in my head.") By the
end of the next day he had verified that the entire process did indeed
work—just as it had been revealed to him in that brief moment of illumination (Snyder, personal communication, September 28, 1976). In
the words of the official report, moreover, the results "proved to be
far better than had been hoped" (Smyth, 1945, p. 182).

That the solution was instantly grasped as a whole is especially
noteworthy in this case because the process that it represented possessed a complex temporal as well as spatial structure: Under specially controlled variations of temperature, concentric sleeves of the
constituent metals were caused, by their own different coefficients of
expansion, to come together in the proper sequence and pressure and
later to separate, leaving the desired bonded composite core. That a
process drawn out in time in this way should be pictured, as Snyder
emphasized, instantaneously suggests a possible abstract connection
with Watt's "indicator diagram," in which, too, dynamic changes in
temperature, pressure, and spatial configuration are captured in a static
picture. It also reminds one of the famous passage in a letter attributed to Mozart in which the composer speaks not only of musical
themes spontaneously arising within him but also of the point when,
according to one translation of his words,

> the whole, though it be long, stands almost complete and finished in my
> mind, so that I can survey it, like a fine picture or a beautiful statue, at
> a glance. Nor do I hear in my imagination the parts successively, but I
> hear them, as it were, all at once (gleich alles zusammen). What a de-
> light this is I cannot tell! All this inventing, this producing, takes place
> in a pleasing, lively dream. (Mozart, in Ghiselin, 1952, p. 45)

James D. Watson

A twentieth-century development with perhaps the profoundest
implications for the future of humankind was the "cracking" of the
genetic code. Considering that the discovery of the three-dimensional
double helical structure of DNA, for which Watson and Francis H. C.
Crick shared the Nobel Prize, represented in large part the solution of
a complex geometrical problem, it would be surprising if spatial visualization did not play a significant role. In fact, according to Watson's account of the discovery, it was achieved by adopting a

methodology previously exploited with great success by another Nobel Laureate, Linus Pauling: "Instead of proceeding deductively or
trying to infer the underlying structure by "staring at X-ray pictures,
the essential trick . . . was to ask which atoms like to sit next to each
other. In place of pencil and paper, the main working tools were a set
of molecular models superficially resembling the toys of preschool
children" (Watson, 1968, p. 38).

Watson makes clear that visualization played a role both in his
own thought processes and those of his collaborator, Francis Crick.
As he writes in one place, "For over two hours I happily lay awake
with pairs of adenine residues whirling in front of my closed eyes" (p.
118) and, in another, "I wandered into the lab to see Francis, un-
questionably early, flipping the cardboard base pairs about an imaginary line" (p. 128). Moreover, as in other cases we have considered,
the realizations of crucial structural relationships were typically quite
precipitate: "Suddenly I realized the potentially profound implications of a DNA structure in which . . . each adenine residue would
form two hydrogen bonds to an adenine residue related to it by a 180-
degree rotation" (p. 116); and at the later and most critical juncture of
all, "Suddenly I became aware that an adenine–thymine pair held together by two hydrogen bonds was identical in shape to a guanine–cytosine pair held together by at least two hydrogen bonds" (p.
123). In view of the structural complexity of shapes involved (see
Watson, 1968, p. 119), it seems reasonable to suppose that the processes leading to this sudden awareness were more holistic and analogical than atomistic and logical (cf. Cooper & Shepard, 1978).

Friedrich A. Kekulé

The theory of chemical bonds and molecular structure, which was
subsequently to be brought to its present elegant state of elucidation
by Pauling and others and which has formed the foundations for Watson and Crick's discovery of the molecular structure of the genetic
code, owes much of its earliest development to the highly visual
thinking of the German chemist Kekulé. From time to time, over a
period of seven or eight years, Kekulé, during idle reveries, experienced images of what he took to be atoms dancing before his eyes.
Then, as he was returning home by bus through the deserted streets
"one fine summer evening," he perceived how atoms join to form
molecules. His own description of the incident has been translated as
follows:

> I fell into a reverie, and lo! the atoms were gambolling before my eyes.
> Whenever, hitherto, these diminutive beings had appeared to me, they

had always been in motion; but up to that time, I had never been able to discern the nature of their motion. Now, however, I saw how, frequently, two smaller atoms united to form a pair; how a larger one embraced two smaller ones; how still larger ones kept hold of three or even four of the smaller; whilst the whole kept whirling in a giddy dance. I saw how the larger ones formed a chain. . . . I spent part of the night putting on paper at least sketches of these dream forms. (Findlay, 1948, p. 42)

Later, after years of trying to discover the molecular conformation of benzene, Kekulé made the signal discovery of its hexagonal ringlike structure, and thus revolutionized organic chemistry, through a dream image of a snake swallowing its tail. While dozing in a chair before the fire one afternoon in 1865, he again found that, as he put it,

the atoms were juggling before my eyes . . . my mind's eye, sharpened by repeated sights of a similar kind, could now distinguish larger structures of different forms and in long chains, many of them close together: everything was moving in a snake-like and twisting manner. Suddenly, what was this? One of the snakes got hold of its own tail and the whole structure was mockingly twisting in front of my eyes. As if struck by lightning, I awoke. . . . (In a report of his discovery in 1890, Kekulé concluded): Let us learn to dream gentlemen, and then we may perhaps find the truth''[2] (MacKenzie, 1965, p. 135).

Kekulé was not alone in making a fundamental discovery through dream imagery. Like Newton and Cardan much earlier (Lombroso, 1901, p. 21), a majority of mathematicians responding to a questionnaire by Howard Fehr reportedly believed that they had at one time or another solved problems in their dreams (Krippner & Hughes, 1970). Moreover, the solutions to a number of concrete scientific and technological problems that allegedly first emerged in dreams appear to have emerged in an essentially visual form. Among those mentioned by Krippner and Hughes are Elias Howe's dream that, because he had not yet perfected his invention of the sewing machine, he was being attacked by spears with holes through the points—which led to the crucial step in his invention of drilling the "eye" near the point of the needle rather than at the other end where it had previously always been; Louis Agassiz' thrice-repeated dream of the appearance of a fossilized fish—which finally revealed how to extract the fossil from the slab of stone on which he had been working; and James Watt's re-

[2]A translation of words by F. A. Kekulé from *Dreams and Dreaming* by Norman MacKenzie, Copyright 1965 by Aldus Books, London.

current dream of being showered with solid pellets—which led to his discovery of a much simpler method of manufacturing lead shot by splashing molten lead through the air so that the droplets of lead themselves cooled and solidified into the desired spherules. Even more remarkable is the case, recounted by MacKenzie (1965, p. 135), in which an elaborate dream finally provided the geometrical clue that the Assyrian scholar H. V. Hilprecht had needed in order to decipher the cuneiform characters on two small fragments of agate thought to have been finger rings. This was the clue that the fragments were not finger rings at all, but two of three pieces of a single votive cylinder—a fact that Hilprecht later confirmed when, as a result of his dream, he tried for the first time to fit the pieces together. Similarly, a plastic surgeon recently told me that sometimes, when confronted with a particularly difficult case, he discovers how a skin graft can best be translated, rotated, folded, and temporarily joined from one part of the patient's body to another by trying out various alternatives in a dream. A different kind of spatial problem that was solved in a dream of a primarily tactual-kinesthetic nature was reported by Ann Faraday (1972). According to her, it was during his sleep that a gynecologist "discovered how to tie a surgical knot deep in the pelvis with his left hand" (p. 303).

Geometers

Within the field of mathematics, the various branches of geometry might be expected to call upon especially well-developed powers of spatial visualization. Consider, for example, such problems of differential geometry as the problem of the classification of the "elementary catastrophes" solved by Rene Thom (1975), or the problem of the explicit construction of a continuous deformation for turning a sphere inside out, first proved to be possible by Stephen Smale (see Phillips, 1966). In both cases, advanced methods of computer graphics are used to facilitate the visualization of these extraordinarily convoluted structures by the less spatially perspicacious (see Godwin, 1972; Max & Clifford, 1975; Woodcock & Poston, 1974). It is, incidentally, an intriguing fact that the French mathematician, Bernard Morin, who originally conceived the particular method of eversion of the sphere chosen for computer animation by Max and Clifford (1975), is himself blind!

Another branch of geometry that, perhaps even more clearly, seems to require a rather special kind of spatial visualization is that concerning structures in spaces of four or more dimensions. It appears to be the case, anyway, that many of the most original discoveries in this particular branch were made by isolated individuals quite outside the mathematical mainstream who, by dint of some powerful spatial intuition of their own, were able to establish facts and relationships that had eluded the most advanced mathematicians using more standard, formal methods.

In his book on regular polytopes, Coxeter (1973) has included relevant biographical information about some of the higher-dimensional geometers, as follows: John Flinders Petrie, who discovered the properties of the skew polyhedra and polygons bearing his name, manifested an early ability "in periods of intense concentration [to] answer questions about complicated four-dimensional figures by 'visualizing' them" (p. 31). (He may have come by this ability through his father, the great British Egyptologist Sir Flinders Petrie, who, according to Galton (1883), performed addition by mentally setting one scale against another on an imaginary slide rule and then reading off the sum with his mind's eye.) His set of drawings of stellated icosahedra also reveal a considerable talent for drafting. Thorold Gosset, upon finding that he had no clients after taking a degree in law, "amused himself by trying to find out what regular [and, then, 'semiregular'] figures might exist in n dimensions." However, because the mathematician who reviewed the manuscript in which he reported his novel findings found his methods too "intuitive" and his generalizations too "fanciful," only the "barest outline" was published, and Gosset, being a modest man, returned to his career as a lawyer, leaving his geometrical results to be rediscovered by other, later researchers (p. 164). Ludwig Schläfli completed his pioneering work on four-dimensional polytopes at a time when the great mathematicians Cayley, Grassmann, and Möbius "were the only other people who had ever conceived the possibility of geometry in more than three dimensions." And Schläfli's work "was so little appreciated in his time that only two fragments of it were accepted for publication" (p. 142). Interestingly from our standpoint, Coxeter notes that Schläfli "never managed to speak German properly." Finally, Alicia Boole Stott, the middle of five daughters of the renowned inventor of the algebra of logic, George Boole, must have developed her singular "power of geometrical visualization" quite on her own, since her father died when she was only four and circumstances thereafter precluded any "education in the ordinary sense." In any case, a set of wooden cubes brought into the house by a family friend, though proving a bore to her sisters, "inspired Alice (at the age of about eighteen) to an extraordinary intimate grasp of four-dimensional geometry." Having never learned analytic geometry, she determined by purely synthetic methods the

sections of the four-dimensional polytopes—well before the mathematician Schoute published descriptions of a subset of these, which he
had determined by more orthodox methods (p. 258).

Designers of Particle Accelerators

Within the science of physics, it is not just the orbits, fields, and
waves of the physical phenomena themselves that place heavy demands on our spatial intuition. Geometric visualization is at least as
crucial in the design of the machines used to study these phenomena.
In 1930, Ernest O. Lawrence conceived the idea of the cyclotron,
which opened the door to the modern era of high-energy particle accelerators and gained him the Nobel Prize, as a result of reading a report of an experiment (by Wideroe) in which charged particles moving
in resonance with a radio-frequency electric field emerged with twice
the energy. Lawrence pictured how, by placing the whole apparatus
within a strong magnetic field, the path of the charged particles would
be curved into a circular spiral, enabling the particles to be subjected
to a further accelerating kick with the completion of each successively larger orbit, in resonance with the alternating electric field (Livingston, 1969, p. 13).

Just as in the case of four-dimensional geometry, contributions
in high-energy physics, too, can come from outside the mainstream of
the field. The most remarkable case in point is the invention of the alternating gradient synchrotron, which came about in the following curious way: In 1952, a team of top accelerator physicists, engineers, and
mathematicians working toward the design of a new-generation (10
GeV) accelerator at the Brookhaven Laboratory attempted to improve on the efficiency of the magnets used in the preceding synchrotron. In an effort to reduce the effects of asymmetric saturation of the
yokes of the magnets inherent in their C-shaped configurations, a new
design arose in which every other yoke was oppositely oriented. A
mathematical analysis then yielded the unexpected discovery that the
weak alternations in the gradients of the field that resulted from this
change—far from making the orbits of the particles less stable, as had
been feared—actually made the orbits more stable and tightly confined. Indeed, further analyses revealed that, by properly shaping the
poles of the magnets (into steeply inclined rectangular hyperbolas) and
thus maximizing the contrasts between the successive positive and
negative gradients, the transverse orbital oscillations could be mini-
mized, making possible in turn (a) a smaller vacuum chamber, (b)
smaller magnets, (c) a much larger radius of curvature of the entire

machine, and, hence, (d) acceleration of the particles to much higher energies. The geometrical basis of this breakthrough, which resulted in machines whose performance surpassed even the favorable predictions, is evident in the numerous complex diagrams that accompany the published reports (see Livingston, 1966, Chapter IV).

Then, about a year after the initial reports by this prestigious American team reached the scientific community with much fanfare, a remarkable fact came to light: Buried in a "crackpot file" at the Lawrence Radiation Laboratory of the University of California was a letter, received there well before the Brookhaven team had even initiated its study, in which a Nicholas Christofilos set forth the entire concept and design of such an alternating gradient synchrotron, which he had developed entirely on his own in his spare time while employed as an elevator engineer in Athens, Greece (Livingston, 1966, p. 269; 1969, p. 69; Omar Snyder, personal communication, April 5, 1977). The fact that the importance of the development described in Christofilos' letter was not recognized by the American physicists until after such a machine had been independently worked out in full detail in this country points, once again, to the limitations of verbal encoding.

Some Factors that May be Associated with the Development of Exceptional Powers of Imagination

In reviewing what information we have about the childhoods of many of the cases considered here, I have been struck by the recurrence of certain suggestive patterns. Putting together a kind of composite caricature, we might say that the genetic potential for visual-spatial creativity of a high order seems especially likely to be revealed and/or fostered in a child (a) who is kept home from school during the early school years and, perhaps, is relatively isolated from age-mates as well, (b) who is, if anything, slower than average in language development, and (c) who is furnished with and becomes unusually engrossed in playing with concrete physical objects, mechanical models, geometrical puzzles, or, simply, wooden cubes. In addition, the inspiration to press relentlessly and concertedly toward the highest achievements that such a creativity makes possible may require the stimulus or model provided by a previous great thinker of a similar turn of mind. Thus, Einstein may require his Maxwell and Maxwell his Faraday; Watt may require his Newcomen; Watson and Crick, their Pauling, and so on.

Some Reasons for the Special Effectiveness of Mental Imagery

The effectiveness of nonverbal processes of mental imagery and spatial visualization in the kinds of creative works just reviewed can perhaps be explained, at least in part, by reference to the following interrelated aspects of such processes: their private and therefore not socially, conventionally, or institutionally controlled nature; their richly concrete and isomorphic structure; their engagement of highly developed, innate mechanisms of spatial intuition; and their direct emotional impact.

To amplify a bit on the first of these aspects, it seems reasonable that the most novel ideas and radical departures from traditional ways of thinking are not likely to arise within the very system of verbal communication that is the primary vehicle for maintaining and perpetuating established ideas and entrenched traditions. Rather, the challenges to such a system are likely to come from outside the system itself—perhaps particularly from the idiosyncratic probings of a few unique individuals who, for reasons of a congenital predilection for visual–spatial over verbal thinking, often together with a degree of early isolation from the standard socialization afforded by the peer group and/or formal schooling, are less constrained by tradition.

Second, the richness of concrete visual imagery, together with its structurally "isomorphic" relation to the external objects, events, or processes that it represents (Cooper & Shepard, 1978; Shepard, 1975; Shepard & Chipman, 1970; Shepard & Podgorny, 1978; Sloman, 1971), may well permit the noticing of significant details and relationships that are not adequately preserved in a purely verbal formulation. As Galton (1883) well put it, "A visual image is the most perfect form of mental representation wherever the shape, position, and relations of objects in space are concerned" (p. 113). Thus Watson's sudden and crucial realization that adenine–thymine and guanine–cytosine pairs form identically shaped overall configurations could hardly have come about as a result of processes of purely verbal deduction; rather, it is an example of exactly the kind of thing that my associates and I have found can be done with considerable speed and accuracy by "mental rotation" (Cooper, 1975; Cooper & Shepard, 1978; Metzler & Shepard, 1974; Shepard & Metzler, 1971).

Third (and intimately connected with the immediately preceding aspect), the spatial character of visual images makes them directly accessible to powerful competencies for spatial intuition and manipulation that have developed during the eons of evolution of our prehuman ancestors in a three-dimensional world—long before the first appearance of any sort of linguistic competency. The ability to carry out mental rotations is presumably illustrative of one such competency (see Shepard, 1975, pp. 112–116). As another example, consider that, because of the very great rate of exponential expansion of possible branches of the proof trees, it has been suggested that even the elementary theorems of plane geometry would be largely inaccessible in the absence of the heuristics of spatial intuition possessed by the average high school student (Marvin Minsky, personal communication, July 1958; see also, Shepard, 1964, p. 59).

And fourth, vivid mental images, because they provide psychologically more effective substitutes than do purely verbal encodings for the corresponding external objects and events, have a greater tendency to engage the affective and motivational systems. This is undoubtedly why powerful emotions of fear, anger, and desire tend to be more strongly determined by the vividness with which one concretely pictures the relevant object or event (a plane crash or a terminal illness, in the case of fear) than by the probability that one abstractly assigns to that event by verbal reasoning. This is also why many current methods of behavior modification (such as systematic desensitization and implosion) make such heavy use of imagery to extinguish fears, overcome phobias, and so on. Likewise, the scientist or inventor who vividly envisions the problems, paradoxes, and possibilities implicit in a situation (whether a steam engine, a rotating magnetic field, a helical molecule, or an observer traveling at the speed of light) may thereby possess a more insistent inner incentive for continuing to struggle with those problems or paradoxes and to pursue those possibilities.

Related to several of these aspects is the further possible factor, noted in connection with Einstein, Maxwell, and Watson, that the search for invariances and symmetries, which has proved so productive in theoretical physics and molecular biology, may be traceable to the responsiveness to structural symmetry that seems to have reached an unequaled degree of development in the visual system. The preoccupation with structural symmetry as such, as in the cases of the geometers of the four-dimensional polytopes, may seem to be too esoteric to be of any broad significance. However, we should remember that four-dimensional geometry is basic to the special theory of relativity, and that the tensor calculus, which seemed equally esoteric and remote from significant application when it was originally invented by the mathematicians Ricci and Livi-Civita, turned out to provide exactly the tools that Einstein later needed to characterize the gravitational curvature of the four-dimensional space-time continuum in his general theory of relativity. Moreover, the regular polygons, polyhedra, tesselations, and honeycombs of the pure geometers contain, as a subset, the symmetrical structures that have proved so handy in the representation of the relationships among the subatomic particles—as in the meson octet or the baryon decuplet within the quantum-number space of "isospin" and "hypercharge" (Capra, 1975, pp. 253–4; and, for more general discussions of the role of symmetry in science and art, Boardman, O'Connor, & Young, 1973; Critchlow, 1976; Shubnikov & Koptsik, 1974; Weyl, 1952).

Clearly, many of the greatest conceptual advances of modern science—including electromagnetic theory, special and general relativity, the theories of atomic structure and of subatomic particles, and the discovery of the molecular structure of DNA—have a strongly geometrical component. Consider also the appeal of pictorial representations such as the Minkowski diagrams for the space–time manifold in special relativity, the Feynman diagrams for quantum electrodynamics, or the "crossing" diagrams of Heisenberg's quantum-mechanical S-matrix formalism for particle interactions. The appeal of such diagrams is, in part, that the underlying physical invariances are preserved geometrically under those pictorial mental transformations, such as rotation or reflection, that come most naturally to the human mind (cf. Capra, 1975, p. 271; Cooper & Shepard, 1978).

FURTHER CASES, IMPLICATIONS, AND CONCLUSIONS

The preceding self-reports from the survey that I published almost a decade ago (Shepard, 1978a) seem to me to exhibit certain consistent patterns that warrant the attention of anyone interested in understanding or promoting scientific creativity. In the ensuing years, moreover, further cases that have come to my notice have only reinforced my impression of these consistent patterns. Before turning to a consideration of these patterns, and to the implications they may have for educators, I will briefly mention three additional, especially pertinent cases.

Three Further Cases

Richard Feynman

In a popular account of the work of contemporary physicists, theoretical physicist Freeman Dyson has made some relevant comments about the highly pictorial approach to physics taken by the principal architect of modern quantum electrodynamics—Richard Feynman, Nobel Laureate and inventor of the "Feynman diagrams" that physicists now find so indispensable for work in that field. Concerning Feynman, Dyson says: "Dick was . . . a profoundly original scientist. He refused to take anybody's word for anything. This meant that he was forced to rediscover or reinvent for himself almost the whole of physics. It took him five years of concentrated work to reinvent quantum mechanics. He said that he couldn't understand the official version of quantum mechanics which was taught in textbooks, and so he had to begin afresh from the beginning. This was a heroic enterprise. He worked harder during those years than anybody I have ever known." (Dyson, 1979, p. 69).

Feynman's novel approach to physics was at first very difficult for his elders to grasp. Most theoretical physicists working in that field (Dyson mentions, in particular, Bethe, Oppenheimer, and Schwinger) had been accustomed to proceeding analytically, by writing down some equations and then laboriously calculating their solutions. In contrast, Dyson tells us that Feynman, without writing down any equations, "had a physical picture of the way things happen, and the picture gave him the solutions directly, with a minimum of calculation." Dyson says he was reminded, by this aspect of Feynman, of a statement by John Maynard Keynes that Isaac Newton's "peculiar gift was the power of holding continuously in his mind a purely mental problem until he had seen straight through it" (1979, p. 70). One might make the connection, too, to Einstein's statement that his own "particular ability" did not lie in mathematical calculation but in "visualizing . . . effects, consequences, and possibilities" (Holton, 1972, p. 110). Indeed, Dyson attributes to Feynman the opinion that in the long continuing effort of Einstein's later years to achieve a unified field theory, "Einstein had failed because he stopped thinking in concrete physical images and became a manipulator of equations" (1979, p. 75).

Stephen Hawking

Prospects for the kind of grand unification that Einstein sought now appear much brighter thanks to remarkable advances in theoretical physics, astrophysics, and cosmology during the last few decades. We seem to be poised on the threshold of a new synthesis in which gravitation, which is currently described by Einstein's theory of general relativity, will at last be subsumed with the other three basic forces of nature (the recently unified electromagnetic, and the weak and strong nuclear forces), which are currently described by the very different quantum-mechanical theories of electrodynamics and chro-

modynamics. Many feel that such a synthesis will also bring an unprecedented understanding of the origin and ultimate fate of the
universe as a whole. The single individual who is regarded by many
as most likely to achieve this awesome synthesis is Stephen Hawking,
the theoretical physicist who holds Isaac Newton's Lucasian Chair of
Mathematics at Cambridge University.

The theoretical results that Hawking has already achieved include: (1) a demonstration that general relativity implies that the universe must have emerged from a geometrical singularity of space–time;
(2) a demonstration that general relativity implies that black holes, once
formed, can neither divide nor diminish but, as they insatiably suck in
all matter and energy that comes within their range, can only become
even larger and more rapacious; (3) his later, surprising qualification
of this result, which for the first time took fully into account the quantum-mechanical properties of the gravitationally contorted space–time
surrounding a black hole—that in the absence of a continuing supply
of external matter and energy, black holes are in fact destined to lose
their mass through what has come to be called "Hawking radiation"
until ultimately (if the universe itself does not first succumb to total
gravitational collapse) the last vestige of each hole self-annihilates in
a final, explosive flash; and (4) his further discovery that contrary to
the prevailing view that black holes could be formed only by the gravitational collapse of objects of substantially larger mass than the sun,
"primordial" black holes of far smaller mass could have been formed
during the earliest, highly condensed moments of the universe (and
may even now be flashing out of existence here and there throughout
the universe).

An aspect of Hawking's case that seems particularly relevant here
is that all of these astonishing theoretical results were achieved after
Hawking had developed, while still a graduate student, a progressive
motorneuronal disease (diagnosed as amyotrophic lateral sclerosis),
which has left him confined to an electrically controlled wheelchair,
unable to write or even to turn the pages of a book, and with so little
control of his speech that only a few close associates are now able to
understand and transcribe his vocalizations for the scientific community. When Michael Harwood, who interviewed Hawking through such
an interpreter, asked Hawking how he was able to keep in mind all the
equations with which his written reports are filled, Hawking replied:
"I tend to avoid equations as much as possible, I simply can't manage
very complicated equations, so I have developed geometrical ways of
thinking, instead" (Harwood, 1983, p. 19). Hawking indicated that he
has by necessity had to leave much of the detailed mathematical cal-

culation to his collaborators. In a remark reminiscent of what Keynes said of Newton, and of what Dyson said of Feynman, Harvard's William Press told Harwood that "Stephen's genius is in piercing through to the solution without having to calculate non-essential pieces" (Harwood, 1983, p. 59), and that "it makes him one of the greatest physicists of our age" (p. 53). As Harwood puts it well, Hawking, in his search for the origin and ultimate fate of the universe, "has followed a path marked by signposts that so far are invisible except to the imagination" (p. 54). Indeed, could there be a more striking illustration of the power of imagination?

Mitchell Feigenbaum

A significant shift of focus is now taking place in all the physical sciences from the previous almost exclusive concern with the deterministic evolution of physical systems as prescribed by classical, relativistic, and quantum mechanics, to a realization that in the far-from-equilibrium conditions that largely prevail on earth and, indeed, throughout the universe, two kinds of qualitatively different phenomena emerge: first, the onset of cascading "bifurcations" resulting (even in simple Newtonian systems—see Lighthill, 1986) in nondeterministic, chaotic behavior, such as turbulence; and, second, the emergence, out of such chaos, of new kinds of order, called "dissipative structures," such as the highly regular hexagonal lattice of toroidal convection cells (Bénard cells) and, presumably, life itself (Prigogine & Stengers, 1984).

Contributing to this shift, the young physicist Mitchell Feigenbaum made the remarkable discovery that in the most diverse physical, chemical, and presumably biological systems, chaos often ensues as the limit of a sequence of increasingly complex periodic behaviors of the system with periods of successively doubled lengths, T, 2T, 4T, ... Moreover, Feigenbaum found that this progression, now called the "Feigenbaum sequence," is characterized by a new universal constant, or "Feigenbaum number," 4.559201609 . . . . The manner in which Feigenbaum arrived at his discovery is reminiscent of the manner in which Einstein began his journey toward the theory of special relativity by imagining a light wave. According to Gleick (1984), inspiration came to Feigenbaum one day at lunch: ". . . it was in the form of a picture, a mental image of two small wavy forms and one big one . . . no more, perhaps, than the visible top of a vast iceberg of mental processing that had taken place below the waterline of consciousness. It had to do with scaling, the way the small features of a

thing relate to the large features, and it gave him the path he needed"
(Gleick, 1984, pp. 49, 66).

The social isolation of Feigenbaum's youth and the difficulty that
he later experienced in getting his ideas accepted also have a familiar
ring. Sometime after second grade, Feigenbaum told Gleick, he became so absorbed in learning new things that he neglected friend-
ships. By college, he said, he was working all night, totally preoccupied
and totally without friends. Then, after obtaining his doctorate, Feigenbaum struggled for several years without coming to much in the
way of publishable results before he finally achieved his breakthrough. Even then, the first papers in which he reported his new results were rejected for publication (Gleick, 1984, p. 49). Although these
results eventually came to have a wide impact (e.g., see Prigogine &
Stengers, 1984), they had their origin in the earlier protracted period
of seemingly unproductive rumination.

The Nature of Scientific Imagination

The end product of a scientist's work is of course the published
papers that present the new discoveries of theoretical synthesis in some
language that is shared by the scientific community at large—usually
in the form of written words and, often, mathematical equations. However, as we have seen, many of the greatest scientists have emphasized that the processes that led to their inventions, discoveries, and
theories were neither linguistic nor mathematical and, indeed, even
when they knew that they had reached the crucial insight, they often
had to struggle in order to cast their insight into the communicable
form of words or mathematical symbols. These self-reports by scientists, together with the results on mental transformations that my associates and I have obtained in the psychological laboratory (to say
nothing of my own introspections!), have convinced me that an important part of the process of scientific imagination is a kind of internal "analog" simulation of possible events in the world (Shepard, 1984;
Shepard & Cooper, 1982). I have argued that such a process makes use
of perceptual mechanisms that have, through evolutionary eons, deeply
internalized an intuitive wisdom about the way things transform in the
world. Because this wisdom is embodied in a perceptual system that
antedates, by far, the emergence of language and mathematics, imagination is more akin to visualizing than to talking or to calculating to
oneself.

A Challenge for Educators

The skills of written communication, of calculation, and of logic and mathematics are based on relatively recent developed conventions of society and yield externalized, shareable, written products. Such skills are the subject of formal instruction in school. In contrast, imaginative skills guide inherently unseen and unexternalizable processes of perception and representation. Those skills, to the extent that they are developed, are not developed by formal schooling. Their development evidently occurs before, outside of, or perhaps in spite of such schooling—apparently through active but largely solitary interaction with the physical objects of one's world.

I have already remarked on the fact that many of the most creative scientists manifested an early preoccupation with such solitary explorations of the ways in which physical things fit together or work (building blocks, mechanical contrivances, and the like) and, whether by choice or by circumstance, underwent periods of less-than-usual involvement with school subjects or with other children. Among others, the scientists Newton, Maxwell, Helmholtz, Einstein, and Feigenbaum; the inventors Watt and Tesla; and the geometer Alicia Boole Stott provide particularly salient illustrations of one or more of these tendencies. Even when they became adults, the novelty of the approaches of a number of creative thinkers prevented their work from obtaining early or full acceptance by the establishment. Among many others, I think here of the scientists Feynman and Feigenbaum; the inventors Tesla and Christofilos; and the geometers Gosset and Schläfli.

I have already pointed to some possible reasons why highly original thinkers might be particularly subject to these tendencies and problems: Insights into the deep invariances that lie behind the superficial variations of objects and events in the world may be most likely in those who, sufficiently early in life, (1) become engrossed in a direct, interactive exploration of such objects and events and (2) do so unconstrained by conventional, verbalized, and rigidly compartmentalized interpretations (or dismissals) of those objects or events. If so, we face a difficult challenge. On the one hand, science and technology have advanced to the point where, except in rare cases (such as that of Christofilos), major developments are seldom achieved by the likes of a Faraday, an Edison, or a Tesla, working in the relative absence of an administrative organization, scientific colleagues, and technical or mathematical training. On the other hand, individuals who adapt well to the mastery of conventional school subjects and to working with other individuals within an established organization seem less likely to question accepted ideas or to break new paths.

As educators, perhaps particularly in a country, like the United States, that has long taken pride both in maintaining itself at the forefront of technology and in guaranteeing a formal education for all of its citizens, we increasingly confront a dilemma: Young people who show early indications of unusual scientific curiosity and talent evidently require two things, but these two things appear to stand in mutual conflict. On the one hand, such individuals need to develop basic verbal and social skills (to say nothing of humanitarian values!) as well as to master the enormous and still growing body of essential scientific and technical knowledge. On the other hand, they evidently need an opportunity, beginning at an early age, for complete absorption in a free, direct, and nonverbal exploration of the natural world. I say "natural world" to contrast it with the artificially contrived, conventional world of television and ready-made plastic toys, which leaves so little to the imagination! The challenge, in short, is this: Without sacrificing formal education, can we find a way to encourage the kind of unconstrained early exploration of the world that appears to be crucial for an individual's development of scientific intuition and creative imagination?

REFERENCES

Ashvaghosha, (1900). *The awakening of faith*. (Trans. D.T. Suzuki). Chicago: Open Court.

Beveridge, W. I. B. (1957). *The art of scientific investigation* (3rd ed.). New York: Vintage.

Boardman, A. D., O'Connor, D. E., & Young, P. A. (1973). *Symmetry and its applications in science*. New York: Wiley.

Cannon, W. B. (1945). *The way of an investigator*. New York: Norton.

Capra, F. (1975). *The tao of physics*. Boulder, CO.: Shambhala.

Cooper, L. A. (1975). Mental transformation of random two-dimensional shapes. *Cognitive Psychology, 7*, 20–43.

Cooper, L. A., & Shepard, R. N. (1973). Chronometric studies of the rotation of mental images. In W. G. Chase (Ed.), *Visual information processing* (pp. 75–176). New York: Academic Press.

Cooper, L. A., & Shepard, R. N. (1978). Transformation of representation of objects in space. In E. C. Carterette & M. P. Friedman (Eds.), *Handbook of perception*, Volume VIII, *Space and object perception*. New York: Academic Press.

Cooper, L. A., & Shepard, R. N. (1984). Turning something over in the mind. *Scientific American, 251*, 106–14.

Coxeter, H. S. M. (1973). *Regular polytopes*. London: Methuen, 1948; 3rd ed., Dover.

Critchlow, K. (1976). *Islamic patterns: An analytical and cosmological approach*. New York: Schocken.

Dyson, F. (1979, August 13). *New Yorker*, pp. 64–88.

Faraday, A. (1972). *Dream power*. New York: Coward, McCann & Geoghegan.

Ferguson, E. S. (1977). The mind's eye: Nonverbal thought in technology. *Science*, *197*, 827–36.

Findlay, A. (1948). *A hundred years of chemistry* (2nd ed.). London: Duckworth.

Galton, F. (1883). *Inquiries into human faculty and its development*. London: Macmillan.

Ghiselin, B. (1952). *The creative process*. New York: New American Library.

Gleick, J. (1984, June 10). Solving the mathematical riddle of chaos. *The New York Times Magazine*, pp. 31–71.

Godwin, A. N. (1972). Three-dimensional pictures for Thom's parabolic umbilic. *Institut des Hautes Études Scientifiques. Publications Mathématiques*, *40*, 117–38.

Gregory, R. L., Wallace, J. G., & Campbell, F. W. (1959). Change in the size and shape of visual after-images observed in complete darkness during changes of position in space. *Quarterly Journal of Experimental Psychology*, *11*, 54–6.

Hadamard, J. (1945). *The psychology of invention in the mathematical field*. Princeton, N.J.: Princeton University Press.

Harwood, M. (1983, January 23). The universe and Dr. Hawking. *The New York Times Magazine*, pp. 16–64.

Herschel, Sir J. F. W. (1867). *Familiar lectures on scientific subjects*. London: Strahan.

Holton, G. (1972). On trying to understand scientific genius. *American Scholar*, *41*, 95–110.

Hunt, I., & Draper, W. W. (1964). *Lightning in his hand: The life story of Nikola Tesla*. Denver, CO.: Sage.

Hutchinson, E. (1949). *How to think creatively*. New York: Abingdon-Cokesbury.

Kendall, J. (1955). *Michael Faraday, man of simplicity*. London: Faber & Faber.

Koenigsberger, L. (1965). *Hermann von Helmholtz*. (Trans. F. A. Welby). New York: Dover.

Koestler, A. (1964). *The act of creation*. New York: Macmillan.

Krippner, S., & Hughes, W. (1970, June). Genius at work zzz. *Psychology Today*, pp. 40–3.

Lighthill, Sir James. (1986). The recently recognized failure of predictability in Newtonian dynamics. *Proceedings of the Royal Society London A*, *407*, 35–50.

Livingston, M. S. (Ed.) (1966). *The development of high-energy accelerators*. New York: Dover.

Livingston, M. S. (1969). *Particle accelerators: A brief history.* Cambridge, MA.: Harvard University Press.

Lombroso, C. (1901). *The man of genius.* New York: Scribner's.

MacKenzie, N. (1965). *Dreams and dreaming.* London: Aldus Books.

Max, N. L., & Clifford, W. H., Jr. (1975). Computer animation of the sphere eversion. *Computer Graphics*, *9*, 32–9.

Maxwell, J. C. (1873). *A treatise on electricity and magnetism* (2nd ed.). Oxford: Clarendon.

Metz, W. D. (1978). Midwest computer architect struggles with speed of light. *Science, 99*, 404–9.

Metzler, J., & Shepard, R. N. (1974). Transformational studies of the internal representation of three-dimensional objects. In R. Solso (Ed.), *Theories in cognitive psychology: The Loyola Symposium*, pp. 147–201. Potomac, MD.: Lawrence Erlbaum.

Myers, F. W. H. (1903). *Human personality and its survival of bodily death* (Vol. I). New York: Longmans, Green.

Newman, J. R. (1955). James Clerk Maxwell. *Scientific American, 192*(6), 58–71.

O'Neill, J. J. (1944). *Prodigal genius: The life of Nikola Tesla.* New York: Ives Washburn.

Patten, B. M. (1973). Visually mediated thinking: A report of the case of Albert Einstein. *Journal of Learning Disabilities*, *6*, 415–20.

Phillips, A. (1966). Turning a surface inside out. *Scientific American, 214*(5), 112–20.

Planck, M. (1933). *Where is science going?* (Trans. J. Murphy). London: Allen & Unwin.

Platt, W., & Baker, R. A. (1931). The relationship of the scientific "hunch" to research. *Journal of Chemical Education*, *8*, 1969–2002.

Prigogine, I., & Stengers, I. (1984). *Order out of chaos.* New York: Bantam Books.

Randhawa, B. S., & Coffman, W. E. (Eds.). (1978). *Visual learning, thinking, and communication.* New York: Academic Press.

Richardson, A. (1969). *Mental imagery.* New York: Springer.

Shepard, R. N. (1964). Computers and thought: A review of the book edited by E. Feigenbaum & J. Feldman. *Behavioral Science, 9*, 57–65.

Shepard, R. N. (1975). Form, formation, and transformation of internal representations. In R. Solso (Ed.), *Information processing and cognition: The Loyola Symposium*, pp. 87–122. Hillsdale, N.J.: Lawrence Erlbaum.

Shepard, R. N. (1978a). Externalization of mental images and the act of creation. In B. S. Randhawa & W. E. Coffman (Eds.), *Visual learning, thinking, and communication* (pp. 139–89). New York: Academic Press.

Shepard, R. N. (1978b). The mental image. *American Psychologist, 33*, 125–37.

Shepard, R. N. (1984). Ecological constraints on internal representation: Resonant kinematics of perceiving, imagining, thinking, and dreaming. *Psychological Review, 91*, 417–47.

Shepard, R. N., & Chipman, S. (1970). Second-order isomorphism of internal representations: Shapes of states. *Cognitive Psychology, 1*, 1–17.

Shepard, R. N., & Cooper, L. A. (1982). *Mental images and their transformations*. Cambridge, MA.: MIT Press/Bradford Books.

Shepard, R. N., & Metzler, J. (1971). Mental rotation of three-dimensional objects. *Science, 171*, 701–3.

Shepard, R. N., & Podgorny, P. (1978). Cognitive processes that resemble perceptual processes. In W. K. Estes (Ed.), *Handbook of learning and cognitive processes*. Hillsdale, N. J.: Lawrence Erlbaum.

Shubnikov, A. V., & Koptsik, V. A. (1974). *Symmetry in science and art*. (Trans. G. D. Archard). New York: Plenum.

Sloman, A. (1971). Interactions between philosophy and artificial intelligence: The role of intuition and non-logical reasoning in intelligence. *Artificial Intelligence, 2*, 209–25.

Smyth, H. DeW. (1945). *Atomic energy for military purposes: The official report on the development of the atomic bomb*. Princeton, N.J.: Princeton University Press.

Sullivan, W. (1972, March 27). The Einstein papers: Childhood showed a gift for the abstract. *The New York Times*, p. 1.

Tesla, N. (1956). *Nikola Tesla: Lectures, patents, articles*. Beograd: Nikola Tesla Museum.

Thom, R. (1975). *Structural stability and morphogenesis*. (Trans. D. H. Fowler). Reading, MA.: W. A. Benjamin.

Thompson, L. J. (1971). Language disabilities in men of eminence. *Journal of Learning Disabilities, 4*, 34–45.

Thurston, R. H. (1878). *A history of the growth of the steam-engine*. New York: Appleton.

Tyndall, J. (1868). *Faraday as a discoverer*. London: Longmans, Green.

Warren, R. M., & Warren, R. P. (1968). *Helmholtz on perception: Its physiology and development*. New York: Wiley.

Watson, J. D. (1968). *The double helix*. New York: New American Library.

Wertheimer, M. (1945). *Productive thinking*. New York: Harper.

Weyl, H. (1952). *Symmetry*. Princeton, N.J.: Princeton University Press.

Woodcock, A. E. R., & Poston, T. A. (1974). A geometrical study of the elementary catastrophes. *Lecture notes in mathematics*, Vol. 373. New York: Springer-Verlag.

10 ◇ The Philosophical Imagination in Children's Literature

GARETH MATTHEWS
University of Massachusetts

This chapter explores four children's stories that, each in its own way, illustrate how philosophical imagination can give richness and meaning to literature written for children. "The Garden," from the collection, *Frog and Toad Together*, raises questions in the logic of scientific reasoning. *Yellow and Pink* introduces us to natural theology and the philosophy of religion. *Albert's Toothache* raises interesting questions in metaphysics and the philosophy of mind. *Tuck Everlasting* explores ethics and the meaning of life.

By way of contrast, I will begin with a children's story that conveys a different message. This story, called simply "Questions," comes from the very popular series of stories about Oliver and Amanda Pig by Jean Van Leeuwen. The volume from which it is taken (*More Tales of Oliver Pig*, 1981) is attractively illustrated by Arnold Lobel and is advertised as "A Junior Literary Guild Selection." Following is a shortened version of the story.

> Oliver and his father go walking in the snow.
> "How many snowflakes are up in the sky?" Oliver asks.
> "So many that no one can count them all," his father replies.
> Oliver boasts that he can count to a hundred. His father assures him that there are more snowflakes than that—in fact, that there are "millions and millions."

In my discussions of Arnold Lobel's *Frog and Toad Together*, Barbara Williams' *Albert's Toothache*, William Steig's *Yellow and Pink*, and Natalie Babbitt's *Tuck Everlasting*, I use material that first appeared in my column, "Thinking in Stories," in *Thinking: The Journal of Philosophy for Children*, vols. 2 (1980–1), 5 (1983–5), and 6 (1985–6). I wish to thank the editor of *Thinking* for permission to reuse this material.

Oliver asks where the garden goes when the snow comes.

"It is still there, sleeping under the snow until spring comes," Oliver's father answers.

"When spring comes, will my flowers come back?" Oliver wants to know.

"Not the same ones," his father admits; "but under the ground the beginnings of new flowers are waiting."

There are more questions, and more answers. Then Oliver and his father go inside to get warm.

Oliver complains of cold toes. His father offers to help warm them with hot cocoa.

"When you were little," Oliver asks his father, "did your father know just how to warm you up?"

"Yes, he always did," Oliver's father assures him.

Oliver and his father look at a picture of Oliver's father and grandfather together. "Why does that picture look just like my father and me?" Oliver asks.

Oliver is told that they all—Oliver, his father and his grandfather—belong to the same family.

"Why do you ask so many questions?" Oliver's father asks.

"I want to know a lot of things," Oliver replies.

"Someday I think you will know a lot of things," Oliver's father reassures him.

Suppose I pick up this volume at my local bookstore and take it home to read to my child. What message will my child get from "Questions"?

The message is clearly a very conventional one. Children, like Oliver Pig, are endlessly curious. Fathers, like Father Pig, are endlessly patient—well, if not quite endlessly, still admirably so. More important, children are naively ignorant. They know very little about the world and they lack the sophistication required to hide their ignorance so as to keep themselves from looking foolish. Childish naivete is attractive, up to a point. It is something to be patronized by adults, and even by older children. In fact, a girl or boy of six or seven who reads or hears this story can be expected to smile indulgently at Oliver's questions, all the while realizing, or half-realizing, that her or his own best questions may well sound "stupid" to a child of ten or eleven. Childhood, even relative childhood, is something we all indulge and condescend to.

The contrast to Oliver's naive ignorance is, of course, his father's wisdom. Father knows the answers. He also knows how to break them to Oliver—understandingly, gently, a little bit at a time, never more than Oliver can handle. This reassuring picture is finished off with the specific promise that Oliver, when he grows up, will also be wise. Just as flowers grow and bloom in the spring, children grow and blossom into wise and patient parents.

There is much about this conventional picture I would like to call into question, but I shall concentrate here on only one point. It is the phony contrast between naive ignorance in children and patient wisdom in adults. The fact is, Oliver's father is not really interested in Oliver's questions. (Nor, of course, is the author of the story.) The father uses his position of natural advantage to put Oliver down, as most adults do most of the time to their children, and as older children are encouraged to do to their younger peers. To be sure, it is with a kind and gently condescension that Oliver's father puts him down, but that only makes it more effective.

How many snowflakes are there up in the sky? For almost all of us the honest answer would be "I don't know," or even "I haven't any idea." In any case, it is not "Too many to count." It would certainly be possible to take a photograph with a high-speed camera of a cubic foot of falling snow, enlarge the picture sufficiently to get a good flake count, estimate the volume of a given snowstorm, and come up with the estimate that at t there were n snowflakes over area a. Doubtlessly no one is interested enough in learning the answer to do the research required, nor would the National Science Foundation fund it. But that is another matter.

In the story, poor Oliver boasts of his prowess in being able to count up to a hundred. We smile indulgently at the obvious inadequacy of this ability. Even a six-year-old will smile indulgently. We admire the father's all-knowing patience. But we shouldn't. The putdown is uncalled for.

"Will my flowers come back?" Oliver asks later. The question needs to be clarified. Perennials like roses will produce new blossoms. Is that what you mean, Oliver? Annuals like petunias and sunflowers will have to be grown from new seeds.

Admittedly, Oliver's father may not be a gardener. But what does he mean by saying that "not the same ones" will come back? Does he mean that there will be *new* blossoms on the old mum plant? Surely Oliver wasn't expecting the return of the very same blossoms. Or was he? Or does Oliver's father mean that, for example, new sunflower plants will have to be grown from seeds produced by last year's sunflowers? We never learn. Instead we move on quickly to other questions.

The topic of family resemblance is a wonderful subject to investigate. A child may have had the recent experience of seeing a new litter of pups or kittens. Sometimes a litter will provide a clear illustration of Mendel's Laws. (Father may not remember Mendel's Laws, but he could consult the encyclopedia.) Another interesting issue that family resemblance raises is the difference between inherited and acquired characteristics. One of my old teachers used to say, "Wooden legs are not inheritable, wooden heads are." Thinking about which features of a person, or a pig, can be inherited and which cannot, can be stimulating for all. But as a way of developing a discussion of family resemblance, Oliver's father's response, "We all belong to the same family," is a non-starter.

REASONING ABOUT CAUSALITY

Are there ways to make Oliver-like naivete an invitation to reflection and exploration, rather than a justification for father-like condescension? Of course there are. One is through animal stories written for children. The illustrator of the Oliver stories, Arnold Lobel, is wonderful at using his characters, Frog and Toad, to do just that. The story, "The Garden," from his collection, *Frog and Toad Together* (1972), will serve as an example. An abbreviated version of this story follows.

> Toad admires Frog's garden. "What a fine garden you have," he says.
> "It is very nice," agrees Frog, "but it was hard work."
> Toad decides to plant a garden. He plants the flower seeds Frog gives him. "Now seeds," he says, "start growing."
> Not surprisingly, the seeds do not start to grow—at least not visibly. So Toad puts his head close to the ground and says loudly, "Now seeds, start growing!" Still seeing no result, Toad puts his head *very* close to the ground and shouts, "NOW SEEDS START GROWING!"
> "You are shouting too much," advises Frog, "these poor seeds are afraid to grow." Frog suggests leaving them alone for a few days.
> When night comes Toad looks out his window and moans, "My seeds have not started to grow; they must be afraid of the dark." Toad decides to read the seeds a story so that they will not be afraid. The next day he sings songs to his seeds. The next day he reads poems to his seeds. The next day he plays music to his seeds. Still he can see no growth.

> "These must be the most frightened seeds in the whole world!" says Toad.
>
> Feeling very tired Toad falls asleep.
>
> "Toad, wake up," says Frog; "look at your garden!"
>
> Toad looks at his garden. Little green plants are coming up in the garden. "At last," he shouts, "my seeds have stopped being afraid to grow!"
>
> "And now you will have a nice garden too," says Frog.
>
> "But you were right, Frog," says Toad, "it was very hard work."

This time, too, there is a contrast between naivete and sophistication. Toad is naive; Frog is sophisticated. But this is not a generational difference. Frog and Toad are friends.

Moreover, although we laugh at Toad—even six-year-olds laugh at Toad—it is he, not Frog, who provokes our thought. We ourselves don't think seeds respond to songs, poems, or stories, but how do we know? After all, some gardeners are said to have "green thumbs." Some of them think it important to have a positive attitude toward the plants they want to grow and especially important not to say negative or threatening things in the presence of those plants. Do *we know* this is just superstition?

The punch line, "You were right, Frog, it was very hard work," makes it clear that Toad thinks his singing and reading not only preceded, but also helped cause, the outcome. The textbook name for Toad's error in inductive reasoning is given in the Latin phrase, *post hoc, ergo propter hoc* ("after this, therefore because of this"). Even very small children laugh at Toad's comment and thus show some awareness that *post hoc, ergo propter hoc* is a fallacy. But it is difficult for even a sophisticated adult to be clear about what makes the reasoning fallacious. David Hume (1894) said at times that causation is conjunction plus a certain human expectation. "We may," he wrote in *Enquiry* 7.2, " . . . form another definition of cause, and call it, *an object followed by another, and whose appearance always conveys the thought of that other*." So why won't singing to seeds in the fervent expectation of flowering plants be the cause of flowering plants, since the first "conveys the thought to that other"?

Hume also spoke of "constant conjunction" (singing over seeds always followed by the appearance of flowering plants) and even suggested a stronger requirement: Singing won't be the cause of the appearance of flowering plants unless, if one *were* now to sing over seeds, flowering plants *would* appear, after a suitable interval, of course.

In the story it is Toad's naivete that provokes reflection on the nature of causality. We laugh at Toad, but doing that is not a way of laughing at children. Moreover, we are prevented from being completely condescending even to Toad, since we are all hard pressed to explain exactly what is required for true causality.

The genius of the philosophical imagination in children's literature is that it avoids condescension to children, whether children in the stories or children in the audience, by raising provocative questions that engage and tax the acumen of adults as much as of children.

NATURAL THEOLOGY
AND THE PHILOSOPHY OF RELIGION

I can think of no better example of the philosophical imagination at work in a children's story than the delicately exciting reasoning in *Yellow and Pink* by William Steig (1984). Here is the story in brief:

Two wooden figures, one painted pink, the other yellow, lie on newspapers in the sun, perhaps to dry. They look like marionettes. The pink one is short and fat, whereas the yellow one is straight and thin.

Each starts to wonder what he is doing there on the newspaper in the sun. When Yellow notices Pink beside him he asks, "Do I know you?"

"I don't think so," Pink replies cautiously.

"Do you happen to know what we're doing here?" Yellow asks. Pink doesn't know.

"Who are we?" asks Yellow. Pink doesn't know that either. "Someone must have made us," Pink surmises.

Yellow produces all sorts of difficulties with Pink's hypothesis and himself concludes, "We're an accident, somehow or other we just happened."

Pink starts laughing. "You mean these arms I can move this way and that," he asks, "this head I can turn in any direction, this breathing nose, these walking feet, all of this just happened, by some kind of fluke? That's preposterous!"

Yellow is unmoved. He admonishes his companion to stop and reflect. "With enough time," he says, "a thousand, a million, maybe two and a half million years, lots of unusual things could happen. Why not us?"

Patiently Pink takes up one feature of their construction after another. In each case he challenges Yellow to suggest how that feature could have been the result of an accident. For each feature Pink mentions Yellow tries to say how that feature could, indeed, have been the result of an accident.

Finally a mustachioed man shambles up, examines Pink and Yellow, and announces, with satisfaction, "Nice and dry." As the man takes Pink and Yellow away, tucked under his arm, Yellow whispers in Pink's ear, "Who is this guy?" Pink doesn't know.

In the fifth century B.C., Empedocles speculated that animals and human beings could have been the accidental concatenations of bits of matter, concatenations that just happened to function well as units. The ideas of Empedocles and, after him, those of Democritus, Epicurus, and Lucretius are quite Darwinian, except that the ancients had no genetic theory to explain how a chance concatenation of bits and parts that happened to function well as a whole could reproduce itself, so that the type would survive.

Plato, with his picture of the Master Craftsman creating the world and all its inhabitants according to eternal blueprints, was Pink to Empedocles' Yellow. Plato's pupil, Aristotle, was at least Pinkish, and also a clear opponent of Yellow.

The debate continues, right down to the present day. David Hume and Charles Darwin refined the terms of the debate, but they did not settle it.

In Steig's story, the mustachioed man at the end vindicates Pink, even though, not recognizing his maker, Pink doesn't realize he has been vindicated. But is Steig's story also the story of our world? And how can we find out?

Yellow and Pink is a gem. Not a question, comment, or descriptive detail in it is wasted. And the illustrations, also by Steig, do much more than illustrate; they embody the story they help tell.

Someone will ask who the story's audience is meant to be. (Someone always does.) No doubt that question is almost as tricky and intriguing as the story's own question, "Who are we?" Perhaps Mr. Steig will say he wrote the story for himself. But I shall be dogmatic and insist that his story is as much for the child philosopher in every reflective adult as it is for the aspiring scientist and incipient theologian in every curious child.

METAPHYSICS AND THE PHILOSOPHY OF MIND

Yellow and Pink actually incorporates philosophical reasoning in its story line. But a story can be philosophical without doing that; indeed, it can be philosophical without even stating the philosophical question or questions that it provokes. Arnold Lobel's "The Garden" is a good example of philosophy by indirection. *Albert's Toothache* by Barbara Williams (1974) is another. It has a philosophical richness of ideas and questions. The story is largely paraphrased below.

Albert is a turtle, who complains that he has a toothache. Albert's father is quite unsympathetic. "That's impossible," he says; "it is impossible for anyone in our family to have a toothache."

Though Albert's father does point to his own toothless mouth (Does he also point to its toothlessness? Can one?) to establish the impossibility of a turtle's having a toothache, he never actually says to Albert, "To have a toothache you need to have a tooth and turtles like you and I don't have teeth."

Wouldn't it have been much better to tell Albert that he can't have a toothache because he doesn't have any teeth? Perhaps Albert can have a *tailache*; but he doesn't have the right equipment for having a toothache.

It isn't even enough just to have a tooth (for example, under one's pillow). One can't have an ache in x unless x is a part of one's very own body. Indeed for y to be able to have an ache in x at a particular time, t, x must be an integral part of y's body at t.

But is that last claim really satisfactory? Descartes was impressed by the fact that amputees sometimes report having aches and pains in their amputated limbs (the phenomenon of the "phantom limb"). Suppose that, while I am unconscious, my last remaining tooth is extracted and, when I wake up, I report having an awful toothache. Is it false that I then have a toothache, since I then have no tooth? And what do I have instead? A jawache? But suppose it doesn't feel like a jawache? (I've had those, too.) "It's just in your head," someone might say. Perhaps so. But it's not a headache. (Nor, of course, is it a brainache!)

Albert's grandmother is the only character in the story who is sympathetic to Albert. To her he explains that his "toothache" is on his left toe. Albert's explanation makes it hard to avoid the conclusion that he simply doesn't know what a toothache is.

How does one learn what a toothache is? By having one? And how does one first know it is a toothache one has?

Doesn't it go this way? I come to learn that I have various anatomical parts, including teeth. Once I know a little about my own anatomy, I immediately know where I hurt without having to learn how to tell. Then, so long as I know I have a tooth, I am in a position to recognize that an ache or pain I have is in my tooth.

But there are complications. Suppose the dentist says there is nothing wrong with my tooth? Can the dentist tell me I don't have a toothache?

Perhaps the dentist will say (as a dentist said to someone I know) that, my tooth being sound, what I have is a *simulated* toothache. Is this something Albert could have had?

Then there is the ache in the phantom tooth. If one can have an ache in a tooth one no longer has, why not in a tooth one never had?

Albert's grandmother takes a handkerchief from her purse and wraps it around Albert's toe. I don't know whether that treatment would help a simulated toothache, or an ache in a phantom tooth, but it seems to have been just what Albert needed.

ETHICS AND THE MEANING OF LIFE

For my final example of the philosophical imagination in children's literature, I turn to ethics and the meaning of life. The story is Natalie Babbitt's classic, *Tuck Everlasting* (1975). Packed with surprise, suspense, and adventure, this wonderful story is held together by a remarkably sustained and eloquent effort to convince Winnie that the ordinary life of childhood, adulthood, old age, and death is vastly preferable to an everlasting life arrested at 10 or 17 or 42. The story is summarized below.

> Winnie Foster, ten years old, who is about to drink from a spring in her family's wood, is suddenly kidnapped by Mae Tuck and her two sons. The Tucks eventually explain to Winnie that they all—father, mother, and two sons—drank from that spring 87 years ago. The result was that they all stopped aging. "If you'd had a drink of it today," Mae tells Winnie, "you'd stay a little girl forever. You'd never grow up, not ever."
>
> One thing the Tucks point out is that they don't fit into the society around them. They can't even stay in one place for long. "People get to wondering," as Mae puts it.
>
> More basically, the Tucks don't fit into the world. Out in a rowboat on a summer's evening, Mae's husband, Tuck, tries to explain. "Everything's a wheel," he says.
>
>> turning and turning, never stopping. The frogs is part of it, and the bugs, and the fish, and the wood thrush, too. And people. But never the same ones. Always coming in new, always growing and changing, and always moving on. That's the way it's supposed to be. That's the way it is. (p. 56)

When their rowboat gets stuck, Tuck takes up the analogy. "But this rowboat now," he points out,

> it's stuck. If we didn't move it out ourself, it would stay here forever, trying to get loose, but stuck. That's what we Tucks are, Winnie. Stuck so's we can't move on. We ain't part of the wheel no more. Dropped off, Winnie. Left behind. And everywhere around us, things is moving and growing and changing. (p. 56)

At one point Winnie blurts out, "I don't want to die." "Not now," Tuck replies,

> your time's not now. But dying's part of the wheel, right there next to being born. You can't pick out the pieces you like and leave the rest. Being part of the whole thing, that's the blessing. But it's passing us by, us Tucks. Living's heavy work, but off to one side, the way *we* are, it's useless, too. It don't make sense. If I knowed how to climb back on the wheel, I'd do it in a minute. You can't have living without dying. So you can't call it living, what we got. We just *are*, we just *be*, like rocks beside the road. (p. 57)

Tuck Everlasting gradually nudges its readers toward the conclusion that any life worth living has a beginning, a middle, and an end. Given the choice between an unendingly arrested childhood and a life of the normal sort, the heroine of the story finally chooses mortality. The reader, whether eight or eighty, is likely to approve the choice, or, if not, at least to understand it.

Of course this story does not exhaust the ways of conceiving immortality. In particular, it does not address the ancient idea that one might live a succession, perhaps even an endless succession, of discrete lives. (Perhaps it is worth noting, however, that many traditions that include the idea of transmigration regard reincarnation as a curse to be obviated eventually by one's coming to peace with oneself and one's desires.) Nor does this story consider what it would be like to live a life where everyone, not just a "lucky" one or few, is 17 or 42. In his *Summa Theologica* Thomas Aquinas suggests that we shall all revert, in the resurrection, to the state of youth, "the state of ultimate perfection" (IIIa Suppl. q. 84 a. 1).

Still, *Tuck Everlasting* presents an engrossing thought experiment that forces us to reconsider the attitudes that most of us have toward death. It encourages us to think freshly about whether, to use John Wisdom's way of putting it, such attitudes are "well placed" (1955).

Some adults who most need the consolation of philosophy in confronting their own mortality may recoil from the suggestion that a book for children should confront this topic, or that children can reflect with profit on a thought experiment of this sort. "Leave them in their blessed ignorance," such people may say. But what passes for innocence is, too often, the unspoken agreement not to mention what one has not yet come to terms with. Discussing death with children is frequently more difficult for the adults than for the children.

CONCLUSION

Can one say anything helpful about what distinguishes stories like these four, which exhibit a genuinely philosophical imagination, from those that don't? I think so.

Typically, a philosophically sensitive story presents a thought experiment that exposes something problematic about a concept, an hypothesis, or an attitude. Thus "The Garden" provokes us to consider what there is to the concept of causality besides temporal precedence and spatial contiguity. It does this by giving us a thought experiment in the form of a good joke, which is funny to a child as well as to an adult. *Albert's Toothache* gets us to think about the most private of mental phenomena, pain, by giving us a thought experiment in the form of another joke. Lying behind the joke is this profound question: If I never really know what is in the mind of another, how can I know that a turtle doesn't have a toothache?

Yellow and Pink pursues the design hypothesis. Am I the product of design, rather than the product of accident? It does this by asking us to imagine marionettes arguing about their origin on the basis of their own paltry evidence base. *Tuck Everlasting* asks us to reconsider our attitude toward death. If that attitude is truly well placed, we should envy the Tuck family. But we don't, or at least it's not clear that we do or should.

Some people think there is something inevitably inauthentic about children's literature, especially stories conceived, written, published, and sold by adults for an audience of children. (See, for example, Jacqueline Rose, 1984.) I disagree. Children's stories need not be sentimental, moralistic, or condescending. And even if the author's motivation is so complex as to tax the diagnostic skills of the most sophisticated psychotherapist, a story written in respect for both its audience and its subject matter will be authentic.

One way, though certainly not the only way, for a writer of children's literature to write a story in full respect for children is to write with philosophical imagination. Addressing the ageless questions of philosophy is itself a renunciation of condescension; it is also a celebration of the humanity we share with our children.

REFERENCES

Aquinas, St. Thomas. *Summa theologica*. Garden City, NY: Image Books.

Babbitt, Natalie. (1975). *Tuck Everlasting*. New York: Farrar, Straus and Giroux.

Hume, David. (1894). *An enquiry concerning human understanding*. Oxford: Clarendon Press.

Lobel, Arnold. (1972). *Frog and Toad Together*. New York: Harper & Row.

Rose, Jacqueline. *The case of Peter Pan or the impossibility of children's fiction*. London: Macmillan.

Steig, William. (1984). *Yellow and Pink*. New York: Farrar, Straus and Giroux.

Van Leeuwan, Jean. (1981). *More Tales of Oliver Pig*. New York: Dial Press.

Williams, Barbara. (1974) *Albert's Toothache*. New York: E. P. Dutton.

Wisdom, John. (1955). "Gods." In Antony Flew (Ed.), *Logic and language*, First Series (pp. 187–206). Oxford: Blackwell.

11 ◇ Visual Imagery, Imagination, and Education

DAN NADANER
Palo Alto, California

It would be too simple to declare that visual images and the imagination are equivalent, or that a study of visual imagery is the surest route to an enhanced understanding of the imagination. Within this book, there is ample evidence that the imagination also takes musical and dramatic forms, and Barrow argues that the imagination is a quality of conception, thus encompassing the logical and metaphorical capacities of mind as well.

Yet the visual image is such a strong focus of imaginative activity that it is difficult to ignore. Dreams, daydreams, and creative visualizations begin with visual imagery as their substance. A focus on the image–imagination connection helps to shed the layers of mystification that surround the imagination. In place of supernatural or other mysterious sources of the imagination, the mental image is a plausible basis of imagination, open to the introspection of everyone.

The visual arts offer a vast body of tangible evidence of the role of imagery in human thought. The visual arts have always been central to civilization, and they serve as direct documents of the diverse visual conceptions that humans have applied to their experience. From the intricate cosmological schemas of Mayan painting to the rough sensuality of a Rodin sculpture, the arts represent the use of imagination by all peoples to more fully grasp their worlds.

It is worth exploring, therefore, the nature of the visual image and its role in imagination—not just as it functions for great artists, but as it functions in everyday life.

NATURE OF THE VISUAL IMAGE

The introspective and anecdotal evidence for visual mental images is strong. In the late nineteenth century, Francis Galton developed a questionnaire to investigate the intensity and flexibility of mental images. Asking a wide range of people to imagine their table at breakfast that morning, he discovered rich imagery among the general public. The scientific community remained skeptical of Galton's work, doubting that images existed at all (Sommer, 1978). When Piaget (1971), however, challenged a group of similarly skeptical scientists to represent their concepts of whole numbers, the results were rich in imagery, ranging from vertical batons to escalators to zig-zag lines and curves. Roger Shepard collected autobiographical reports from generative scientists such as Faraday, Maxwell, Einstein, Tesla, Kekulé, and James Watson, all attesting to the central role of imagery in their discoveries (Shepard, 1978).

Simple tests allow anyone to document the existence and variety of mental imagery at first hand. Robert McKim's "apple" exercise, for example, asks a group to imagine an apple and "project" that image onto a blank sheet of paper (1980). The group is then asked whether it was a green or red apple, what shape and texture it had, what background it sat against. A wide variety of apples usually emerges.

Given this wide variety of introspective evidence, the existence of mental images does not seem problematic. But what precisely is a mental image? Certain advocates of imagery and image therapies are not particular on this point. Sommer (1978), for example, equates the mental image to mental "pictures," or "private cinemas." Most psychologists, however, disown the photographic analogy. They prefer to compare the image to perception: Imagery is perception in the absence of an external stimulus that could have caused that perception (Gordon, 1972).

For Rudolf Arnheim (1969), images are like percepts in the sense that both are abstractions of significant visual features in the environment. Arnheim's book *Visual Thinking* remains the seminal contribution to our understanding of the place of imagery in thought. For Arnheim, the image is not a picture in the literal sense, but a record of the mind's activity in structuring significant visual information. The image is never a complete record of perceived reality (except in the special case of eidetic, or "photographic memory," imagery), yet it appears complete to the subject because it contains the features that are relevant to the subject.

Arnheim refutes the philosopher's contention that images interfere in rational thought (Hannay, 1971). The philosopher's argument is that images are too concrete and sensation-bound to permit the abstraction and synthesis of central meanings, causes, and consequences. Arnheim counters that images may exist at several orders of abstraction. At lower orders of abstraction, the image may be as concrete and sensual as a photograph. But at the higher orders of abstraction, images may provide the internal representations of very abstract concepts, such as "freedom," or of casual relations. In this respect they are quite different from photographs or paintings. Images interact with perception by showing the underlying forces that animate what we see, and in this way they contribute to cognition. Through imagery, the mind performs operations such as exploring, selecting, simplifying, completing, and putting in context (Arnheim, 1969).

Cognitive psychologists such as Neisser and Piaget support Arnheim's view of the function of the image in thought. For Neisser (1972), imagery stands between perception and memory. Imagery is a process of actively constructing knowledge about the world. For Piaget (1971), images are symbols, and as such are necessary to thought. Images supplement language by evoking and making possible thought about what has been perceived. It is worth noting the difference between Piaget's view and Paivio's (1971), who hypothesized that visual thinking was an alternative to verbal thinking. Piaget, like Arnheim and Neisser, proposes no such bifurcated system: Imagery is a constituent part and mediator of the larger cognitive system, not a specialized pathway within it.

SKEPTICS: THE PICTORIAL FALLACY

Contemporary North American cognitive psychology is dominated, however, not by the gestalt, environmental, and interactive models of Arnheim, Neisser, and Piaget. It is dominated by the information-processing model, which appeals to computer simulations of intelligence for both hypotheses and replication of findings. The information-processing model seeks to define how "data" is "processed" and "stored" in the "shallow" or "deep" structures of "short-term" and "long-term" processing. The terms in quotation marks here are indicative of the extent to which an analogy with cybernetic systems guides the information-processing model, and resists an image- or vision-centered model.

Predictably, then, the topic of mental imagery is surrounded by controversy in contemporary cognitive psychology. Two issues are most central in the literature. First, regarding the nature of the image: Is it pictorial or descriptional in nature? Second, regarding the cognitive function of the image: Is it a primary constituent of cognitive functioning, or merely an epiphenomenon of other processes?

Dennett (1981) sets forth the polemic against "pictorial" mental images. For Dennett, pictorial accounts of mental imagery are unsatisfactory because they are hedged in so many ways: The image is not like a photograph, not like a painting, not a point-for-point analogue of the object it represents. If the image is unlike pictures in so many ways, Dennett reasons, then it is more like a verbal description than a picture. Descriptions, unlike pictures, highlight key points of information and leave out less significant details. Descriptions can refer to the personality or actions of a man without representing every article of clothing he is wearing. Pictures, on the other hand, must (in Dennett's view) represent the full visual array. Although Dennett does not discuss Arnheim's conception of imagery, we can infer that he would agree with Arnheim's emphasis on abstraction and interpretation, but disagree that this kind of imagery is therefore closely related to visual perception. Dennett would reimpose the separation of verbal/information-processing cognition from visual/sensory perception, the very separation against which Arnheim so adamantly argues.

Against this skeptical attitude toward imagery, there remains the substantial weight of introspective evidence and common sense. What of the dreams, daydreams, mental maps, and other commonly reported pictorial images? To this the information processor would reply that visual images, if they exist, are no more than epiphenomena of more primary cognitive mechanisms (Block, 1981; Pylyshyn, 1981). Block argues that images are often mistaken for sources of thought, when in fact they are only side effects. Kekulé, for example, thought that the image of the snake caused the recognition of the structure of the benzene ring. The epiphenomenalist, however, would argue that an underlying brain state caused both the image and the idea. This theory has best been developed by Pylyshyn in the form of the "tacit knowledge" position. Using the tacit knowledge position, Pylyshyn challenges the view that imagery plays a role in cognition. For Pylyshyn, imagery can always be penetrated to reveal more primary knowledge-representing mechanisms. When people report visual images or spatial rotations or other imagistic processes, what they are really reporting (in this view) are properties of real-world objects, not images, as informed by tacit knowledge of the real world.

For me, Arnheim resolves the pictorial–descriptional polemic masterfully with his idea that visual images give an "incomplete representation but in a complete way." Abstract painting is a good analogue of this kind of imagery. Imagery can represent qualities, values, and selected idiosyncrasies without describing every detail in the visual array. Abstract imagery is less descriptional, in fact, than the conventional picture, not more descriptional, as Pylyshyn would have it.

The information-processing model stretches credulity by assuming that research in human cognition should be guided by the model of artificial intelligence. One simple failing of this radical cyberneticism has been demonstrated here: a failure to draw upon human cultural achievements to form the most robust conception of mental imagery. While the contemporary cognitive literature has demonstrated its power to curtail irresponsible claims about imagery, it has proven less successful in generating its own hypothesis. It is to Arnheim's credit that he has generated an informed response to fill this conceptual void.

LINKING IMAGERY AND IMAGINATION

With some understanding of the nature of the mental image, the relationship between imagery and imagination becomes more tangible. If, as Arnheim argues, imagery is an active process of structuring significant visual features, then the leap from imaging to imagining may require only the "adjective" that Barrow suggests, that is the quality of expanded conception that separates the random image from the special or powerful one. This notion is borne out, I think, by the process of making art. Typically, the artist begins with the raw material of sketches and rough ideas, and works toward something deeper, more essential, and clearer. Any painting by Van Gogh or Cézanne is a good example of a work that has been shaped to the point that it represents a very specific aspect of the artist's experience: in *Starry Night*, for example, Van Gogh's dynamic but clear elegy to the harmonious action of heaven and earth. The painting is imaginative because it conveys imagery that is strong and essential to the artist. Rosemary Gordon (1972) has defined well the sense in which the artist's most private images are essential to his or her art:

> Finally, imagery is the raw material of man's capacity to imagine and to symbolize. In this last function imagery reveals itself as the basis and the essential origin and reason for man's need to make art. His apparently inexhaustible and, as far as we know, ever-present wish to make art seems to rest on man's need to embody and to bear witness to the existence and to the validity of his inner world. It is, as it were, a defiant assertion that this carapace of images is real and essential, that it is complex and varied and that this is his personal experience of reality. (p. 79)

Art remains the homeground of the visual imagination, providing a concrete form through which to observe the workings of the imagination. But imagination can also be observed introspectively, as Galton did, and through such forms as play, daydream, and structured imagination activities. In his delightful book *Put Your Mother on the Ceiling*, Richard De Mille (1976) has invented imagery exercises that encourage young children to develop more intense and flexible imagery in all sensory modalities. (Now you see the mice on each corner of the ceiling; but what color are their shirts? What songs are they singing?)

IMAGINATION AND EDUCATION

The need for expanded visual conceptions enters into every part of education. In formal schooling, imagery plays a role in many areas, including mathematics, writing, and reading. Words, in Arnheim's view, are labels placed on meanings that we know through experiences more direct than words, of which visual experience is the prime example. In order to read well we need to form images that we can hold in memory; in order to write well we need to have a rich imagination and be able to control it at will.

As Shepard's reports of Faraday, Tesla, and others illustrate, imagery is essential to the sciences. It is essential both to grasping the raw evidence in detail (as a biologist draws a cell through a microscope) and to seeing the forces that underlie the subject. In order to know a glacial valley, we need images of the contours and textures of rocks, earth, and flora that have been moved and shaped by the glacier. Those are the details, the nuances of observation, with which we can say we know a glacial landscape in comparison to, say, a volcanic mountain range or a windswept desert. But the details by themselves may still be quite incoherent; so we want an integrating, organizing image that puts the big picture together and shows us the glacial movement that no longer exists; or, if it does exist, that shows us in a fleeting moment of thought the movement and changes that would take millions of years to occur in chronological time. We could almost say that science is nothing but a process of forming more accurate images of forms and forces in the world (which makes science very similar to art).

SOCIAL IMAGERY

Perhaps the most important application of imagery is in the social studies. I focus on the social applications of the visual imagination because they are a good example of how imagery extends throughout everyday life. Social imagery can be likened to a map, with full detail and high relief for some parts of the world and blank spots for others. There may be a large space reserved for professional sports, and small peripheral areas for other kinds of human problems and activities. Or, there may be a neat grid of downtown streets for work routines, chores, and shopping, with a set of distant country roads for the rest of the world. It is only natural to construct a selective, and therefore limited, view of the world. Selectivity can be a positive attribute, when it allows the mind to function in a state of equilibrium. If, however, selectivity leads to rigidity and oversimplification of imagery, then it can be an intellectual liability, producing damaging stereotypes instead of useful images.

Stereotypes—or rigid, oversimplified, overemotional versions of mental images—are most clearly a problem in the area of understanding people and cultures different from one's own. The conflict between Israel and Egypt provided a classic example of stereotyping of others (Eldridge, 1979). During the Seven Days War, the Arab media characterized the Israelis as conducting illegitimate, imperialistic, illegal aggression. Leaders, not the people, were blamed: what some call the "black top" image of national politics. At the same time, the Israeli media saw the Arabs as criminal, inhumane, barbaric against civilians, guilty of genocidal policies. For each, the self was strong and right, the other was weak and wrong. This of course is black-and-white thinking, and has been recognized as a major precondition for war (Eldridge, 1979).

One of the distinctive features of the twentieth century is that we are surrounded by visual images that suggest social constructions of reality, including many stereotypes. In order to sell their products, advertisers use their own brand of visual imagination to define the "look" of the good life. Inevitably, television or magazine images specify the ethnicity, class, clothing, and mannerisms of those to whom the good life belongs. It is not known, by scientific means, exactly to what extent a television viewer's images of society match the television program's images. But surely these omnipresent images are seductive, and they serve to support very specific and limited views of the world.

The counterforce to the prefabricated image is the individual's own habit of actively forming imagery. Through the exercise of the imagination, the view can become more broad, more flexible, and therefore more resistant to demeaning stereotypes and unproductive fixations of attention. In an early study of stereotyping, Rosemary

Gordon hypothesized that students who had poor control over their imagery would tend to rely more readily on ethnic stereotypes, while those with better controlled (that is, more flexible) images would be more open to impressions gathered from direct experience. And this was exactly what she found. In Gordon's study, those who had vague, uncontrollable imagery often relied on stereotypes of Chinese, German, and Jewish people formed at an early age from parents, pictures, and films. Those with vivid and well-controlled imagery formed less stereotyped images from recent personal experience (Gordon, 1949).

Gordon's early experiment has been followed up on by educators who have invented role plays to help students identify with the perspectives of others (Nadaner, 1983). While a description of such curricula is beyond the scope of this chapter, the chapter by Degenhardt and McKay in this volume reports on this kind of activity. Educational activities like these have given encouraging evidence that the conscious elaboration of social imagery can be a counterforce to stereotypes formed unconsciously through exposure to the media.

CONCLUSION

The social use of the visual imagination is but one example of the function of visual imagery beyond the art studio. I have focused on social imagery because it is a good way to see quickly the connection between the three terms under discussion here: imagery, imagination, and education. Imagery is a mental activity that pervades most forms of thought. Imagination is a qualitative condition attached to the functioning of imagery and specifies a breadth of conception.

Education too is a special quality. Education means that learners expand their cognitive horizons and strengthen their capacities for further action. So there is a strong overlap between the concepts of imagination and education, having much to do with broadness of view. In the area of social imagery we can see at a glance the connection between the private image, its imaginative extension so as to reduce stereotyping and include the views of others, and the status of this imaginative act as education, by virtue of its having broadened the individual's world view.

The same close connections between imagery, imagination, and education could be demonstrated in poetry, mythology, and of course the visual arts. Each area requires a strong habit of visual imagining to support its form of understanding.

Because of the dominance of behaviorist conceptions of the mind in educational psychology, there is much catch-up work to be done to restore the function of imagery in education. If visual imagery functions as Arnheim suggests it does, then psychology texts and school curricula need extensive revision. And if, as Arnheim also argues, art is the "homeground of visual thinking," then the role of art in cognitive development and education is far more central than has been supposed.

I have tried to outline the strong affinity between the visual imagination and education; but I do not want to leave the impression that the value of the imagination is found only through its educational benefits. The imagination, like art, has value by virtue of its own unique character and the history of it functioning across human cultures. Education too, as schooling, has its own character (image: a typical classroom), but it is hard to see it functioning very well without the exercise of the imagination. The imagination makes thought more personal and gives the individual a more authentic kind of participation in his or her environment. Personal images of feelings and problems might stand up well to the totality and impenetrability of media images, but they need a chance to be developed first, and to make this chance possible the educational system has much work to do.

REFERENCES

Arnheim, R. (1969). *Visual thinking*. Berkeley: Univ. of California Press.
Block, N. (1981). *Imagery*. Cambridge, MA.: MIT Press.
De Mille, R. (1976). *Put your mother on the ceiling*. New York: Penguin.
Dennett, D. C. (1981). The nature of images and the introspective trap. In Ned Block (Ed.), *Imagery*, pp. 51–61. Cambridge, MA.: MIT Press.
Eldridge, A. (1979). *Images of conflict*. New York: St. Martin's Press.
Gordon, R. (1949). An investigation into some of the factors that favor the formation of stereotyped images. *British Journal of Psychology, 39*(3), 156–87.
Gordon, R. (1972). A very private world. In Peter Sheehan (Ed.), *The function and nature of mental imagery*, pp. 64–80. New York: Academic Press.
Hannay, A. (1971). *Mental images: A defence*. Atlantic Highlands, N.J.: Humanities.
McKim, R. (1980). *Experiences in visual thinking*. Monterey: Brooks-Cole.
Nadaner, D. (1983, November). On art and social understanding: Lessons from Alfred Schutz. *Journal of Multi-Cultural and Cross-Cultural Research in Art Education, 1*(1), 15–22.

Neisser, U. (1972). Changing conceptions of imagery. In Peter Sheehan (Ed.), *The function and nature of imagery*. New York: Academic Press.

Paivio, A. (1971). *Imagery and verbal processes*. New York: Holt, Rinehart & Winston.

Piaget, J. (1971). *Mental imagery in the child*. New York: Basic Books.

Pylyshyn, Z. (1981). The imagery debate: Analog media versus tacit knowledge. In Ned Block (Ed.), *Imagery*. Cambridge, MA.: MIT Press.

Shepard, R. (1978). The mental image. *American Psychologist*, *33*, 125–37.

Sommer, R. (1978). *The mind's eye: Imagery in everyday life*. New York: Dell.

12 ◇ In Search of a Child's Musical Imagination

ROBERT WALKER
Simon Fraser University, Canada

OVERTURE

In searching for a child's musical imagination, some questions spring to mind as being important preliminaries. If we identify musical imagination in adults, can we draw some conclusions that would be applicable to children? Furthermore, can we expect the same type of behavior as manifests musical imagination in adults to occur in children? Do we expect children to do the same things as adults? What kind of behavior contains evidence of musical imagination as far as both children and adults are concerned?

Some would be tempted to agree that a child of preschool age who could play an unaccompanied violin sonata by J. S. Bach displayed more musical imagination than one who could merely bang tin cans and play-bricks together, accompanied by shouts and screams, or even a reasonably well-sung song. Yet if we can recognize children's musical imagination only in behavior we call musical in the adult sense, then there are certain implications. First, and perhaps most important, is the odd position this gives music in a child's range of behaviors. We might accept "childish" drawings on their merit as important sources of information about children's mentality and visual representation in the way Rudolf Arnheim has done, but "childish" musical actions would be rejected as such. And it would mean that as far as musical behavior is concerned, we expect children to be like little adults; that is, we can take them seriously only when they play or compose adult music like a Bach violin sonata. Applied to visual art, it would mean looking for children who could paint a *Blue Boy* or *The Adoration of the Magi*, and so on. Such a view would mean that very few children are capable of either displaying or even possessing musical imagination. One feels intuitively that something must be wrong with this view of music and children.

THEME 1

Gardner (1983) regards what he calls musical intelligence as one of man's finite number of intelligences, along with spatial, logical-mathematical, and others. Interestingly, he explains the term by reference to the behavior of unassailably musical adults. In claiming that no other intelligence "emerges earlier than musical talent" (p. 99), he cites examples of precocious behavior in children as the manifestation of musical intelligence, at least in Western culture or, more precisely, recent Western culture.

But, as if aware of the problem inherent in the precocity argument, he goes on to explain that the music of other cultures contains different acoustic emphases than that of the Western traditions. This is quite a crucial point, which needs exploring further.

Some African tribal music contains enormously complex or tediously repetitive (to the Western ear) rhythms played on sticks, drums, and voices chanting pitches that Western music does not utilize. Some North American Indian music uses different vocal timbres and minute frequency changes near the threshold of auditory functioning in humans, which have never been employed in recent Western traditions, except in the work of some of today's avant-garde musicians. Many singers in other cultures across the world can produce more than one note simultaneously, a practice never used in the West, and in some South Pacific islands there is a flute that is played with the nose. Some cultures revere the sound of the rattle above all else as possessing special powers, particularly when it is shaken by the most powerful persons in their society. Thus the rattling together of bits of metal, slivers of bone or shell, or dried seeds is thought by many to contain deep spiritual significance. Similarly, in some societies dried skins from the backs of humans, seasoned with the urine of descendents, are thought to make drums of frightening power and the ability to communicate with spirits of the dead (Sachs, 1942).

Considering music in such a world context, it can be argued that for some cultures, at least, a child banging tin cans and play-bricks may well be regarded as displaying musical imagination in a more comprehensible manner than a child playing a violin. But there is another point: The type of technique required to make some of the musical sounds of cultures outside the Western tradition of high art is of a different order than that needed to play a Bach violin sonata. So the role of specialized training and access to it assume some importance. Little technical training appears necessary to make some of the sounds heard in some non-Western cultures, compared with the rigor and scope of that needed to play the violin, and certainly little training appears necessary for success in the pop-rock scene—a form of musical communication that seems to transcend cultural barriers in a way no other musical behavior may be capable of doing. Therefore, apart from any lingering nineteenth-century notions of Western cultural superiority, there seems little to suggest that mere skill acquisition through rigorous training can contribute much to the development of musical imagination. Irrespective of the possibility that preschool children who can play Bach sonatas are "freaks," ipso facto, it must follow that precocity cannot be the only behavioral attribute in which musical imagination is manifest. If that were so, musical imagination would be found only in such freaks. It is, of course, quite conceivable that some freaks, like any other subgrouping, may display musical imagination, but it is surely unaccceptable that only musical freaks can.

In fact, it is possible to illustrate this point through reference to child prodigies and musicians in history. One of the most celebrated of all time was Wolfgang Amadeus Mozart. At least this is how history has brought him down to us. Those in the eighteenth century might have seen things differently! There were literally hundreds of child prodigies at the time, of whom Mozart was but one, even though he was highly regarded. In England, for example, there was William Crotch of Norwich, who in 1778, at the age of three, was giving recitals in London and Cambridge. The 1954 edition of Grove's Dictionary of Music states that "Crotch's precocity is almost unparalleled in music; even Mozart and Mendelssohn hardly equalled him in this respect." He was also precocious in drawing and painting and was the subject of an enquiry by the Royal Society at the age of five.

If anyone can be said to display musical imagination, it must be Mozart, whose compositions and legendary fame at improvising and making fun of others' musical mannerisms earned him, respectively, posthumous and contemporaneous reputations. He even made fun of the young Beethoven, much to the latter's annoyance, imitating his excessively loud playing and furious sounds. The same cannot be said of William Crotch, who has been all but forgotten as a prodigy and is not known at all as a composer, except in the organ lofts of some English cathedrals. If we contrast this with a most unprecocious French composer, Hector Berlioz, whose music is discussed under headings like "Berloiz and the Romantic Imagination," we are surely able to draw some conclusions!

Berlioz could almost be said to have been the antithesis of a precociously talented youngster. He could not play any instrument really well, and he showed a certain lack of aptitude at his musical studies. One of the professors (Cherubini) at the Paris Conservatoire actually had him thrown out. Berloiz attempted to study music somewhat illegally, while a student of medicine, and his angry father cut off his allowance on hearing of his musical activities. Yet few now would disagree that the mature Berlioz displayed outstanding musical imagination in his compositions.

From this we can say with some assurance that precocious behavior in music is by no means a sine qua non for manifestations of musical imagination. We might even say that it should be possible to identify musical imagination in nonprecocious children. Berlioz was certainly not the only imaginative musician to lack a precocious beginning.

THEME 2

It is no easy task to identify musical imagination in adults, even within an artistic tradition like Western high art. For example, would we consider a composer whose music was described by his contemporaries as "obscene" or "obscure, idle balderdash" an imaginative? These were just some of the opinions expressed about Berlioz' symphonies (Strunk, 1950). If we read the terms "madness" and "muscial contortions" about someone's music, would we be likely to say the composer displayed musical imagination? A prominent nineteenth-century German music critic wrote such things about Tchaikowsky's music for orchestra, and Liszt's piano music was described as "the invitation to stamping and hissing" (Sitwell, 1967).

DEVELOPMENT AND VARIATIONS

Today, in contrast, no one would have any compunction at agreeing that all three composers displayed what can be called musical imagination, and not just in comparison with any mediocrity that surrounded them. We say things like Berlioz' music plumbs the depths of individual sensibility pitting itself against the collective insensitivity in unique ways, and that Liszt and Tchaikowsky provide musical transportations into realms of consciousness not achieved or even attempted previously. We might also add that their imitators in this century have earned millions by providing diluted resemblances of such musical imagination for the movies and television.

Judging by these contemporary opinions of the three composers, we can say that they represented disturbing departures from acceptable norms of musical expectation to some people in the nineteenth century, even though to their supporters they exemplified the epitome of musical and romantic imagination. It is significant that the names of those many musicians who tended to conform to societal expectations do not appear in retrospect as exemplars of musical imagination in the commentaries of those who write about such things. We do not see chapter headings such as "Cherubini and the Romantic Imagination." One supposes this has nothing to do with the fact that it was this gentleman who was responsible for getting Berlioz thrown out of the Paris Conservatoire library, not only as a nuisance but as an "untalented wastrel."

There certainly seems something worth following up in the observation that those who conform to expected norms in music do not earn reputations for being imaginative in the way that those who create their own independent expressions do. Many could learn to write music like Cherubini, and still do in some music academies, but few, if any, could learn to write like Berlioz, Tchaikowsky, or Liszt. It is this presence in music of a disparity between the mediocre and the unique and brilliant that has fired people's imaginations for two or three centuries in Western European musical culture. Mozart delighted or infuriated his contemporaries with his brilliant powers of mimicry as he exposed unimaginativeness, mannerism, and transparency in others, while producing music incapable of such imitation himself. The very fact that his music was so unassailable in this way is testimony to its perfect synthesis with his entire being, his whole consciousness, and single-mindedness. He could not have written music for someone else's tastes if he tried. In fact, he did try without success.

At the age of 14, he visited Bologna and met the eminent teacher Padre Martini. It was suggested that he sit the examination for the Diploma in Music, Bologna's highest academic honor. The task involved writing three parts above a given antiphon melody "in istile osservats"—strict counterpoint. Mozart failed miserably (Einstein, 1945). He was unable to write in any style save his own, and Martini had to show him the correct answers. The archives of the Accademia Filarmonica and Liceo Musicale at Bologna retain the manuscripts of this event (Einstein, 1945, p. 147).

These examples do not mean that anarchy and a total lack of any continuity and uniformity characterize musical imagination, but they do suggest that we are not able to draw any conclusions about identifying musical imagination simply by looking for norms. We could almost make a case for looking for deviations from norms as a first prerequisite to discovering musical imagination. We certainly cannot derive any clear relationship between actions that may contain evidence of musical imagination and laws of musical art distilled from musical practices at a given time or place. We can no more recognize a Mozart until he is dead than we can an Elvis Presley or a John Lennon until the sales figures tell us. It is against this background of an apparent uniqueness and a nonconformity with established norms that I want to suggest alternative ways of viewing musical imagination as it might appear in children.

EPISODE AND FUGUE

Generally speaking, not many people associate music with children making their own compositions, in the way they associate visual art with children drawing and painting, or myth and literature with children telling their own stories. To claim that music is different, or is regarded differently, may seem like a lame excuse for being unable to explain why all children are not regarded as capable of composing a piece of music in the way they are of drawing a picture. Nevertheless, it is a fact that adults in Western culture generally either regard musical activity as something that has to be taught or consider that to make up his or her own music, a child would have to be a genius.

Look around any school and there will be evidence of children's activities in drawing, painting, and writing stories, but virtually none of their musical inventions. So the first thing to establish is that, apart from trying to identify how imagination manifests itself in children's music making, there is the problem of actually finding and observing the musical equivalent to children drawing and telling their own stories. Children are not encouraged to make up their own music; instead, they are made to play someone else's, who always happens to be an adult.

This is not to suggest that there is universal regard for children's inventions in visual art and storytelling, but none for music. To many, all such activities appear to be a category of "things children do" until they grow up, rather like listening to pop-rock, wearing jeans, getting dirty frequently, or throwing stones at birds or into ponds. Despite the work of many researchers into children's behavior, there is still a lack of general understanding of what is seen by some people as disorganized, un-adult creative play that should perhaps be tolerated, at least until children learn something of greater value. This is a far cry from regarding children's behavior in producing "scribbly" drawings or cacophonous sounds as a category that might be different from mere worthless children's play. Yet it is probably not an exaggeration to claim that far more attention has been paid by researchers to children's drawings and storytelling than to their exploration and expression using sound, despite the work of Harvard's Project Zero team between 1977 and 1987. There is no large corpus of research into children's musical behavior among psychologists, in spite of the growing numbers who are now entering the field of music psychology. Those who do attempt to fill this gap have the difficulty of dealing with an historically biased population among both musical practitioners and observers. This bias is largely because of the nature of musical art: It is a performance activity in which a composer cannot be heard without performers, many of whom have spent years perfecting historical techniques. Musical taste and preference consequently tend to oscillate between classical rigidities founded upon notions of quality derived from Plato and Aristotle, and a bewildered acceptance of anything, in the face of the overwhelming influence of pop-rock music. The feeling of safety in attributing musical imagination to the precocious four-year-old who can play Bach is a product of ancient Greek views of music buried deep in Western belief systems.

In the *Republic*, Plato warns that we must

> identify those rhythms appropriate to illiberality and insolence or madness or other evils so that we can use the opposite . . . good speech, then good accord and good grace and good rhythm wait upon a good disposition . . . music has power to affect his spirit, his soul, disposition, and abilities in all things. (Strunk, 1950, pp. 7–11)

And Aristotle, in *The Politics*, explains that "rhythms and melodies contain representations of anger, mildness, courage, temperance and all their opposites and other moral qualities" (Strunk, 1950, p. 18).

Upon such foundations there developed a belief in a relationship between character, personality, or moral worth and types of musical sound. In such a belief system, music actually represented these various qualities. Thus it was possible for American jazz to be outlawed in the 1920s and 1930s. Similarly, there was the outrage that greeted the rise of rock and roll in the 1950s, when one governor in the United States issued a warrant for the arrest of Elvis Presley on the grounds of corrupting the morals of minors. The eminent cellist Pablo Casals summed up the feeling of many when he described rock and roll as "poison put to sound."

The obverse of such attitudes is exemplified in the sanctification of "great" composers, such as Beethoven, who was almost deified by some because of his noble music and a belief in an inextricable link between his personal behavior and his music. We still do not like our musicians to be as revolutionary or antisocial as our visual artists, in whom we tolerate such behavior. The musician is expected to be dressed in a dinner suit; the visual artist can wear jeans and sloppy sweaters.

This has remained in our education systems as a legacy from history. And so it is perhaps not so much a desire to see every child play a violin sonata by Bach that motivates such views, as a lingering belief in the connection between the music one plays and type of person he or she is. We still tend to believe in a relationship between a noble or saintly exterior, as someone plays a "great" piece of music, and his or her inner being. It is the same legacy that makes us prize logical thought, in the fashion of the ancient Greeks, above all other types of mental activity. This in turn causes us to pay more attention to a child's music making that most nearly resembles an adult's rationalizations about music than to his or her expressive use of sound not conforming to such notions.

Many obviously unique talents have suffered throughout recent history from such attitudes. They prompted some of William Blake's contemporaries to regard his paintings and poetry as the daubings and rantings of a madman; similarly, some people were convinced Beethoven had lost his wits, when they heard his later quartets and piano sonatas. It is not just the battle between the rational and intuitive that is referred to here, but rather a modern legacy of this ancient debate. Children's activities in music today are regarded by some people in much the same way that music of the Romanticists was regarded by the empiricists and rationalists of the nineteenth century. In fact, many attempts at explaining artistic activity of any kind in a logical framework have produced a number of theories and formulae.

Joshua Reynolds, for example, was convinced that blue was a cold color and could never be used as the center of a successful painting. Thomas Gainsborough's response was to paint the now celebrated *Blue Boy* (Saw, 1972). Birkhoff (1933), inspired by ancient Greek notions of balance, proportion, and harmony, produced the formula $M = 0/C$, where M is the aesthetic measure, 0 the degree of order, and C the degree of complexity. There are obvious difficulties is assigning a number to concepts like order or complexity in a painting or piece of music, yet later researchers have modified the equation to $M = O \times C$ (Eysenck, 1968; Smets, 1973). Such ideas can be traced back to Euclid, from whom the notion of the "Golden Section" was developed. This is expressed as a ratio of approximately 62:38 between opposing elements.

It is difficult to see how such applications of mathematical methodology can yield anything of significance as far as artists are concerned. Certainly, there has been no such measure applied to real art, and it is doubtful that any will be attempted. Art cannot be measured in such a way, and such methods seem of little value in identifying imagination at work.

Of more use, it is suggested, are questions about the content of actual art works. For example, does musical imagination lie in the fury of a last movement of a Beethoven piano sonata, or the almost static harmonies and rhythmic motionlessness of Erik Satie's "Gymnopedies" or "Sarabandes," or the elegant sonata structures of Mendelssohn, or the wit and clarity of Mozart, or the musical happenings of John Cage? Can it lie in the mixture of blues, country, and hillbilly that is Elvis Presley's style or the throaty patriotic sounds of Bruce Springsteen? Or does it in fact lie in the very diversity of musical practices all these represent? Illogicality, arbitrariness, contradiction, and the unexpected seem far more helpful clues to seeking out imagination in the music of Western culture than logical explanations or mathematical formulae. But this is the problem of aesthetics: It is more a matter of looking at what artists do than of applying some external measure.

SONATA

In describing music from a more multi-cultural standpoint, Wachsmann (1971) explains it as a "special kind of time, and the creation of musical time is a universal pre-occupation of man." The notion of the creation of musical time, one's own personal musical time, seems far more applicable to what actually happens in music than does anything mathematical. It also seems far more appropriate in trying to understand what children may do with sound when they create their own "musical time" than does looking for evidence of incipient greatness or adult behavior.

Children can do with sound what they do with two-dimensional space in drawing and painting or with words in creating their stories. But to a child, the texture of a sound is more important than an adult concept like pitch or melody, and the duration of a sound is more significant than the concept of rhythm. Sergeant (1983) demonstrates that the basic unit of pitch in Western music, the octave (a frequency ration of 2:1), is a concept, not a percept. He explains that young children tend to identify similarities between tones by listening for similarities of sound rather than for a more logical octave generalization. In other research (Walker, 1978, 1981, 1985) there is evidence that visual matchings for sound textures, durations, and loudness yield more consistency in young children than do those of pitch differentiation.

This would seem to point in the direction of children having greater involvement with elements of musical textures, durations, and loudness than with concepts like pitch, derived from high art, in the early stages of their activities in music. It also suggests that musical imagination in children should be sought in observing their use of the basic parameters of musical sound (loudness, timbre, duration, and pitch) in creating their own "musical time." In such observations, one should bear in mind the relationships between the great artists of the past and the norms of expectancy from which they diverged, each in their own unique manner as they created their own musical time.

Looked at in this way, some of the extant studies of children's musical explorations provide some relevant insights. John Paynter (1971) describes an experiment in which he observed a number of five- and six-year-olds in an open-ended task. The children were given freedom to explore a variety of tuned and untuned percussion instruments over a period of several weeks. Paynter reports that after an initial exploration in apparently random and somewhat chaotic manner, the children began to settle down to purposeful activities. These are described in the children's own words. A little girl explained that she was looking out of the window and watching the rain falling off the roof of the bicycle sheds into a puddle, so that she could play the rain on her chime bar. A pair of children described how they were "playing" a conversation between themselves on their instruments. Other children were composing stories or describing events in music.

In another set of observations, Bamberger (1982) describes how a fourth-grade class invented their own drawings for the rhythm of a class composition. The class took about ten minutes to produce the drawings, which were categorized into two types by Bamberger: figural and metric. A second experiment included more children and a greater age range. Although the two types of drawing were to some degree confirmed, there were some interesting deviations, particularly among younger children aged around four years. Bamberger describes them as "the children's invention for externalizing their 'knowledge in action'—that is what they know how to do but had not before tried to put down in some external, static way" (1982, pp. 193–194).

Bamberger hypothesizes in some detail about the motivations for the various drawings, using Piaget's models of children's behavior. These include imitation of the movements needed to produce the rhythm acoustically. The interest for this writer lies in the clear indication that the children could perceive movements in musical time that contained varied loudness due to rhythmic accents, as well as repetition, and could externalize the mental images that resulted. The rhythm used was a simple four-beat pattern with an accent on the first beat. Many children tended to write a larger shape for each first beat, with correspondingly smaller ones for the remaining three. Thus there was evidence of a proclivity to use figural representations of loudness rather than metric representations of rhythm. Bamberger comments that musicians will tend to see rhythms in purely metric terms, having forgotten their own earlier figural interpretations because of their musical training. In Bamberger's view, these conflicts between figural and metric domains "remain tacit barriers, especially to effective teaching" (1982, p. 225).

Other studies (Walker, 1978, 1981) indicate that children will readily provide drawings that faithfully represent, in visual metaphors, auditory movement in the basic parameters of sound: frequency, wave shape, amplitude, and duration. A consistency of visual representation was reported in all age groups from five-year-olds to adult, though age was clearly a factor in maintaining the consistency of representation of frequency by vertical placement, wave-shape by visual pattern or texture, amplitude by size, and duration by horizontal length. The same consistency was observed in congenitally blind subjects (Walker, 1985) and across different cultures (Walker, 1986).

This seems to imply that children respond to the sensuous parameters of sound rather than to adult musical concepts, and that musical sounds are perceived by children as auditory expressions. In fact, there is some indication in these studies that children are attracted to the sensuous properties of sound and by their potential for personal expressive use. It is to this latter aspect that I finally want to turn, for this, it is maintained, constitutes a basic ingredient of musicality.

It is a fairly reliable assertion that if children are asked to invent some music—may be just "a piece" or might describe their friends or their parents—they will use the sounds available rather than search for some Mozartian melody or Bach-like counterpoint. In one such session observed by the writer, a six-year-old described her friend by a loud, long continuous tapping on a variety of instruments. When asked why, she replied that her friend was always talking, and never stopped even in her sleep. Another girl described her mother as alternately like a glockenspiel played softly on a variety of notes and a loud banging on a drum. This related to her perception of her mother as often calm and loving, but sometimes angry.

In using stories as a basis for making music with children, the same proclivity to use what was available, but with as much variety in sound as possible, was noticed. For example, the story of Beowulf fighting the monster Grendel elicited an interesting range of sounds. Young children depicted the walk of the monster Grendel by a combination of cymbal, drum, and woodblocks to indicate its weirdness, unnaturalness, and terror. An older group, including some well-educated and accomplished musicians, produced a five-beat ostinato pattern with accents shifting at random to any of the five beats in a measure, and a combination of cello, double bass, piano, drum, trumpet, and clarinet playing a fugue-like structure above this.

These and many other examples serve to illustrate a dichotomy in musical education. It lies between what Bamberger calls the figural and the metric in rhythm—what is referred to earlier in this chapter as the adult conception of music based upon Greek notions of refinement and the perception of the auditory parameters of sound that comprises musical expression—and what Langer (1969) calls expressive form as opposed to the abstraction of a concept for discursive thought (p. 139).

CODA

In case this might seem like an argument in favor of educational strategies in music that are based on progressions from concrete to abstract experiences, it is important to emphasize the nature of musical communication. It is not like verbal language. The letters *c-a-t* have a specific symbolic and syntactic function of communication in language. In contrast, a musical element such as the chord of C major has no symbolic function and no syntactic constraints of the kind the noun *cat* has. Moreover, the word *cat* can be translated exactly into other languages whose speakers will instantly recognize the small, four-legged domestic pet it symbolizes. There is no equivalent to a C major chord in any other music save the tradition of the West. Moreover, it just isn't possible to translate musical elements from one culture to another by means of identifying their symbolic function and meaning. In Western music, slow, sad music is played at funerals, and gay, happy music at weddings. In Dervish music, fast, happy-sounding music is played at funerals as well as at weddings. There is no matching of musical variety with occasion. They never had a Plato to categorize musical sounds and attribute specific representational qualities to them.

The point is that the kind of abstract and concrete experiences referred to by writers on educational development, while clearly relating to language or mathematical activity, have no relevance to music. When a child hears a tune in C major that modulates to the dominant and back, the meaning he or she derives has nothing to do with C major or the dominant. It has to do with the sound being what Langer calls "expressive form." How different it is with language or mathematics! The child does not abstract meaning from the expressive form of the sound of words in a story, for example, but from the fixed meaning of words. He or she may note the tone of voice and manner of delivery, but it is the ideas symbolized in the words that contain the meaning. Entirely the opposite is true of music. There are no ideas as such expressed in the symbolism of tones, chords, or rhythms. They express only themselves, in the opinion of many musicians and writers about music. But it must be added that there was, historically, some support for a capacity of music to express a certain level of generality of meaning. This was found particularly in the nineteenth-century tradition of Romantic music following the writings of Schopenhauer. The arguments are long and tedious on both sides. Suffice it to say that few composers actually believe that what they write in music has any significance outside of the sounds and structures of music (see Langer, 1969; Strunk, 1950), in the way that words do.

So for this reason, despite the nineteenth-century belief in music having some representational powers, it seems reasonable to say that current educational practices, based as they seem to be on notions of language acquisition, not only are inappropriate to an activity like music, but are possibly inimical to the true nature of musical expression and perception as it occurs in cultural tradition. The very lack of children's musical compositions in schools is testimony to the misconceptions about music referred to here, and to the timorous attitudes toward children's activities with sound, particularly those that do not result in recognizable rhythms or melodies.

REFERENCES

Bamberger, J. (1982). Revisiting children's drawings of simple rhythms: A function for reflection-in-action. In Sidney Strauss, *U-shaped behavioural growth*. New York: Academic Press.

Birkhoff, G. (1933). Cited in D. E. Berlyne, *Studies in the new experimental aesthetics*. (1974). New York: Wiley.

Einstein, A. (1945). *Mozart*. London: Oxford University Press.

Eysenck, H. J. (1968). Cited in D. E. Berlyne, *Studies in the new experimental aesthetics*. (1974). New York: Wiley.

Gardner, H. (1983). *Frames of mind*. New York: Basic Books.

Langer, S. K. (1957). *Problems of arts*. New York: Charles Scribner's Sons.

Langer, S. K. (1969). *Philosophy in a new key*. Cambridge, MA.: Harvard University Press.

Paynter, J. (1971). *Creative music in the classroom*. Unpublished Ph.D. thesis, University of York, England.

Sachs, Curt. (1942). *The history of musical instruments*. London: Dent.

Saw, R. L. (1972). *Aesthetics: An introduction*. London: Macmillan.

Sergeant, D. (1983). "The octave—percept or concept?" "Psychology of Music, *2*, (1), pp. 3–18.

Sitwell, S. (1967). *Liszt*. New York: Dover.

Smets, D. (1973). Cited in D. E. Berlyne, *Studies in the new experimental aesthetics*. (1974). New York, Wiley.

Strunk, O. (1950). *Source readings in music history*. New York: W. W. Norton.

Wachsmann, K. P. (1971, September). "Universal perspectives in music." *Ethnomusicology*, *15*(3). Middletown, CT: Wesleyan Univ. Press.

Walker, R. (1978). "Perception and music notation." *Psychology of Music*, *6*.

Walker, R. (1981). *The presence of internalized images for musical sounds and their relevance to music education*. Council for Research in Music Education U.S.A. Bulletin 66/67.

Walker, R. (1985). *Mental imagery and musical concept formation*. Council for Research in Music Education. Special issue of papers read to the tenth International Research Seminar on Music Education.

Walker, R. (1986). *Some differences between pitch perception and basic auditory functioning in children of different cultural and musical backgrounds*. Paper invited to the eleventh International Research Seminar on Music Education, Frankfurt, West Germany, July 1986. Council for Research in Music Education.

13 ◇ Symbolic Inventions and Transformations in Child Art

CLAIRE GOLOMB
University of Massachusetts

Child art refers to a pictorial reality invented by the child and for the child, a reality that exists only in a special frame of mind. Drawing with crayons, magic markers, or pencils is a solitary activity that creates an imaginative representation of an aspect of the child's world. The child who discovers the magic power he or she can wield over the blank page engages in a uniquely human activity that transforms our ordinary experience of the world and represents it on a new and perhaps mythical plane of action and thought. Unlike the temporal world of children's stories, drawing leaves a visible record, a tangible trace that can be examined, talked to, and understood quite independently of the temporal and spatial sequence of actions that gave rise to it. For young children, drawing can be an absorbing and gratifying activity, which adults watch with bemusement and a touch of awe.

Child art has held our interest for approximately the last 100 years, with spurts of intensive activity in several of its decades. Most of the interest in child art has been limited to young children's drawings. This is not surprising, since the drawing activity of a child can easily be followed and documented, and its product, the drawings, can be collected, catalogued, and stored. This may account for some of the interest in child art, and it certainly has facilitated the establishment of large collections of drawings (Kellogg, 1968); (Kerschensteiner, 1905; Levinstein, 1905).

The first drawing efforts usually begin with a variety of scribbles, created quite effortlessly, which consist of whirls, zigzags, and overlapping diagonals. They are the result of motor actions performed with very little guidance. The scribble-patterns tend to be dispersed across the page, and their placement is largely determined by the orientation of the paper, the marker, and the mechanical construction of

222

arm, hand, and wrist. Whether the child pays attention to what his or her hand is doing with crayon and paper, or looks elsewhere during the production process, the child seems pleased that his or her actions have had an effect, that a mark has been left where none was before. The next distinctive phase in the evolution of drawing skills emerges with the appearance of relatively clear *contours*. To create such an outline figure, the unruly swirls of the continuous scribble motion must be controlled. Drawing a single line that encloses an area and arrives back at its starting point demonstrates a remarkable visual-motor control. It speaks of an effort to subdue the impulse to make rotational swirls, and thus to subordinate a preferred motor gesture to visual dictates. It is an *intentional* action, and it creates the first stable and meaningful shape. The successful drawing of a contour illustrates a new degree of mastery and the deliberate use of lines to create a stable and meaningful shape. It is interesting to note that two- and young three-year-old children who only scribble in their free drawings, create circular and ovalish figures when they are asked to draw ''specific'' objects, for example, a mommy, a kitten, or a giraffe.

Many authors have commented on the significance of clear outlines for graphic development, and Rudolf Arnheim (1974) and Schaefer-Simmern (1948) have pointed to the figure-ground characteristics that the circle on its paper background represents. According to Arnheim, the contour is not impartial; the circle bounds the *inside* area, which attains a solid-looking and figural quality that makes it useful for representational purposes. Once the clear outline figure has emerged, it draws attention to itself in a number of ways and elicits interpretation of its meaning. The child tends to label the form according to a perceived likeness to a known object, a mental activity of ''reading off'' the figure what it might refer to (Golomb, 1974). The child infers the meaning of the drawn shape by searching for a resemblance between it and an object in the real world. Once the circular shapes have been drawn, the figural quality of the shape seems to invite further action on the part of the child, who now endows the inside area with a few simple markings. These figures begin to look like huge heads, and we might best define them as ''Global Humans'' (see Figure 1).

It makes good sense to begin the story of child art with the invention of the circle, since it represents the first shape that is both visually expressive and representationally useful. It is a form that can carry symbolic meaning and thus lends itself to representational purposes. Almost from the moment the clear circular form emerges, it becomes endowed with internal markings that usually represent a human. Indeed, in the spontaneous productions of young children, the

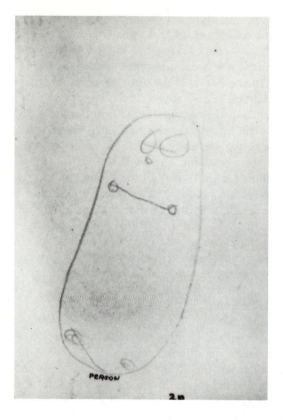

FIGURE 1. The
Global Human
is the earliest
representation of a
person. It consists of
a global unit, usually
a large oval, with
some differentiation
of facial features
inside its contour.

human tends to be one of the first figures to be drawn, either inten-
tionally or labeled after inspection of the drawn circle.

In quick succession, see the appearance of the ''Tadpole Man,''
and a variety of trunkless creatures that puzzle and provoke us since
they so clearly deviate from our usual conception of what a human
figure should look like. These peculiar figures are characterized by sins
of omission as well as commission: The body seems forgotten, the arms
misplaced, the head too large—and we could catalogue a long list of
what seems wrong with these drawings (see Figure 2).

Most adults tend to greet this tadpole creature with a mixture of
wonder, amusement, and uneasiness. There is first the moment of
surprise when we discover and recognize this figure that bears so little
resemblance to the picture-book humans and animals or the photographs that the child is likely to have seen. We marvel at the child's
inventive mind that has produced this simple, visually meaningful figure. But beyond the initial surprise and appreciation, we feel uncer-

FIGURE 2.   The Tadpole Man represents an early step toward figural differentiation, with arms and legs extending from the primary global unit.

tain about the representational meaning of the drawing. Our wariness concerns the originality of the figure, its deviation from widely accepted norms of what a figure ought to comprise. Most adults seem to rely on a standard list of items they deem essential for the portrayal of a human. This list usually includes a head with facial features, torso, arms, and legs. On first inspection, the tadpole figure is quite deficient in the number of its drawn parts. Most striking is the absence of a trunk, while fingers tend to vary from a few to a superabundance. Additional faults concern the misplacement of arms and legs, and a disregard for body proportions. One could easily extend this list of peculiarities and errors.

When the figure is judged in terms of numbers, proportions, and the depiction of essential body parts, the tadpole drawing presents a somewhat disturbing deviation from an hypothesized norm or standard. Indeed, the puzzle of the tadpole figure has provoked a great deal of theorizing. Most students of children's drawings have seen in this simple figure the workings of an immature mind. According to this view, the tadpole drawing reflects the primitive, prelogical mentality of the young child. Various processes have been considered that may predispose the child to drawing mistakes. At times, blurred mental or memory images have been implicated (Eng, 1931), and the inadequacy of the perceptual analysis of the object has also been considered (Piaget, 1951; Piaget & Inhelder, 1956, 1971). With a few notable exceptions, most writers have argued that the child's immature reasoning processes lead to the defective drawings (Goodenough, 1926;

Harris, 1963; Kerschensteiner, 1905; Luquet, 1913, 1927; Piaget & Inhelder, 1956). This emphasis on faulty knowledge was captured in the popular phrase that "the child draws what he knows, not what he sees." Thus, despite the widely held view that young children are perception-oriented, that their attention is turned toward the outside world and captivated by the immediate appearance of objects and people, their knowledge was deemed inadequate, the product of pre-logical reasoning that distorts the perceptual information. It is this emphasis on distortion, and Piaget has contributed the concept of "distorting assimilation," that leads to the paradoxical view that the perception-bound child does not draw what he or she sees but what he or she knows, and that the child's conceptions are incompatible with the world as adults know it.

With the passage of time, we observe gradual changes in the child's drawings, which can be interpreted as steady improvements in the ability to depict objects. Such findings seem to provide support for the notion that progress in drawing goes hand in hand with the growth of conceptual skills. As the drawn figure gains in detail and its proportions appear less idiosyncratic, we assume that this graphic achievement reflects the child's increased conceptual competence. This position has been taken by Goodenough (1926) and Harris (1963), and is embodied in their Draw-a-Man test, which credits each drawn part and the manner in which it is depicted with a score that can be summed to yield an index of the child's conceptual maturity. It is a position that comes close to considering the drawing as a print-out of the child's cognitive status. To use a contemporary figure of speech, the drawing provides a kind of X-ray or CAT scan picture of the child's mental activity.

The simplicity of this assumption has for many decades made it an attractive, albeit somewhat circular, proposition: We know that young children are conceptually immature, and their drawings confirm this inferior cognitive status. However appealing this simple account of the relationship between drawing and concept formation might be, its adequacy has been seriously challenged by Rudolf Arnheim in his book *Art and Visual Perception*, first published in 1954 (second edition, 1974). Arnheim has exposed the fallacy of adopting a stylistic, culture-bound convention, for example, realism, and the tendency to measure the child's graphic achievements by this standard. Psychologists, somewhat unwittingly, have elevated an era-specific accomplishment to a near-universal principle and applied it to child art. If we follow this line of reasoning, we misconstrue art making as a process of replication, and judge early art by its failure to establish a one-to-one correspondence between the object's realistic properties and its graphic representation. Arnheim's analysis of the nature of the two-dimensional medium, and of representation as a search for equivalences, has focused our attention on the *graphic logic* that determines the evolution of early forms and their gradual differentiation. As an example of graphic logic, we might consider the huge circle of the tadpole figure to represent the head as well as the body, to encompass both in its boundary.

From Arnheim's perspective, then, the tadpole figure is not incomplete or defective; it is a simple rendition of a human. Art is not concerned with a replication of all the artist knows about the object; it is concerned with equivalences of a structural and dynamic kind, and it obeys rules of a visual logic that has little in common with an enumeration of parts. In this conception of adult as well as child art, nothing is, strictly speaking, "missing" from the tadpole figure. The simple, relatively undifferentiated structure of the tadpole figure is typical of an early stage in representational development.

This analysis, which stresses the meaningfulness of the tadpole figure and insists on its representational intactness and logic, rests on a sophisticated analysis of the psychology and history of art. Its position is in stark contrast to the conception of child art as an imitative activity in which progress is measured in terms of approximations to "realism" in art. We are faced with two opposing conceptions of art and its relationship to cognitive processes. How do we choose between them? In an age that values empirical evidence, we tend to design experiments.

It is fortunate that the positions, briefly sketched above, lead to different predictions about the effects of media, task demands, and instructions. In the case of the defect hypothesis of art, we ought to predict that the child's representation of the human figure is determined as well as constrained by *what* he or she knows and *how* he or she knows, that is, by the child's concept of the object. It follows that the child's representation of the object as a kind of print-out of his or her conceptual status should be fairly uniform across a wide range of tasks. The same number of parts should be represented in two- and three-dimensional media, in tasks that demand completion or copying of figures, in drawings on dictation, and on form-puzzles that require the construction of a figure. In the case of Arnheim's representational theory, we would predict that the properties of the specific medium and the demands of the task would lead to a considerable degree of variation in the representation of the human figure.

Such a reformulation of the theoretical issues enables us to marshall empirical evidence to support one of the two competing hypotheses and to reject the other. Accordingly, I set out to clarify the relationship between the child's drawing and his or her underlying conception of the object (Golomb, 1969, 1973).

To adequately address the controversial issue of the status of the tadpole drawing, it seemed essential to select young children who are at the beginning phase of their representational explorations. To assess developmental change, it was also important to include older children. With this goal in mind, children ranging in age from three to seven years were presented, on an individual basis, with sets of tasks that differed in the choice of media and task properties, while holding the theme of the human figure constant. I was interested in children's performance when asked to draw a person, to model a person and a snowman out of playdough, to complete a series of incomplete drawings of a human, to dictate to me all the parts I would need if I were to draw a person, to identify a series of incomplete drawings and to select the "best" among them, to construct a puzzle-figure out of a collection of flat wooden forms, and, finally, to draw a human figure as I verbally dictated the various parts.

The results were straightforward: The human figure varied as a function of the task, the medium, the instructions, and the provision of parts. For example, on the task that presented the child with an array of wooden pieces, of which some were familiar-looking and could be identified as head or coat, not a single child constructed a tadpole figure. When the array consisted of relatively unfamiliar flat wooden geometric shapes, only 2 out of the 27 three-to-four-year-old preschoolers constructed a tadpole figure. This finding is quite remarkable, since the majority of these youngsters drew scribbles, global humans, or tadpole figures when asked to draw a person. On the completion task, the child was presented with a figure that consisted of a head with facial features. Almost all the children completed this incomplete figure in greater detail than the figure they produced on the draw-a-person task, and 69 percent of the three-to-four-year-olds now included the trunk section. On the playdough modeling task, children who included the trunk in only 33 percent of their drawings, modeled the trunk in 52 percent of their sculptures of a person and in 70 percent of their snowmen. Similar differences emerged when the results of the free-drawing task were compared with drawings made on dictation and with the children's selections from a series of incomplete figures. Some children progressed on the dictation task from random scribbles to drawing a full-fledged figure, while others made remarkable progress on the free-drawing task. Without receiving any instructions, they responded to the repeated request "to try again" and moved in quick succession from scribbles to differentiated and expressive forms (see Figure 3).

Clearly, the results of this study indicate that the hypothesis of the print-out process and of the simple correspondence between an immature concept and a graphically simple drawing is no longer tenable. The old dictum that "the child draws what he knows" has not been supported, and thus we reject the notion that the tadpole drawing is a case of faulty imitation due to conceptual immaturity. We may now be ready to abandon simpleminded standards of realism and to reaffirm Arnheim's position that the tadpole figure is relatively undifferentiated and represents its object at a very basic level. From this perspective, the concept of "completion" is not very meaningful, since various graphic models can adequately represent their object. Arnheim substitutes the concept of "differentiation of form within its medium" for notions of incompletion or errors of representation. This approach to early child art endows the young child with an intuitive problem-solving intelligence.

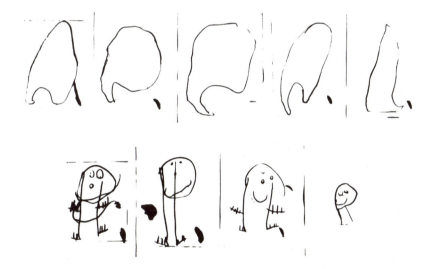

FIGURE 3. First representational efforts of a three-year-old girl. These drawings, in response to a request to draw a person, were made in quick succession, beginning with the upper left figure, and culminating in the successful invention of forms that clearly represent a human (Golomb, 1974).

Our analysis of children's drawings points to an important principle of early representation, namely, *simplicity* or economy. Children attempt to use as little as will do and to adopt a *minimalistic* approach to representation. In drawing a human, the head and the vertical length dimension suffice to create a basic structural likeness to the intended object. Playdough is a less expressive medium than paper and pencil; hence a separate trunk is more likely to be modeled, or an elongated mass shaped to represent the "body."

Another application of the principle of economy of forms can be seen in figures that either include the arms or omit them. At an early stage of representation, when overall forms are deemed to be sufficient, the arms add little to the general definition of the human figure and hence are frequently omitted. In situations, however, where arms are essential to an *activity* or are otherwise necessary to convey the meaning of the drawing, they are included. And so we find drawings in which some figures are equipped with arms, while others lack them; where one arm is sufficient, often a single arm in the desired orientation or direction is drawn (see Figures 4 and 5).

So far we have spoken about the principle of *simplicity*, which states that simple, global forms suffice. Next we must mention the rule that seems to guide developmental change, namely, the law of *differentiation*. The early figures, the tadpole humans that were described as conveying their subject matter with simplicity and clarity, appear on reflection to represent merely an "animate" figure. The early humans and animal drawings are much alike, and it is this *lack* of differentiation that prompts the child to alter the figure, to add defining marks that distinguish between humans and animals. In the case of humans, the differentiation occurs along a vertical axis; in the case of animals, it is mostly along a horizontal axis (see Figure 6).

As our figures demonstrate, there is a tension between the utilization of simple and preferred forms, such as the circle and straight line, and the need to do justice to the looks of the object. The forms that the child uses to represent objects are indeed *forms of equivalence*; they serve a symbolic function, and in some fundamental way they must do justice to the referent. To the extent that the child feels that he or she has failed to capture a likeness to the object, the child might at first use *words* to bridge the gap between what was produced and what it fails to convey, between his or her perception of the object and the inadequate representation. We find a whole range of verbalizations to accomplish this "bridging" (Golomb, 1974). But ultimately, verbalizations are only transient means, and they don't accomplish the real objective, which is to represent an object using

FIGURE 4.   A drawing of three children playing ball. The three players are placed in a triangular arrangement, with a single ball located in the middle of the players. Each of the players is equipped with one arm, pointing in the direction of the ball, ready to throw or catch it. The fourth child is *not* a player, but a mere observer of the game, and thus does not need any arms.

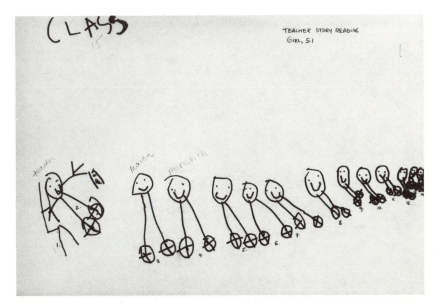

FIGURE 5.   The depiction is of a teacher reading a story to the children in her class. The teacher, seated in a chair, is equipped with two arms, and holds a book in her left hand. The children, all armless, are neatly aligned along the horizontal axis.

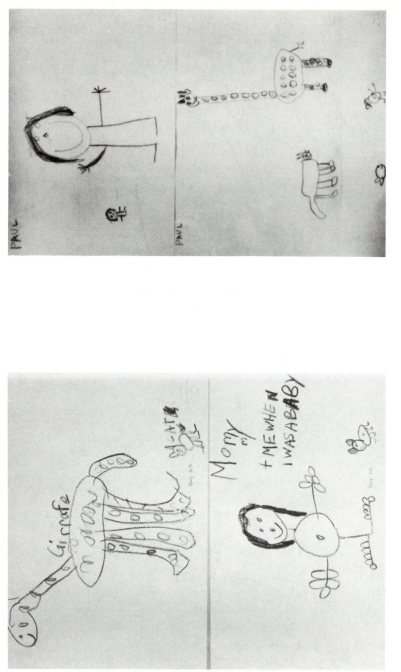

FIGURE 6. The human figure becomes differentiated along the vertical axis, the animal along the horizontal axis. When the animal is a giraffe, the long neck helps to differentiate this figure from other kinds of animals.

graphic means. It is the urge to capture a "likeness," to eliminate the ambiguities of the global figures, that propels the child to search for better means, that is, to graphically differentiate the figures.

The child's prime concern, at each phase of development, is to create acceptable equivalents. The child's concern is with visual likeness to the object—we hear exuberant claims such as "it looks like . . ." or complaints of "it doesn't look like . . . ." It is this symbolizing tendency that establishes a graphic order, fosters articulation, and governs the process of further differentiation. The simple forms are now utilized in a more discriminating fashion. Altogether, the evolution of representational forms is *more* than combining earlier practiced forms and subroutines; it is more than the sum of graphic exercises. It is the object and its visual characteristics that codetermine the graphic organization and the choice of forms. This is not to say that child art over night, so to speak, becomes realistic. We can clearly see that forms are used economically and that the tendency toward simplicity predominates for a long time. But the urge to represent has a referent out there in the real world, and it guides the process of differentiation to an important degree. The solutions to the problem the child faces are worked out, quite autonomously, determined by the nature of the medium, the simple visual logic that guides the child's explorations, and the dialogue that ensues between the child's drawing and his or her satisfaction as well as dissatisfaction with the outcome. I would like to suggest that the child's drawing is determined by the search for *meaning* and *likeness*, but that it is also constrained by the child's experience with the medium and his or her interest, motivation, and attention span.

This view of the development of graphic representation is *not* congruent with the traditional, by now outdated analysis of the drawn figure that overemphasizes the importance of the number of parts, types of omission, and kinds of displacements, and the attention paid to size differences and the lack of proportionality of the body parts. The rules that determine whether a feature is to be included or to be omitted are grounded in a *visual-graphic logic*, which, in the case of the human figure, specifies that the head and vertical length dimension are important defining characteristics, while arms, for example, play a subsidiary role. I have argued that graphic differentiation is not simply a function of the child's greater knowledge of the parts that constitute the human body. We might conceive of the change as a desire to delineate graphically, and with some degree of clarity, what the child conceives as the essential characteristics of the figure. Experience with the medium, repeated practice, and a visual dialogue with the forms created make the child aware of the ambiguities inherent in his or her early work. In those early drawings, lines and contours serve multiple functions such that the large oval comprises head and body, and the lines that extend downward from the circle represent legs as well as torso. The desire to eliminate ambiguities is a major motive for further differentiation of the figures.

We ought to be extremely cautious when interpreting missing features from the drawings of children of all ages: (a) the child may not consider them essential when figural likeness is the issue; (b) there may be insufficient space to accommodate the features; (c) the item may be difficult to represent so the child substitutes a verbal designation for a missing part. Just as armless humans are quite common in the early years, so the human figure does not assume realistic proportions before the end of childhood. Head size, for example, is either over- or underestimated, and thus presents a glaring example of deviation from "realism." As a further example of medium-specific problems and solutions, consider the attachment of arms. As long as the figure is drawn in a relatively "schematic" manner consisting of a head and torso, there is no ideal solution for arms attachment. If the child attaches them to the mid-section of the trunk, a figure is created that is quite acceptable to the adult viewer, although the child violates "realism" since arms certainly do *not* extend from the region of the navel. If the arms are attached to the head, particularly to the lower third of the head-contour, the arms are closer to where they belong "anatomically," although we tend to characterize such attachments as "mistakes." Finally, if the child extends the arms from the intersection of head and torso, a peculiarly imbalanced configuration emerges. Under those conditions, arms misplacement is perhaps a "misnomer." Indeed, from the point of view of what makes a figure "look right," precise measurement is a poor criterion. It follows that questions that focus excessively on such symptoms as omissions, misplacements, and disproportionate sizes are not really the significant ones, at least not at early stages of graphic development. So long as the process of form differentiation is the most important item on the agenda, sizes, proportions, and even colors remain subordinate to the major aim—to create recognizable and meaningful figures. Once the struggle to create forms that adequately represent the intended object has been successful, the child also begins to pay attention to other variables.

In summary, research regarding the emergence of the earliest representational forms indicates that they are self-generated, the outcome of a dialogue among the hand, the eye, and the urge to symbolize reality. The evolution of the earliest forms is a spontaneous, universally observable process, which creates its own momentum and provides its own motivation toward the differentiation of forms and the articulation of meaning (Golomb, 1969, 1973, 1974, 1981; Golomb & Farmer, 1983). We are witnessing in young children a highly sophisticated process, marked by a spontaneous awareness of equivalences that differ vastly from one-to-one correspondences. We are faced with a capacity to symbolize in a domain that, unlike language, has no real outside model that can be closely imitated, but seems to be largely self-taught and to evolve its own formulae. The child is continually experimenting with the medium until adequate models are discovered. The notions of "adequacy" change with age and experience, and they propel the child further until, at each level, order, clarity, and mastery have been achieved. This process, in its early stages, is universal: It overrides culture, social class, race, and history (Haas, 1978; Harris, 1963; Kennedy, 1983; Millar, 1975). We are dealing with a uniquely human *symbolic activity,* which defines the human species. Certainly, our image of the human child has changed, as we acknowledge her or him as a complex human being, endowed with ingenuity and symbol-making propensities. It is this symbol-making capacity that allows human beings to leave a record of their activity and to go beyond reality as immediate experience.

REFERENCES

Arnheim, R. (1974). *Art and visual perception.* Berkeley, CA.: Univ. of Calif. Press.

Eng, H. (1931). *The psychology of children's drawings.* London: Routledge & Kegan Paul.

Golomb, C. (1969). The effects of models, media and instructions on children's representation of the human figure. Ann Arbor, MI.: University Microfilm, 69–16, 308.

Golomb, C. (1973). "Children's representation of the human figure: The effects of models, media and instruction." *Genetic Psychology Monographs, 87,* 197–251.

Golomb, C. (1974). *Young children's sculpture and drawing: A study in representational development.* Cambridge, MA.: Harvard Univ. Press.

Golomb, C. (1981). "Representation and reality: The origins and determinants of young children's drawings." *Review of Research in Visual Art Education, 14,* 36–48.

Golomb, C., & Farmer, D. (1983). "Children's graphic planning strategies and early principles of spatial organization in drawing." *Studies in Art Education, 24*(2), 86–100.

Goodenough, F. (1926). *Measurements of intelligence by drawings*. New York: Harcourt, Brace & World.

Haas, M. (1978). Private communication on drawings by Bedouins in the Sinai Peninsula.

Harris, D.B. (1963). *Children's drawings as measures of intellectual maturity*. New York: Harcourt, Brace & World.

Kellogg, R. (1968). *Analyzing children's art*. Palo Alto, CA.: National Press.

Kennedy, J.M. (1983). "What can we learn from pictures of the blind?" *American Scientist, 71*(1), 19–26.

Kerschensteiner, G. (1905). *Die Entwicklung der zeichnerischen Begabung*. Munich: Gerber.

Levinstein, S. (1905). *Kinderzeichnungen bis zum 14 Lebensjahre. Mit Parallelen aus der Urgeschichte, Kulturgeschichte und Voelkerkunde*. Leipzig: Voigtlaender.

Luquet, G.H. (1913). *Les dessins d'un enfant*. Paris: Alcan.

Luquet, G.H. (1927). *Le dessin enfantin*. Paris: Alcan.

Millar, S. (1975). "Visual experience or translation rules? Drawing the human figure by blind and sighted children." *Perception, 4*, 363–71.

Piaget, J. (1926). *The language and thought of the child*. New York: Harcourt & Brace.

Piaget, J. (1951). *Play, dreams and imitation*. New York: W.W. Norton.

Piaget, J., & Inhelder, B. (1956). *The child's conception of space*. London: Routledge & Kegan Paul.

Piaget, J., & Inhelder, B. (1971). *Mental imagery in the child*. New York: Basic Books.

Schaefer-Simmern, H. (1948). *The unfolding of artistic activity*. Berkeley, CA.: Univ. of Calif. Press.

14 ◇ Imagination and Education for Intercultural Understanding

MICHAEL DEGENHARDT and ELAINE McKAY
University of Tasmania, Australia

Teachers are often urged to develop curricula that are "relevant" or "meaningful" or that match children's needs and experience. Such invocations typically come in loose and ambiguous terms such that either of two distinct educational principles may be intended. One principle equates relevance with close proximity. Clearly this is false, and in a way that both insults the youthful intellect and licences a curriculum to restrict rather than extend mental horizons. Contrary to familiar facts, it asserts that children can be interested in understanding only things close to their existing experience. Acceptance of this view hinders the development of curricula that extend children's imaginations through studies of different and remote cultures. Indeed, it has licensed abandonment of school subjects like history and classics. This chapter is intended to be a modest contribution toward reversing such tendencies.

The other principle is sound. It asserts the importance of engaging children's minds fully and actively, so that they will find their studies "relevant" and "meaningful." Emphasizing familiarity is only one, and not necessarily the most effective, way in which teaching can achieve this. One can also engage a mind by giving it things to do—puzzles to solve, facts to find and interpret, judgments to develop. Or one can set the imagination to work, asking pupils to transport themselves to other times and places, perhaps using limited clues and intimations to build up rich, concrete images.

For many reasons, curricula that teach children about people in other times and places are often in decline. Such curricula may not commend themselves to those who look to education for economic returns and narrow utility. Bad teaching often discredits whole disciplines. A less obvious factor may be a failure to understand the nature and value of imagination. Not only does imagination rouse or enliven the mind; it is indispensable to understanding many things, including people in other cultures. Today there is widespread commitment to imaginative development as an educational aim. Yet this lacks practical force if educational theorists fail to back up such commitment by carefully elucidating the various kinds of imaginative exercise and development and working out how to nurture them.

HISTORICAL PERSPECTIVE

Such neglect may be due to more than the notorious difficulty of the task. According to Theodore Roszak (1972), our most fundamental cultural malaise is a three-centuries-old tradition that denies imagination its proper place and importance in human life. His somewhat extravagant claims include important truths, and a brief sketch of the anti-imagination tradition and of the reaction against it will prepare the ground for us to stake a claim for just one of many ways in which imagination is culturally and educationally significant.

What Roszak has in mind is nicely illustrated in the educational writings of a seventeenth-century French bishop, François Fenelon.

> Girls who are badly educated and indolent have an imagination which is always straying. Lacking solid nourishment, their curiosity turns eagerly towards vain and dangerous objects . . . . They develop a passion for novels, for plays, for fanciful tales of adventure with a romantic love interest. They give way to empty ideas and grow accustomed to the high flown language of the heroes of fiction. By so doing they even spoil themselves for ordinary life; for all these fine, but airy sentiments, these noble passions, these adventures which fiction writers invent in order to please, have no relation to the motives which hold sway in real life and which decide actual events. (Barnard, 1966, pp. 5–6)

Fenelon seems to be prejudiced against literature and women. In fact, however, he loved literature and was advocating an education to help women protect their much abused interests. Moreover, similar views about poetry are found in Locke's recommendations for the education of boys (Axtell, 1968, p. 284). The prejudice here reflects typical seventeenth-century views of mind and knowledge—and it is a prejudice against imagination.

European thinkers of the seventeenth and eighteenth centuries, of the age of the scientific revolution and the "Enlightenment," typically believed that in the new science human beings had learned how to achieve knowledge and to liberate themselves from superstition and irrational authority. Life must improve with every advance in knowledge of ourselves, of our world, and of how we should live in that world. The basis of the new science was seen as twofold. It studied things experimentally and it mathematicized its findings. Experimental observation and mathematization were functions of two fundamental powers of mind: the power of observation by the senses and the power of reasoning by the intellect. No important role was left for imagination. At best, it afforded mental ornament and diversion; at worst, fantasy and illusion to hinder the pursuit of true understanding. Here was common ground between empiricists like Locke and rationalists like Descartes, who wrote, "This power of imagination which I possess is in no way necessary to my essence . . . for although I did not possess it I should still remain the same that I now am" (1917, p. 127).

Certainly many thinkers of the age allowed imagination importance insofar as they tended to equate concepts with mental images. Beyond that they rarely esteemed it highly. In time, however, strong counterclaims came to be made. These were naturally associated with Romanticism, a powerful, broad-based, and thoroughly unsystematic movement of art and ideas that challenged just about every tenet of the Enlightenment. Romantics valued imagination for many reasons. They were impressed by the mystery of things rather than their comprehensibility, and imagination is a mysterious power that can point to further mysteries. They were interested in individuality and subjectivity, and there is something very personal about the workings of imagination. They asserted human freedom against scientific determinism, and human freedom is evident in artistic creation and in the imaginative response of aesthetic enjoyment. They thought particular cases were more important than general abstractions, and mental images are of the concrete and particular. At the same time, they hoped imagination's synoptic power would restore wholeness to the world view that had been fragmented in the "dark satanic mills" of Newtonian analysis.

Yet the Romantics probably did imagination as much disservice as service. Their claims for it were many, varied, and not entirely compatible. Their piecemeal insights reveal imagination as an extraordinarily complex faculty manifesting itself in many diverse ways and vital to the life of the mind. We may esteem so versatile a faculty, but be at a loss to know how to even begin developing an account of its working. It is important to understand imagination for the very reasons that make it difficult to do so. It is hardly surprising that, as Roszak protests, anti-imagination modes of Enlightenment thought endure and flourish. One instance of this that is of present concern is the impressive and often rewarding development over the last centuries of the empirical social sciences conceived on the model of what is supposed to take place in the natural sciences—aspiring to improve our understanding of human affairs by a more or less exclusive reliance on observation and quantification. Such developments now pervade much of our culture, and many social science curricula teach children that *the* way to understand human behavior and soceites is to survey, quantify, generalize, hypothesize, and test. Influential educational theory is informed by the same belief.

THE ROLE OF IMAGINATION IN SOCIAL UNDERSTANDING

We can now begin to understand why there is much invocation but little guidance regarding imaginative development as an educational aim. We feel in need of a well-articulated theory of imagination, but our present state of understanding seems inadequate to the development of one. For the time being it may make sense to adopt a more piecemeal approach, isolating and reflecting on particular exercises of imagination and considering their educational significance. Among other things, such an approach should reveal that imagination can indeed be a means as well as an obstacle to knowledge and understanding. For example, the analyses and observations of natural science would be impossible unless guided by imaginatively generated theory and hypothesis. Artistic creation and appreciation involve exercises of disciplined imagination rather than indulgent fantasy. And, our present concern, only by "re-enactive imagination" can we achieve anything but a distortingly attenuated understanding of people in societies other than our own.

The mere statement of such a proposal may rouse standard anti-imagination responses. Is it not misleading and irresponsible to teach children to understand other cultures on any basis other than one of good solid facts? Are not the irrationalities of fantasy quite out of place here?

Two general points help to counter this objection: One is linguistic and conceptual and the other is phenomenological. Although we often use the words *imagination* and *fantasy* interchangeably, there is no total equivalence. The distinction is far from clear, but there certainly are instances in which the two words are not equally appropriate. Thus I may talk of imagining I am Superman or of imagining I was a sailor on Nelson's victory. However, in the first case it would seem quite natural to substitute "fantasize" for "imagine"; in the second, it would be inappropriate unless the intended implication was that my imagining of life between decks was being done in an indulgent, ill-informed, or undisciplined way, perhaps proposing an anachronistic coziness or giving myself an improbably heroic role. So we would not normally call imaginings fantastical unless they were undisciplined, ill-informed, or governed by no sense of reality and possibility.

Imagining vs. Perceiving

The phenomenological point is more complicated. One important way in which we exercise imagination is in the entertaining of mental images. In theoretical studies, as well as everyday understanding, we often conceive of such imaging as a kind of inner perception. If I tell someone that I am imaging Ronald Reagan, I intend that person to take it that a visual presentation of Reagan is present to me. It seems appropriate to talk of ''seeing'' Reagan in the mind's eye, even if we feel the need to put quotation marks around seeing. This way of thinking about mental imagery can encourage a poor estimation of the imagination, suggesting that images are things that simply occur, somehow just cropping up in consciousness to be encountered there—something beyond intelligent regulation or mental control.

However, Sartre's celebrated phenomenology of mental imagery shows us that things are not really like this. He reminds us of obvious truths about imagery that we readily forget, and makes it clear why we are right to speak of ''seeing'' rather than seeing. For, notwithstanding their similarities, imaging and perceiving are quite distinct modes of consciousness. Mental images are not really things that we observe. Rather, they exhibit what Sartre calls ''the phenomenon of quasi-observation'' (1972, p. 5). Sartre notes that ''the image teaches nothing, never produces an impression of novelty, and never reveals any new respect of the object. It delivers it *en bloc*'' (1972, p. 9). What this means is that it is impossible to further observe a mental image so as to find out more about it. When I perceive an object, I can go on indefinitely looking and relooking at it to observe new details and features. But images exhibit ''a sort of essential poverty'' (Sartre, 1972, p. 8). However long I ''look'' at them, I will find in them nothing but what I put there. To elucidate the point, Sartre cites Alain's well-known thought experiment: I may be able to form an image of the Pantheon, but I will not be able to count the pillars unless I already know how many there are.

Images are produced *by* consciousness in such a way that image and consciousness are one; so it is not surprising that ''the image teaches nothing.'' The real cause for surprise would be if I did find anything new in a mental image, as I can and do find new things when I observe objects. We form our images and we can change them at will in a way that we cannot change the content of our perceptions. So mental imagery is not some necessarily irrational phenomenon that just happens to the mind; forming images is an activity of mind that can be as rational and informed as any other activity of mind. This point extends to all exercises of imagination and is overlooked by those who dismiss all imagining as wild fantasizing.

Imagination vs. Delusion

A related reason for undervaluing imagination is our tendency to equate it with illusion and delusion, as if imaginings necessarily mislead by being taken for realities. Again Sartre puts us right. The imaginative consciousness, he says, is aware of itself as a creative spontaneity summoning up or generating an image. Being aware of ourselves experiencing images by actively forming them, we know our imaginings for what they are. There may be cases like dreams and hallucinations, in which we mistake images for reality (though Sartre would deny even this), but in general to imagine is not to be fooled or taken in. This is not, of course, to say that in imagining an object I necessarily believe it does not exist at all. I may imagine a unicorn, which I believe not to exist; a giraffe, which I believe to exist elsewhere; or a Tasmanian tiger, concerning the existence of which I suspend judgment. But in all these cases I am aware that I am not seeing a real animal, that I am "seeing" an unreal image. We may sometimes mistake imaginings for reality, but in general we do not.

The Value of Imagination
in Teaching about Other Cultures

Imagination, then, need be no obstacle to knowledge and understanding. In the following section, we want to show how in at least one respect it is indispensable to these ends.

There are, of course, many different views as to what is involved in coming to understand other cultures and their people. One can claim to know about people and cultures in purely observational terms. Such knowledge could consist of descriptions of physical body movements and of the physical composition of the artifacts among which such movements take place. These would contain no references to people's motives and intentions, nor to how they understand things. Some scholars advocate and attempt something like this on the grounds that scientific objectivity requires us to confine ourselves to what is observable. Yet critics point out that if we really did carry through such a program, the result would be a very inadequate description of people's conduct or their culture. Indeed, it is illuminating to reflect on how difficult it would be to develop such a description with total consistency. It is easier to say someone is tilling the soil than to give an intention-free account of that person's body movements; easier to refer to a house or temple than to give an intention-free description of an arrangement of raw materials scrupulously eschewing any purposive term such as "door," "nail," "kitchen," or "altar." What then *could* it be to describe the Roman Empire or Azande village life in such restricted terms?

The point is that we really understand neither people nor their culture unless we know their ideas and intentions as well as their observable movements and artifacts. For ideas and intentions are part of what a person and his or her culture are. This is why, as Charles Taylor shows, even the ablest investigators fail to give the intention-free accounts to which their theory commits them (1964, Part II).

In his classic statement of the view we are advocating, Robin Collingwood, using rather dangerous metaphorical language, contended that historical studies are marked by their concern with the "inside" of events. An historian's inquiry "may begin by discovering the outside of an event, but it can never end there . . . the event was an action and . . . his main task is to think himself into this action, to discern the thought of its agent" (Collingwood, 1961, p. 213). The only way to discern such thoughts is to re-think them in one's own mind.

Many theorists have developed similar views regarding history and other human studies like sociology and anthropology. Such theories are sometimes called hermeneutic because they emphasize the interpretation of evidence (documents, relics, artifacts) for what it tells us of the thoughts or meanings that inform actions, practices, and institutions. There is now an abundance of literature on the subject. Continuing debates between advocates of more or less hermeneutic and positivist orientations are matched by disagreements within each tradition. For Collingwood, historians can and should be concerned only with re-enacting past thoughts, while Dilthey, to whom Collingwood was indebted, talks of re-living feelings and emotions (Hodges, 1944). Winch (1958) puts the emphasis less on re-capturing individual consciousness and more on knowing the language of a culture and the norms and perspectives it embodies. Popper (1972, pp. 183–90) talks of grasping the logic of someone's situation in order to explain his or her conduct.

We do not seek to contribute to these continuing discussions that concern the nature of scholarly investigations and explanation rather than the distinct though related manner of educating children. We would note, however, that re-enactment theorists say remarkably little about the imagination. Collingwood does talk of envisioning oneself in other people's situations, yet this is not the theme of his chapter on historical imagination. Perhaps the re-enactment theorists fear changes like those already discussed. However, our contention is that a highly disciplined exercise of imagination is necessary to such re-enactment and that teaching children to understand people in other cultures by engaging in such re-enactment is one very important way in which curricula should provide for children's imaginative development. How else but by imagination can one pass beyond the observable evidence for people's thoughts to get at the thoughts themselves?

Far from distrusting this informed exercise of imagination, we should recognize its peculiar fitness to this kind of understanding. When we imagine, we present to our consciousness a certain object or state of affairs. Images are of concrete particulars, not of abstract generalizations, and one thing we can mean when we say someone has a good imagination is that he or she is able to form rich, detailed, and coherent mental images. Such images will capture much of the abundant complexity of a particular object or circumstance. An analogous ability to hold present to the mind abundant details (of circumstance, belief, motive, previous experience, and so on) is also needed in order to envision someone's situation and re-enact that person's thoughts. Without it, a historian will not do a good job of re-enacting Caesar's thoughts, a student will not do well at entering the perspectives of people in other cultures, and none of us will be good at emphathizing with the people next door. It is neither necessary, nor possible, that all the details be held in mind in the form of a mental image. Yet the summoning and holding present to the mind of such details is clearly an achievement of imagination analogous to imaging.

This connection is probably educationally important. People like artists, who are much concerned with the appearance of things, usually develop high imaging capacities, which it seems can be increased by appropriate training. So, as we will consider shortly, it is reasonable to suppose that appropriate strategies could be developed to nurture the re-enactive capacity. Empirical research here would surely be rewarding.

The anti-imagination theorist is partly right, of course, in that we will go astray if we rely on imagination alone. To understand other people and cultures imagination must be informed and disciplined by evidence. To rely on introspection alone in an effort to understand people of another culture could be totally misleading. After all, the subjective life of such people may follow patterns quite unlike those in one's own experience; the "obvious" interpretation of an act may be totally erroneous. Consider, for example, the various interpretations of a smile or a wink. Introspection may generate hypotheses, but they have to be tested against the evidence (see Barbour, 1966, Ch. 7; Geertz, 1973, Ch. 1). All this is of educational moment. Lessons to help children imaginatively capture the thoughts of people in other cultures can go wrong in two opposed ways. Too much emphasis on facticity may stifle imagination, while imagination without the support and constraint of facts lapses into fantasy. The right balance is hard to judge. The need to strive for it should be kept in mind as we now consider some of the ways in which teachers can foster this particular kind of imaginative exercise.

Perspective Taking in the Classroom

As we have argued, learning about other cultures is, centrally, a matter of exercising imagination to enter another perspective. The sociologist J. C. van Leur, after surveying Dutch writings about the Indies, realized that

> with the arrival of ships from western Europe, the point of view is turned a hundred and eighty degrees and from then on the Indies are observed from the deck of the ship, the ramparts of the fortress, the high gallery of the trading-house. (1967, p. 251)

Pupils can practice reversing such angles of vision. They might, for example, be asked to take the following sentences by a venerable modern historian and rewrite them from the point of view of the Sultan of Palembang.

> Firm action had to be taken against the Sultan of Palembang, who in 1658 treacherously attacked the Dutch factory, murdering the factors and the crews of two ships lying at anchor before it. The punitive expedition forced him to permit the construction of a Dutch fort close to his town and to grant the Dutch exclusive right to purchase his pepper. (Hall, 1970, p. 321)

Contrasts can also be used to develop appreciation of how differently different people can view the same topic. Thus pupils might compare a Western textbook's view with that of an Indian poem on the subject of the cow (The Asia Society, 1974, pp. 8–9).

> [Nehru] also had to fight ancient Hindu customs. These customs often hindered India's economic progress. One of these customs were [sic] the belief that the cow was a sacred animal . . . Hindus do not eat beef, and the cattle served no useful purpose.

> Living, I yield milk, butter and
>   curd, to sustain mankind.
> My dung is as fuel used,
>   Also to wash floor and wall;
> Or burnt, becomes the sacred ash
>   on forehead.
> When dead, of my skin are
>   sandals made,
> Or the bellows at the blacksmith's
>   furnace;
> Of my bones are buttons made . . .
>   But of what use are you, O Man?

Traditionally, debating has been used to develop appreciation of perspectives. Debates can be designed to achieve at least temporary identification, as when a class divides to debate the merits of living in Sparta or Athens. This can also involve the process that Berthold Brecht called "alienation." For, as well as identifying with the view they are to present, pupils must also "stand aside" to anticipate likely attacks by the opposing team. It can be immensely valuable to have pupils defend views other than their own. We know of a teacher in a white school in southern Africa who in this way was able to get ardently racist pupils to start taking black viewpoints seriously.

Similar processes have been developed in teaching through improvised drama. According to one exponent, Dorothy Heathcote, children (and adults) are eased into roles by a combination of information about the situation and an appeal to self-knowledge. Whenever the necessary knowledge is exhausted or whenever the children's conviction about their roles breaks down, the action must be frozen, the roles dropped, and more research done or the problem resolved (Wagner, 1976). Imagination is centrally involved here, but again it is a demandingly disciplined and informed exercise of imagination.

As Betty Wagner says:

> Drama is never doing your own thing. Everything each person does must be in context of the others in the drama . . . . In a classroom, each in-

dividual must agree to be open to others and to stay with the challenge
of responding relevantly if the imagined moment is to take on the texture of real experience. Ironically, by disciplining themselves to respect
the rules of drama, the participants become more free to discover all of
the possibilities within the art form. (1976, p. 147)

Heathcote is not training professional actors. She is teaching people
"to expand their understanding of life experience, to reflect on a particular circumstance, to make sense of their world in a new or deeper
way" (Wagner, 1976, p. 147). We would add that she also allows children "to try on" roles, to anticipate a range of actions, and to practice a range of responses. By providing opportunities to appreciate
individual diversity, she mitigates stereotyping and generates a need
to know. Her approach can be used to treat of intercultural themes,
but, even when it is not, it will generate qualities of mind appropriate
to imaginatively entering other cultures.

The kind of understanding we are concerned with does not come
easily, and provision must be made for reflection. It is bound to take
time both to grasp the world view of another culture and also to weigh
its significance for one's own world view. Today the media, which can
bring the rest of the world and its cultures into our homes, also bom-
bard us and our children with a plethora of stimuli. Rapid successions
of impressions and ideas come too fast for us to make sense of them,
intellectually or emotionally. What is contemporary is brought to us
immediately, but the event is left distant in space and remote from our
senses. Teachers often feel required to offer children more of the same.
Rather, we should be slowing the pace. We should take responsibility
for greater selectivity of material, reducing quantity in favor of quality
of content, while not, of course, denying children access to information and opportunity to pursue inquiry. Above all, we should ensure
for children time to reflect on both the meanings that inhere in the
subject of their study and the meanings of that study for themselves.

The profundity of learning is a product of more than a student's
capacity and opportunities for reflection. The quality of teaching and
of teaching resources is also vital. Teachers must be educated into a
deep understanding of other cultures if they are to start bringing about
the same in their pupils, and they need to have the support of
thoughtful and informed teaching materials. The point may seem obvious, but the scope for reform is immense. To illustrate this, we ask
the reader to contrast two pieces of work from two different classrooms, both dedicated to the same topic—the clash of two cultures,
Aboriginal and Anglo-Saxon, in the early European history of Australia.

The first was an attempt with a class of ten-to-eleven-year-olds by a teacher who wanted to move beyond the stereotypes of Australian history—Captain Cook, convicts, and gold. Half the time over four weeks was devoted to the Aborigines, and then white settlement was taken up to the present; the methods used were information gathering, discussions, an excursion, and writing activities. At the end of the unit, the children were asked to write "A History of Victoria." One student wrote:

> It all started far back in those years when the Aborigines came to Australia. The Aborigines just did not settle in one place . . . . The Aborigines hunted for food. They lived their life very differently . . . . In 1770 Captain James Cook . . . came to Australia. They met the Aborigines. One month later Captain Cook tried to communicate with them. They couldn't. The Aborigines got a bad idea and they threw some spears. The Aborigines thought [the British] were going to kill them . . . Captain Cook claimed Australia [as] his. (Duggan, 1985, p. 6)

The second example is from a class of twelve-year-olds that was studying the first white settlement in Tasmania in 1803. In that year, a tribe of Aborigines, probably engaged in a hunting expedition, unexpectedly appeared in the small white settlement of soldiers, convicts, and free settlers. Lieutenant Governor Bowen was away exploring on the day in question and the soldiers were drinking. In panic they let off the canon and killed a number of blacks, claiming later that they were being attacked. The teacher planned to re-enact, not the massacres, but the inquiry conducted by Bowen on his return. In order to do this, considerable research had to be done into Aboriginal tribal life; for example, did they take women and children on war missions as well as on hunting expeditions? In addition, the social composition and the nature of authority in the white settlement had to be uncovered. The students read the available records of the event and tried to get to the truth of the happening. They were asked to see the events from the viewpoints of the Aborigines, the soldiers, the convicts, the doctor, and the free settlers who were onlookers. We reproduce one letter from among those written "home" by the class after the dramatization.

Risdon Cove,
September, 1803

Dear Father,

I hope this letter finds you well. I am as well as can be expected, the barracks are more comfortable than the tents, not so drafty. I am in with my friends Joe and Tom. Remember I told you that black aborigines had been sighted close to Risdon where we are billeted, well the other day September the 13 I saw them for myself, a lot of great ugly black brutes came tearing down over the hill with their spears raised and some stupid drunk soldiers opened fire with their maskets and killed a couple. The ones not killed or hurt ran off. It was an awful sight I still hear the screams in my sleep. Torn bodies oozing blood scattered all around. I was part of the burial party and the sight I saw made me sick. I was with doctor Mount Garrett and we found the body of a black child it was a boy about eight years old. The Doctor was very interested in it and he has had it frozen (sic) and sent back to England for studying. Lt. Bowen called a hearing to find out why it all happened. The aborigines claim they were only a hunting party chasing wallaby for food. The whole thing could have been avoided. Funny they don't look so savage when they are dead only innocent like a child. Well its almost lights out give my love to my sister Sally and mother god bless you all.

Love, James

Many things are significant about this second example when compared with the first. Although both teachers' aims were similar, the second focused narrowly on a case study, while the first conducted a survey, focusing, it seems, on the very emphases he sought to criticize. This necessarily involved generalizations. Both teachers shared many teaching strategies, but the second included dramatization and first-person writing. This allowed for identification with the characters making the history and allowed the student to "enter" the context of time and place. The nature of the research that each group undertook was different and so was the quality of the product of their learning. Whereas the first has a tone of blaming the victim, the second has developed a well-informed empathy. Most strikingly, it shows that imaginative re-enactment can yield insights that may not come from straight description. The first example was a survey of events, the second recreated one event. An event is a story to be uncovered. It therefore has a structure and motivates us, because our curiosity demands satisfaction: The story must have an end. The story frames things in time and space; it allows for explanation and invites identification and empathy (see Egan, 1986; Fines, 1983).

As teachers we can learn much from these examples. They show the importance of choosing topics that are themselves important to learn about, that generate a holistic picture, and that are affectively engaging. Teaching strategies must be varied, must encourage sympathetic imagination or empathy, and sympathetic re-enactment, and must leave time for reflection and the development of individual responses. The support materials must be rich and authentic to nourish children's imaginations and to answer some of their best questions.

All this, of course, asks a great deal of teachers who must have a deep understanding of the cultures studied and be well-versed in possible teaching approaches. Again there are important implications for teacher education (Degenhardt & McKay, 1986).

Using Imaginative Works of Other Cultures in Teaching

We will mention one other way in which pupils can exercise their own imaginations to give themselves entry to another culture—that is, by responding to the imaginative creations of that culture. Many artworks reveal something of the outlook, world view, and life-style that constitute the culture in which they were created and of which they are a part. This is most obviously so of literary works that expound and explore perspectives that are made more or less explicit. It is also true of other art forms, but not so obviously. The style of neoclassical portraiture gained its point from motivating views of human virtue. The intimations of mystery and loneliness in a painting by Friedrich, or of power and distance beyond comprehension in a Turner mountain-scape, both instance Romantic transformations of human conscious-ness. Grasping the point of much Chinese landscape painting is inseparable from grasping traditional Chinese values and religious perspectives. Examples can be added from all art forms.

Recent curriculum developments have increased provisions for children to exercise their own creativity, but often to the detriment of learning about and enjoying the creative achievements of others. Un-less we also teach courses to help learners appreciate works of art and what is to be found in them, then many children will leave school largely ignorant of the diversity of artistic achievements, past and present. Thus they will be deprived of profoundly illuminating en-counters with the diversity of human outlooks, values, and sensitivi-ties.

Roadblocks to Effective Teaching Strategies

The development of these and similar teaching strategies may be hindered by features of our own cultural and educational context that are unfavorable to the kind of learning intended. Certainly much is fa-vorable. The principle, if not always the practice, of ethnic tolerance and understanding is now well established. Modern communication technologies facilitate many links between cultures. On the other hand, the broadcasting of silly films and dramas invites undemanding exercises of re-enactive imagination in order to understand shallow characters about whom there is virtually nothing to understand. Competing for attention, teachers are tempted to follow suit and render children's imaginations even more indolent. Fortunately, good literature teachers still wage valiant war against such soporifics.

Also unfavorable to what we propose is the impact of positivistic views on much educational thought and practice. Not only is the content of many school curricula now highly positivistic; positivistic views of the human mind also underpin the development of programmed learning and of teaching by behavioral objectives, which deliberately leave little room for interpretation or imaginative initiative by teacher or student. Many teachers-in-training undergo courses in positivistic educational theory, which could impair their capacity to imaginatively enter into the minds of their pupils, let alone help those pupils to imaginatively enter other cultures.

Finally, we have already noted fashionable and narrowing interpretations of educational "relevance" against which we hope our arguments will have some corrective force. So far we have only adumbrated a view of what is involved in developing an imaginative understanding of other cultures; we have not asked whether this ought to be a curriculum aim. However, our reasons for believing that it should follow naturally from what has been said. We conclude by summarizing the most important of these.

RATIONALE FOR DEVELOPING AN IMAGINATIVE UNDERSTANDING OF OTHER CULTURES

We have argued that imagination is necessary in order to grasp what it is like to see things as they are seen in another culture, to understand another perspective as well as another situation. This is clearly important if education is to help remove antagonisms and develop harmonious relationships between different cultural groups, whether they be rival great powers or hostile religious or ethnic groups living in uncomfortable proximity. Clearly, we often go wrong here. Consider the almost standard response of political leaders to IRA bombings or PLA hijackings. Invariably they come forward to denounce these "cowardly acts." What is wrong here is not just that the supposed cowardliness is treated as more reprehensible than the cruelty; it is also that such acts clearly are *not* cowardly. It must take considerable courage to plant explosives in big cities or take over airliners in flight. Politicians who really think such acts are cowardly are display-ing an outstanding incapacity for imaginative re-enactment. Failing to appreciate that terrorists do exercise courage, they are unlikely to stretch their imaginations far enough to understand why these people think their actions are justified and even obligatory.

Of course, things may not always be as bad as politicians' utter-ances suggest, but the point remains that with no imaginative appre-ciation of opposing views, reasoned resolutions of conflict are hardly conceivable. Our point is well illustrated in one of Freeman Dyson's thoughtful writings on the threat of nuclear war.

> The first and most important fact to remember about Russian generals is that they start out by reading Tolstoy's *War and Peace*. Their whole experience of war and peace in the years since 1914 has confirmed the truth of Tolstoy's vision. War according to Tolstoy is an inscrutable chaos, largely beyond human understanding and human control. In spite of terrible blunders and terrible losses, the Russian people in the end win by virtue of their superior discipline and powers of endurance. All this is entirely alien to the American view of thermonuclear war as a brief affair, lasting a few hours or days, with the results predictable in ad-vance by a computer calculation like a baseball score, so many mega-deaths on one side and so many megadeaths on the other. Assured destruction and limited nuclear war make sense if war is short, calcul-able, and predictable. Counterforce makes sense if war is long-drawn-out and unpredictable . . . . (1984, p. 231).

We do not know if Dyson's analysis is correct. We do suggest that things are more likely to go wrong if people concerned with nuclear strategy and negotiation thoroughly misunderstand the other side be-cause they have made no such imaginative entry into other perspec-tives. So far as Dyson has got things right, this must be because he has balanced his own experiences as a university physicist and U.S. de-fense consultant with readings of Russian history and literature, visits to Russia, and conversations with Soviet citizens, so as to achieve an informed, imaginative reconstruction of how things seem to a Rus-sian. This *has* to be a work of imaginative reconstruction informed by varied clues and data, and developed on the dialectical lines we de-scribed earlier. For Dyson is comparing not two theories susceptible of brief and lucid summary, but two ways of seeing things that are linked to different circumstances, ideologies, and cultural traditions.

Of course, teachers should not plan lessons on the supposition that their classes are full of future leaders and negotiators. They should, however, suppose that their pupils will compose the future citizenry and thus create the context of demands and expectations within which policy makers have to work. And teachers do know that, now or later, many of these pupils will live or work close to other social groups.

The kind of imaginative development we have discussed is likely to enrich learners' understanding of themselves as well as of others. It should do this in three related ways. First, our understanding of ourselves is linked to our understanding of human nature in general. It is easy to take distortingly limited views of human nature by taking our own particular world view and way of life as the universal norm. We are liberated from such myopia by imaginative entry into the perspectives of other ages and cultures and by coming to appreciate how such perspectives can seem as natural as our own. We understand our own perspective better when we view it from another perspective. Second, by using imaginative insight to compare possible perspectives, we are alerted to the importance of subjecting our own perspective to critical scrutiny. We thus advance in autonomy and indeed wisdom. Third, our understanding of ourselves is involved when we plan our lives. Often such planning goes wrong due to a deficiency of imagination plus an excess of fantasy. In envisioning future developments in our lives, in trying to foresee chosen activities and commitments, it is easy to focus on and exaggerate the rewards of a particular life-style. We may then become disillusioned and even bitter when we encounter the realities of such a life-style and our own aptitude for participating in it. This could have been avoided if our initial imaginings had been fuller, more disciplined, and better informed. Developing our imaginations to understand the lives of others should improve our ability to imagine possibilities for our own lives.

Finally, the exercise of re-enactive imagination enriches moral development. Moral development involves understanding both people and values. Learning to better understand people through anthropological, historical, or artistic exercises of imaginative re-enactment should make us better at understanding people in real life. Understanding of values requires sympathetic insight into the diversity of values that people can live by. Wilhelm Dilthey described eloquently how he achieved this through imaginative historial study.

> For me, as for most people today, the possibility of living through religious experiences in my own person is narrowly circumscribed. But when I run through Luther's letters and writings, the accounts given by his contemporaries, the records of the religious conferences and council

and of his official activities, I live through a religious process of such eruptive power, of such energy, in which the stake of life or death, that it lies beyond any possibility of personal experience for a man of our day. But I can relive it. I project myself into the circumstances. And so this process opens up to us a religious world . . . which widens our horizon to include possibilities of human life which are accessible to us only in this way. Thus man, determined from within, can live in imagination through many other existences. Before man limited by circumstances there open out strange beauties in the world, and tracts of life which he can never reach. (Hodges, 1944, p. 123–4)

There is surely no reason why this kind of mental enrichment, with appropriate adjustment for maturation and ability, ought not to be the prerogative of every child in school.

REFERENCES

The Asia Society. (1974). *Asia in American textbooks*. New York: The Asia Society.

Axtell, J.L. (1968). *The educational writings of John Locke*. Cambridge, Eng.: Cambridge Univ. Press.

Barbour, I.G. (1966). *Issues in science and religion*. Englewood Cliffs, N.J.: Prentice-Hall.

Barnard, H.C. (1966). *Fenelon and education*. Cambridge, Eng.: Cambridge Univ. Press.

Collingwood, R.G. (1961). *The idea of history*. London: Oxford Univ. Press.

Degenhardt, M. (1984). "Educational research as a source of educational harm." *Universities Quarterly: Culture, Education and Society, 38*(3), 232–52.

Degenhardt, M., & McKay, E. (1986, October). "On teaching children to understand people in other cultures." *Discourse: The Australian Journal of Educational Studies 7*(1).

Descartes, R. (1917). *A discourse on method and meditations on the first philosophy*. (Trans. J. Veitch). London: J.N. Dent & Sons.

Duggan, S. (1985). "Images of history. The problem with books, convicts and gold." *Primary Education*, pp. 8–10.

Dyson, F. (1984). *Weapons and hope*. New York: Harper & Row.

Egan, K. (1986). *Teaching as story telling*. London, Ontario: Althouse Press.

Elton, G. (1970). *Political history*. London: Allen Lane.

Fines, J. (Ed.). (1983). *Teaching history*. Edinburgh: Holmes McDougall.

Gallie, J.B. (1964). *Philosophy and historical understanding*. London: Chatto & Windus.

Geertz, C. (1973). *The interpretation of cultures*. New York: Basic Books.

Hall, D.G.E. (1970). *A history of South East Asia*. London: Macmillan.

Hodges, H. (1944). *Wilhelm Dilthey: An introduction*. New York: Oxford Univ. Press.

Popper, K. (1972). *Objective knowledge*. Oxford: Clarendon Press.

Roszak, T. (1972). *Where the wasteland ends*. New York: Doubleday.

Sartre, J.P. (1972). *The psychology of imagination*. (Trans. anon.). London: Methuen & Co.

Taylor, C. (1964). *The explanation of behaviour*. London: Routledge & Kegan Paul.

van Leur, J.C. (1967). *Indonesian trade and society: Essays in Asian social and economic history*. The Hague: W. van Hueve Publishers Ltd.

Wagner, B.J. (1976). *Dorothy Heathcote. Drama as a learning medium*. Washington, D.C.: National Education Association.

Winch, P. (1958). *The idea of a social science and its relation to philosophy*. London: Routledge & Kegan Paul.

◇ About the Editors and the Contributors

Robin Barrow was, formerly, Reader in Philosophy of Education at the University of Leicester, U.K., and is currently Professor of Education at Simon Fraser University, Canada. He was awarded his Ph.D. by the University of London for his work on Plato, and was Vice-Chairman of the Philosophy of Education Society of Great Britain from 1980–83. He has authored several books in the fields of philosophy, classics and curriculum, including *The Philosophy of Schooling, Athenian Democracy,* and *Giving Teaching back to Teachers.*

Michael Degenhardt, Ph.D., has taught at schools and colleges in Africa and Great Britain. Since 1978 he has been Senior Lecturer in Philosophy of Education at the University of Tasmania, Australia. He has written on various aspects of education and is the author of *Education and the Value of Knowledge.*

Kieran Egan, (editor), is Professor of Education at Simon Fraser University in Canada. His books include *Educational Development, Education and Psychology, Teaching as Story Telling,* and, most recently, *Primary Understanding: Education in Early Childhood.*

Claire Golomb received her Ph.D. from Brandeis University. She has taught psychology at Wellesley and Brandeis, and since 1974 has been a professor of psychology at the University of Massachusetts, Boston. Her major research centers on symbol formation in child art and child play, and she has published on developmental processes in children's drawings and pretend play, both in normal and developmentally atypical populations. She is the author of *Young Children's Sculpture and Drawing: A Study in Representational Development,* and of *The Child's Invention of a Pictorial World: Studies in the Psychology of Child Art,* currently in progress.

Maxine Greene is Professor of Philosophy and Education and the William F. Russell Professor in the Foundations of Education at

Teachers College, Columbia University. Past-president of the American Educational Research Association and the Philosophy of Education Society, she is also a former editor of the *Teachers College Record*. Her works have dealt with topics ranging from aesthetic education to curriculum problems and moral issues, and include *Teacher as Stranger* and *Landscapes of Learning*. Nearing completion is *The Dialectic of Freedom*. Dr. Greene holds M.A. and Ph.D. degrees from New York University and a D.H.L. from both Lehigh and Hofstra Universities.

Karen Hanson is an Associate Professor of Philosophy at Indiana University. Her A.M. and Ph.D., in Philosophy, are from Harvard University. She specializes in philosophical psychology, ethics, and aesthetics, with both a theoretical and a practical interest in education. Her publications include *The Self Imagined*.

Ted Hughes was appointed Poet Laureate of England in 1984. Previously, he had been a teacher, a rose-gardener, nightwatchman, and script-reader for Pinewood Film Studios. Hughes is the recipient of many awards, including the City of Florence International Poetry Prize, The Queen's Gold Medal for Poetry, and the Order of the British Empire. The author of several books of children's stories and verse (*Meet My Folks, The Earth Owl and Other Moon People, How the Whale Became, The Iron Man,* and *The Coming of Kings*), he was married to the American poet Sylvia Plath.

Gareth Matthews is Professor of Philosophy at the University of Massachusetts. He received his Ph.D. from Harvard in 1961 and has held regular teaching posts at the Universities of Virginia and Minnesota. He has been Santayana Fellow at Harvard; special lecturer at Cambridge University; a member of the School of Epistemics, University of Edinburgh; and a member of the Institute for Advanced Study, Princeton. A recent focus of his work is the philosophy of childhood: conceptions of childhood, theories of cognitive and moral development, children's rights, and the place of children in society. He is the author of *Philosophy and the Young Child, Dialogues with Children,* and some 50 articles.

Elaine McKay, M.Ed., was a secondary school teacher in Victoria before moving to Tasmania, Australia, to work in teacher education. She also worked in Thailand, Indonesia, Malaysia and the Philippines in teacher education, schools broadcasting, curriculum development, and research. She has been active in promoting the inclusion of the study of Asia in curricula at all levels of the Australian education systems. Recently, she was elected President of the Asian Studies Association of Australia and she edits a section of the *ASAA Review.* She also edited *Studies in Indonesian History* and *Indonesian Nationalism and Revolution: Six First Hand Accounts* and has written on Indonesian history, Malaysian education, Asian Studies in Australia and teaching about Asian cultures.

Dan Nadaner (editor) received his undergraduate degree at Harvard and his doctorate in art education at Stanford. He has taught art at the elementary, secondary, and college levels. In 1975–76 he was a Rockefeller Foundation Fellow at the Metropolitan Museum, where he produced two films about the museum. From 1981–85 he was Assistant Professor, Faculty of Education, Simon Fraser University, where he organized the conference *Imagination and Educational Development.* He has published 25 articles on art and education, and is currently a painter living in Palo Alto, California.

Roger Shepard, an experimental/cognitive/mathematical psychologist, received his Ph.D. from Yale University in 1955. He has been a member of technical staff and a department head at the Bell Telephone Laboratories, Professor and Director of the Psychological Laboratories at Harvard University, and, since 1967, Professor of Psychology at Stanford University. He has been the recipient of a Guggenheim Fellowship, the Distinguished Scientific Contribution Award of the American Psychological Association, the Warren Medal of the Society of Experimental Psychologists, and was elected to the National Academy of Sciences and to the American Academy of Arts and Sciences.

June Sturrock, who works in the Centre for Distance Education at Simon Fraser University, Canada, has published articles on Wordsworth, Shakespeare, Samuel Richardson, Iris Murdoch, and C.M. Yonge as well as on Distance Education. She is an associate editor of the *Journal of Distance Education,* and is presently completing a book called *Daughters of the Church: Conflicting Attitudes toward Women in the Novels of Charlotte Mary Yonge.*

Brian Sutton-Smith received his Ph.D. in Educational and Developmental Psychology from the University of New Zealand in 1954. He has taught school in New Zealand; has been a Professor at Bowling Green State University, Ohio, and at Teachers College, Columbia University; and is now Professor of Education and Professor of Folklore at the University of Pennsylvania. He has authored, co-authored or edited 3 children's novels, 11 books on play and games, and 9 works on aspects of child development.

Robert Walker is an Associate Professor in the Faculty of Education at Simon Fraser University, Canada. He received a Ph.D. from the University of London and performer's diplomas from the Royal College of Music and the Royal College of Organists, London, England. He has held posts as director of music at English grammar schools and at a cathedral choir school. He has lectured in music and music education in England, Australia, and Canada, and has authored more than 40 articles and research papers, as well as 2 books. Currently, he researches the music of Inuit and North American Indian peoples through spectral analysis and other acoustic techniques.

Otto Weininger received his Ph.D. in Psychology at the University of Toronto, where he is now Professor of Educational Theory, also teaching clinical child psychology in the Department of Applied Psychology, The Ontario Institute for Studies in Education. Dr. Weininger has been appointed by the Minister of Education for Ontario to the Primary Curriculum Revision Committee, as a member of the Specialist Group, and as a member of the Kindergarten Curriculum Revision Committee. His research deals with readiness, play, treatment models for emotionally disturbed children, school, psychology, and maternal separation. His books include *Play and Education: The Basic Tool for Early Childhood Learning,* and *Out of the Minds of Babes: The Strength of Children's Feelings.*

◇ Index